The M Word

the M 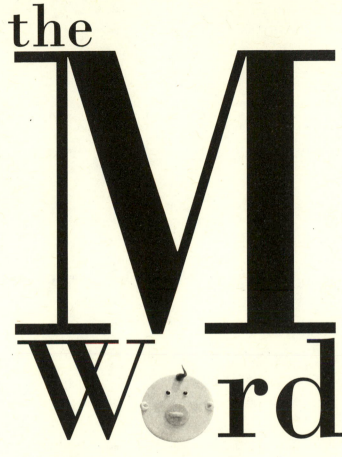 Word

Conversations about Motherhood

Edited by **KERRY CLARE**

GOOSE LANE

Edited by Bethany Gibson.
Cover and page design by Julie Scriver.
Cover image courtesy of Samantha Potter, *Cakes by Samantha*, www.partycakes.gr.
Typeset in Richler, designed by Nick Shinn.
Printed in Canada.
10 9 8 7 6 5 4 3 2 1

Library and Archives Canada Cataloguing in Publication

The M word: conversations about motherhood / edited by Kerry Clare.

Issued in print and electronic formats.
ISBN 978-0-86492-487-2 (pbk.). —ISBN 978-0-86492-797-2 (epub)

1. Canadian essays (English)—Women authors.
2. Canadian essays (English)—21st century. 3. Motherhood. 4. Mothers.
I. Clare, Kerry, 1979-, editor of compilation.

PS8367.M67M22 2014   C814'.608035252   C2013-907597-6
                        C2013-907598-4

Goose Lane Editions acknowledges the generous support of the
Canada Council for the Arts, the Government of Canada through the
Canada Book Fund (CBF), and the Government of New Brunswick
through the Department of Tourism, Heritage, and Culture.

Goose Lane Editions
500 Beaverbrook Court, Suite 330
Fredericton, New Brunswick
CANADA   E3B 5X4
www.gooselane.com

To our women friends,
and all their stories.

Contents

Foreword

The Motherhood Conversation (or "Life With a Uterus")

When I had my first baby a few years ago, I started talking about motherhood, joining a conversation that is buzzing and vital, notwithstanding clichéd headlines about mommy wars, helicopter moms, yummy mommies, even slummy ones. This was a conversation apart from the headlines, one that took place on thoughtful blogs and webforums, in the margins of books like Rachel Cusk's *A Life's Work* and the anthology *Double Lives: Writing and Motherhood*, and with friends over cups of tea as we talked and talked, our babies playing on the floor beside us.

During those early, overwhelming days when I was struggling to find my footing with a screaming babe in tow, it was by talking about motherhood and reading about motherhood that I was able to make sense of my new life and of this whole other world into which the baby and I had landed. These were conversations that took for granted the nuances of love and ambivalence, the exhaustion of the sleepless nights, all the ways that motherhood had changed us, and (even more troublesome sometimes) the ways that it hadn't.

For a while, motherhood was my main occupation, but it was also my preoccupation, one you might have supposed I shared with society in general. After all, motherhood memoirs abound, celebrity motherhood feeds the gossip mills, and there is now such a thing as "bump watch." Motherhood is still widely considered to be a woman's sole path to self-realization — even as mother blaming is a favourite pastime. Amplifying the noise, everybody and their auntie is asking when you're having kids, or when you're having another. This mama saturation all became officially too much for me around the time that the term "momtrepreneur" was coined.

Yet, there is a difference between this pop culture-fuelled din and the motherhood conversation that helped me find my feet after my baby's birth. With the former, motherhood is simplified, commodified, packaged to make most of us feel inadequate. The essence of the motherhood conversation gets drowned out. And as much as these prevailing views of motherhood fail to reflect the reality of so many mothers, women without children must feel particularly alienated against such a cultural backdrop, the exclusivity of motherhood so underlined.

The exclusivity of motherhood is a paradox, however, given that mothers are everywhere. How is exclusivity even possible for an institution with non-existent standards for membership and such low barriers for entry? But all this does little to undermine mothers' set-apartness, the insularity of their order (even in spite of a conspicuous lack of a united front), and the knowing glances indicating that outsiders *just don't get it*.

"Could it be true that one has to experience in order to understand?" asks Rachel Cusk in her seminal book on mothering. "I have always denied the idea, and yet of motherhood, for me at least, it seems to be the case." And it's true that there is something so transformative about the experience of bringing a child into the world. To become a mother by any means is to cross a threshold; it is to shatter one's universe and then have it put back together as a wholly other place. It is difficult to put into words exactly what this transformation feels like, though this hasn't stopped many of us from trying again and again, thereby ensuring the motherhood conversation is perpetuated.

As my baby grew and we settled into life together, my preoccupation with motherhood waned and I started having different conversations. Many of my friends were having babies, too, but others had had miscarriages, were dealing with infertility, were ambivalent about the prospect of motherhood, or had decided against having kids altogether. Other friends were talking about single-parenthood, adoption, step-parenting, and IVF costs, and it began to occur to me that in our most earnest and essential conversations about motherhood, many of us had been missing huge parts of the story.

We were missing it partly because these other experiences involved ideas that people still have a hard time discussing. But we were also missing it due to a presumed gulf between women with children and those without them, one that is usually presented as unbridgeable.

There is among mothers a reflexive tendency to close ranks, which goes a long way toward shutting up blowhards, idiots, baby whisperers seizing on our desperation, and any male doctor-turned-author with bad advice about how one should care for her child. Mothers also continue to be maligned (check out the comments on any online article about big strollers or public breast-feeding to see what I mean), even as they're being sanctified in theory by our mother-obsessed society, and the contradiction is confusing, bolstering mothers' defences. And this is where the exclusivity comes in, enhancing the motherhood conversation not a bit, creating a sense of apartness that leaves so many other women feeling their experiences are outside of the ordinary and, for some, that they are, perhaps impossibly, alone.

Though they aren't. Not least of all because even women with more straightforward relationships to maternity can feel alienated by motherhood, particularly under the influence of those aforementioned clichéd headlines. There isn't a mother alive who hasn't thought of herself as stationed far outside maternity's central zone, that place we all imagine, where all the babies are cooing, the bananas are never bruised, and every woman is comfortable enough in her own skin to disregard magazine covers' blaring provocations: *Are You Mom Enough?*

In fact, it seems that outside the zone are most of us, those whose relationships to motherhood are complicated — we've lost children, we never had the ones we longed for, the children we have are not biologically ours. We are the women who've had too many children or not enough, or we didn't have them properly. Women for whom motherhood is a fork in the road, encountered with decidedly mixed feelings. There are those of us who made the conscious choice not to have children and yet find ourselves defined by what we're lacking instead of the richness of our lives.

Motherhood: the M Word. It means something different to all of us, and exactly what it means is rarely simple.

You might ask if the world needs another literary anthology about motherhood, and I would argue that it needs this one. Here is an anthology that presents women's lives as they are really lived, probing the intractable connections between motherhood and womanhood with all the necessary complexity and contradiction laid out in a glorious tangle. It is a book whose contents themselves are in disagreement, essays rubbing up against one another in uncomfortable ways. There is no synthesis — is motherhood an expansive enterprise or is motherhood a trap? — except perhaps a general sense that being a mother and not being a mother are each as terrible and wonderful as being alive.

These essays show that in this age of supposed reproductive choice, so many women still don't have the luxury of choosing their mothering story or how it will play out. And those who do exercise choice often still end up contending with judgment or backlash.

The essays also make clear that women are not as divided between the mothers and the childless (or between the breeders and the child-free, depending on your point of view) as we might be led to believe. Women's lives are so much more complicated than that. There is mutual ground between the woman who decided to have no *more* children and the woman who decided to have none at all. A woman with no children also endures a similar kind of scrutiny as the woman who's had many, both of them operating outside of societal norms. A woman who has miscarried longs to be acknowledged for her own invisible mothering experiences, for the baby she held inside her. And while infertility is its own kind of journey, that journey is also just one of so many whose origins lie with the desire for a child.

"So, life with a uterus, then?" is how it was put to me once when I was trying to sum up this anthology and its intentions. And in a way the suggestion is exactly right. Except for when it's also about life without one.

—KERRY CLARE

Truth, Dare, Double Dare

HEATHER BIRRELL

for Charles

Truth

What I know about motherhood could fill a book—a book with pages that crumble on contact with the earth's fierce and gentle atmosphere. Or a thimble—a thimble full of fairy tears, a swimming pool for pin-dancing angels. Everything I know about motherhood seems to contain its own bristling contradictions. I cannot think "knowing" without thinking "knowing better." But I didn't know better, and I probably never will.

I knew I wanted to have children from a young age. Or at least I thought I did. But then I decided I wanted to be a writer. It took me a long time to cultivate the selfishness and singularity of purpose required to write. I come from a family of socialists, coal miners, factory workers, hairdressers, and teachers. The women in my family were never shown how to take or make space for themselves. So when I finally had my first child, as a writer and teacher I thought I had managed something incredible—an integration of all best possible worlds.

But when the first person asked me, "Can you even imagine your life without her?" I chose to shake my head mutely rather than lie.

Because I could. And I did. I pined for and mourned that pre-baby life. "I don't think I thought this through," I found myself blurting to my sister, a mother of one child, aged two at the time. "Oh," she replied dryly, "I still feel that way." I got the same response from a friend with three children, ten, thirteen, and sixteen. And when I voiced my dismay to my own mother, she laughed. "I know what you mean," she said. Cold comfort. But I think I understand now what they were getting at. If Motherhood had a slogan, it might very well be the double-barrelled "You should have known better" and "You can't think it through."

Dare

I gave birth, at the age of thirty-seven, in a crowded, faded hospital room—husband, sister, three midwives, a fickle fetal heart monitor, two nurses, and an OB/GYN in attendance. They sucked her out of me with a Hoover-like apparatus, inserted like a plunger. Vacuum extraction is the doctor name for the procedure. They cut me. It was too late for painkillers. The pain was sudden and searing and strange. Unlike the contractions that rocked me from within, this pain was an attack. I felt besieged by baby. I thanked the OB/GYN, a latecomer, an interloper really, for her efficiency. I would feel the wrench of the baby being pulled, unwillingly, from my body for six months afterwards —when I walked, when I sat, when I reached or sneezed. But at the moment, there was only the stark, expansive relief of pain's absence, and a cone-headed bundle nestled in my arms.

Back home, my husband and I did not sleep, too terrified for her. And perhaps she, in turn, took cues from us. She cried, as newborns do. She cried a lot. We were mildly crazed by trauma and intense fatigue. Something was spinning out in both of us. We gazed at each other as if at poorly drawn self-portraits, with a growing sense of both distance and dismay. Three days later, my milk had come in but I was engorged, exhausted—I couldn't get enough of the stuff into the tyke's little maw. Mid-morning, the midwife manhandled my breasts, kneading and pinching, and my husband, overzealous with concern, took cues. I finally began to understand the expression, "Get off my tits." In the afternoon, we discovered the dehumidifier, a white noise maker that lulled the baby into slumber, however short-lived. That night, the baby would not stop wailing, mewing, and writhing in her bassinet. My husband lifted her in her bassinet. We were on the second floor of my mother's house; the dehumidifier was in the basement. He carried her down the stairs. I was half-awake, advised not to walk much, never mind run, so sore and slow.

But I knew he would drop her before he did. I took that first flight of stairs like a champion—all long strides and unselfconscious leaps—and I watched as one of the bassinet's handles slipped from his hand at the top of the basement flight, watched as it happened, the baby rolling, little well-swaddled sausage, bump, bump, down three stairs, coming to a soft thudding stop on the landing. Not crying now. And she was in my arms, on my breast, lips latched like a lock around a key. At the hospital, they pronounced her unscathed, but a bit yellow. Monitor the jaundice, they said. And, they said, wake her up every two hours. To be safe. They used the word concussion. And suddenly I was a mama bear gone mental, claws bared, where before I was merely a wrung-out, strung-out human. I was moody, possessive, unrepentant. I had trouble letting my husband touch our child.

For weeks afterward, I refused to let him carry her up or down stairs. We spun further out and away from each other. There was a terrible murk between us; it was a recipe for mistrust and misfired remarks. The unabated shock of the baby's continued vulnerability and my pointed lack of confidence in my husband's parenting abilities helped send him spiralling downward—plus his own father left when he was four and was generally crummy in the dad department, unreliable, absent. He was beset with doubts. Then there were the practicalities of tending to a baby: the hand offs and jigglings and bum changings and bathings. Oh, the feedings. The skewed biological reality of it all; I had the boobs. I wanted him to do more but I wouldn't let him do anything. He became angry, withdrawn.

We forgot how to be kind to each other.

I couldn't give him what he needed most: the trust that would allow him to grow into being a dad, the assurance and reassurance that he was a good father. He was too distraught to comfort me or encourage my nascent motherly efforts. But we didn't tell each other any of this; we couldn't see it, wouldn't know what to do with it if we could. He fell into a postpartum depression that culminated in an early-morning confession of suicidal thoughts. The baby was crying and we were crying, too. The peak of the crisis was a relief in many ways; we began to discuss ways of moving forward. But the earth still turned, the baby still cried, the nights still rose up, sleepless shifts of darkness in every sense.

I was so tired I could not put coherent sentences together. Sometimes I unwittingly swapped words like "recreation" for "consternation": a strange, perhaps Freudian, conversational dyslexia at play. The baby—so uncooperative!—didn't understand the concept of napping. You must sleep when the baby sleeps, went the chorus of the well-meaning. Except the baby would only sleep when I was holding or pushing her in her stroller, like a royal, along stretches of Bloor Street. It is possible I did not trust myself to venture off this main artery—how would I find my way back again? It is also possible my brain was having difficulty giving orders that extended beyond the impulse toward a certain staggering forward locomotion. The truth is that even when I had a moment or three to myself, the prospect of sleep was so foreign, my bond with my baby so solipsistic and all-consuming, I could only lie awake creating disaster narratives, pining for her as if she had been kidnapped by hostiles, when in reality she was being lovingly lullabied by responsible blood relations in the room down the hall. I hesitate still to use the term post-traumatic stress disorder; it seems a designation best reserved for those who have endured awful losses, witnessed horrible atrocities. I gave birth to a healthy baby in a well-equipped hospital in a developed country, loved ones by my side. What was the matter with me?

I went twice to the emergency room with unbearable stomach cramps. There are gallstones in my family; I yearned for a corresponding diagnosis. Imagine: a few days alone in hospital, cooing nurses on call to tend to my various hurts. Out with the gallbladder! But it was only my heart and head in disarray, my gut a sympathetic cousin; there was nothing "wrong."

Double Dare

When, a little over two years later, I got pregnant again, it was a mistake, an accident, a surprise. A whoops! baby is the cutesy name for it. But there is nothing cute about an unwanted pregnancy. We had talked about another child in an abstract, tentative-yet-positive way, but there was never any orchestrated intent; instead a slip-up, a just-this-once, a gamble.

I was frightened by the baby growing inside of me, the prospect of the birth, the loss of control, but mostly I was frightened by what another baby — days and nights of frazzled repetition, the journey from bed to rocker to couch to stroller — would do to my relationship with my husband, how we would, if we could, weather this particular unpredictable storm.

I considered having an abortion. How selfish and irresponsible —adding an erasure to a fuck-up!—especially considering that, at the time, I had two friends trying desperately to conceive. And in the last few months miscarriages had been blooming secretly around me, the fact of them muffled by the hush of convention—such cloistered, terrible losses. I had no right to end this pregnancy.

But, in the end, the decision did not come down to the baby itself. (And semantics and diction are important here; at this point it was most definitely still an "it," a problem to be solved—as was my first child when she was wedged in the birth canal. "Get it out," I screamed. Except I didn't, I'm told. But the phrase scrolled like an electronic news banner across my mind's eye, somehow louder and more urgent than any voiced imperative.)

You see, it was not a good time. The resentment that had fomented between my husband and me after No. 1 had receded. I had returned to work; my husband was a full-time stay-at-home dad, which tipped and then evened the domestic chore balance. We were filling out our mother and father shapes in the world. I finally had time to rock back on my heels and take a good hard look at my life; I had dreaming and writing space. Oh, we should have known better. We were on the brink of forty—certainly old enough to know better. So why didn't we? Any therapist, indeed, any friend worth her salt, will tell you that a baby is never a solution—not to marital strife, to feeling lovelorn, lost, or lonely. A baby, once born, is purely and stubbornly—actively, even—herself.

And yet.

We found ourselves grappling with this perhaps most fundamental and mysterious intersection of biology, emotion, instinct, and great, complicated need. I know it is easy to find pattern and purpose retro-spectively, from the distance a measured articulation of experience and emotion affords. Still, I hope you will not think me old fashioned or twee if I say it's possible there was something beyond our ken at work in this conception.

But, at the time, what it came down to was choosing the lesser of the evils. Evils? Did I just call my baby-to-be evil? This deserves censure or at least bears discussion. And how sacrilegious it seems, now, to record these thoughts. The baby is ten months old. She is the most remarkable of children. I say this, safely ensconced in my mother pod, shooting out indiscriminate lasers of love. Her birth was intervention-free and quick, as these things go. The baby is good-natured, calm, and serene. An observer, but also a joker. Sometimes she "laughs," heh, heh, heh, not because she finds anything funny but because she anticipates the effect—she can read an audience. The girl elicits joy, deliberately. Showbiz (yet somehow achingly sincere) smile, sumo thighs. An Olympic-calibre cuddler, she naps as though it is a task she has been paid handsomely to perform. When she's sick (rare), her attitude is wry and apologetic: Oh God, what a drag sometimes, this being mortal. But let's endure, shall we? Wise, wise eyes, people (strangers!) remark. But all this we were not to know.

Instead: how would we manage post-abortion at this juncture in our lives, in our relationship? What if we couldn't have another child? What kind of hauntings and recriminations would the decision entail? Easier, no, to give birth, to create, than to destroy? Maybe. How were we to know? Becoming a parent means striking a wager with the gods and goddesses; it is truth, dare, double dare. We decided to have the baby. It was not an easy decision, but it was a decision. As I am writing this, Canada has a prime minister who would prefer this decision were not mine to make. South of us, in the US, women are facing draconian limitations on their access to safe and hassle-free abortions. In other parts of our small, small world, women give birth, against their will, to children they cannot care for, at the expense of their own health (physical and mental), their own families.

A couple of weeks ago, I was walking down the main drag in my comfortably middle-class neighbourhood with my youngest strapped to me in her ergo dynamic carrier, my husband by my side pushing our oldest in the stroller. We were eating ice cream. I was trying to maneuver some of my Very Berry into the baby's mouth without slowing or slipping when we noticed a ruckus up ahead. It was a small but vocal pro-choice demo in front of the local Roman Catholic church on the opposite side of the road. We stopped for a few minutes to observe. We wondered aloud at the impetus for the protestors, but we made no move, tethered as we were to our offspring, to our trajectory, to approach them. Still, I'd like to think we conveyed something more respectful than gawking. When we started up again, we passed an old woman who gazed at the cherub on my person, the ice-cream-covered urchin in the stroller, then toward the slogan-chanters and placard-wielders on the other side of what she imagined was an unbroken divide. She gestured toward the demonstrators then, smiled at me inclusively, making us a team. "You don't need them, dear, do you?" she queried, although it was not a question, not really.

It took me too long to grasp her intent, plus I am often slow to speak at pivotal junctures. "Oh yes, she does," said my husband. And we walked on.

(Promise to Repeat)

The mothers I know often play up their small ineptitudes, the extent of their not-knowing. It is easier than acknowledging—out loud—the terrifying depths of our ignorance, the multitude of mistakes we have made or nearly made, and the transcendent satisfaction and pleasure (yep, I said it) of caring for a child. The trend instead is toward a certain gross-out honesty—a "come join me here in the trenches" mordancy ("I just let her chew on the stroller tire!"), which, although funny and often a welcome release, leaves out the deeper resonances and rewards of being a mother and co-parent. Why is this? Because it's hard to put your finger on the glint of joy in the dirty dishwater of drudgery. It slips away, seems a trick of light, impossible to photograph, let alone articulate. It demands a polite repression or a full-on saccharine aww-fest.

At about the four-month mark, my model second child went through a rocky period, difficult to settle. I had been spoiled; I had forgotten what to do with a baby resistant to routine, to textbook soothing strategies. And then one day, it came to me in a moment of well, duh enlightenment. I just had to be there with her—count to six or seven thousand in my head while I rocked, gazing into her deep, darkling eyes. I was speaking about this to my sister one afternoon, walking through a park in midtown Toronto. I explained that once I let go of my expectations, something strange happened. I was singing to the baby—a song our father, dead now for fifteen years, had sung to us—when I felt him streaming through her. She looks like him, it's true—same rascally squint to the eyes, pointy chin that offsets the chub of the cheeks—but this was different; his presence was so powerfully large in the room. I told her the story, haltingly, averting my eyes. Then I said the only thing I could come up with as closing gambit, snorting a little in apologetic prelude: "Kinda weird to be breast-feeding your dad."

Sometimes I think we talk this way—in hey, what can you do? shrugs or sarcastic aphorisms—to keep ourselves from proselytizing. Motherhood must seem the most irritating of cults when viewed from certain outside angles. I mean, really, who can abide a convert?

And sometimes I think it is easier than trying to explain—or perhaps exclaim—how much we actually, miraculously, have learned. We should have known better but we didn't. Except that, maybe now, for an instant, or a lifetime, we do. Or perhaps we know deeper—our children, our partners, the world, our very selves.

People warned me; they said two is more than double the work. Things are not always rosy at our house, but for us, two has been much more than double the recompense. It would not be inaccurate to say our second child cured us in important ways, made us a different kind of family, stronger, more flexible and resilient.

Am I a more relaxed mother the second time around? Is my husband a less freaked-out father? Are we better parents? Yes and no. True, we have experience on our side, but, on the other hand, we have experience on our side. My oldest, almost four now, is, in general, quiet, sweet, and open. She mostly sleeps through the night. She's crazy about gardening and literally stops to smell the roses whenever the opportunity presents. She adores her little sister and very rarely sits on her "accidentally." Those first few months we spent together as a family feel so far away: a desert island populated by three castaways, veins coursing with hormones and history, a treasure map we'd go cross-eyed trying to decipher.

It has become cliché, and is perhaps gratuitous, to say our children teach us because, of course, their teaching is innocent, unwitting, and random, in no way purposeful. They undo and remake us in fundamental, accidental ways. But becoming parents for the second time—despite (or in deference to?) ourselves—allowed us a path to wholeness that had not existed before. And what is family—at its best—but an assemblage of people with wounds they help each other to heal?

Twin Selves

JULIE BOOKER

There's me under a crisp blue Tibetan sky, walking ahead of the jeep convoy on the plateau, getting some exercise before a long day of travel, before my hair, clothes, and fingernails gather the dusty road. I pass staring yaks, then a wandering nomad, a devout man with pads on his hands, in the middle of nowhere, prostrating with each step. There is a complete absence of sound. The snowy tips of distant mountains lift like surrender flags. Later, our jeeps drive through a Wild West town. Four headless, skinless sheep sit on their haunches as if in conversation with the butcher. Two men are asleep on open-air billiard tables along the main road. We head out to the plateau. The children come, stare as we struggle to light our fire and pitch our flimsy tents. They are a tableau of miniature outlaws: filthy, rosy-cheeked faces; colourful sweatpants, plaid shirts, fedoras; snot caked beneath their noses. They work up the courage to speak: "Dalai Lama Dalai Lama," wanting a banned photo of their exiled leader. Then: "Hello pen, Hello pen," until I give in and produce a ballpoint.

Years later, there's me rolling out flax-filled cookie dough in the kitchen in an apron, and the sun is shining down on the open recipe book, which I read in my leisure time for fun. I can hear the dryer tumbling downstairs, the boys' nonsensical gibberish in the living room, the plonk-plonk, battery-operated version of "Baa Baa Black Sheep." I contemplate mopping the floor before loading up the Tupperware with peeled and diced snacks for the double stroller ride, where they won't be able to see whether I'm angry or crying or blissfully happy. Or swearing as I kick recycling bins mid-sidewalk, muttering about wheelchair rights. Then I look up and it's that blue sky of Tibet. The same crisp cold suddenly settles upon me, like a page turning from across the world, reminding me to step with gratitude, grace.

I still can't believe I'm here. A mother of twins in my forties. Continually tripping over the foreign phrase "my kids." While the other me is still out there, hiking in some equally awe-inspiring, strange place.

Right out of university, I worked with children. Each day, exhausted, I said goodbye to my class of six-year-olds, goodbye to the place where family is everything, and went home to my tiny condo, fridge full of Diet Coke, a few condiments, two rolls of expired Kodak film. A fine layer of dust on the furniture. There were many good reasons not to have children. My lack of interest in anything domestic being one. Also: a lack of partner.

"Why haven't you met Mr. Right?" everyone asked. I realized my pulsing uterus was broadcasting a kind of neediness, attractive only to Mr. Wrong. I went underground and gave birth to Super Independent World Traveller Girl instead. What guy doesn't want to capture the free bird? After a few summer adventures in Australia, I found the courage to backpack alone for a year through Asia and Africa, always keeping an eye out for The One. Came home full of wanderlust pheromones, presenting firmly in the No-Kids camp. The inveterate single gal, collecting stories from around the world, dreaming only of getting published. A visit to a psychic revealed the seesaw star cluster on my birth chart was open to interpretation: a baby or a book, my life would be complete with either act of creation. Not exactly what I wanted to hear.

As my friends dropped into marriage, then kids, I tried not to resent how many showers I'd been to with no return on my investment. I took a few years off to make films at art college with twenty-three-year-old green-haired techno-whizzes whose films were devoid of content. To them, I was the middle-aged lady who wept in the editing room each time the computer "lost" her footage. I realized using a pen and paper was far easier. If I wasn't going to have kids, I'd damn well better write that book. I took another year off and wrote stories about women who don't get what they want.

Time ticked on. I'll buy me some sperm. But I imagined being alone and pregnant, and crying all the time. I pictured the absurdity of something expanding to the point of outgrowing its exit hole. How could I enjoy nine months knowing the inevitable painful finale?

So, in my late thirties, I had a brainwave: adoption. Each week, for three months, I took a bus, then a subway, then a long walk up a hill to the Children's Aid Society. Two-hour classes addressed every worst-case scenario, including drug-addicted birth mothers, fetal alcohol syndrome, attachment disorder. The class was full of what appeared to be supernaturally compassionate couples, many of whom were on their second adoption of a special-needs child. There was one other single woman; I was there to balance out the numbers. She was a lesbian with a wallet full of photos of her niece. She'd call the six-year-old on break and have high-pitched conversations that left me bored and feeling like a complete narcissist. We graduated with a binder heavier than the DSM-IV and an appointment for a home visit from a CAS worker. With my completed thirty-page medical/psychological/social/physical questionnaire on her lap, the lady looked around my condo and gestured toward the sunroom, swooping her hand to show where a curtain would need to be hung for the child's room. She said I was weeks away from being "presented," weeks away from being a mom. "But I have to be honest," she said. "I've written one word in my file: ambivalence." I breathed a sigh of relief.

I never told anyone I did this.

When I turned forty, my mother hooked me up with a Last Chance Man. He was perfect in every way: wealthy, nice car, good job, a pension. Except he was in his late fifties.

"I might still want kids," I whispered.

"What?" she said. "You don't want children."

That shocked me. As an eight-year-old, I compulsively carried around the smallest of the neighbourhood kids, forcing them into my doll carriage, barking orders at the boy-husbands. But I'd successfully fooled the world, including my mother, into thinking I chose childlessness. Finding the man was work enough.

Then, after years spent at singles club events, speed-dating-rock-climbing-line-dancing my way into some very painful blind dates, Boom.

He was forty-five. I was forty-two. We'd known each other from the neighbourhood for years, had often said hello in passing. Fate had finally put us in the same room. Him, a publisher, and me, in need of an opinion on a manuscript.

"Would you look at it for me?" I asked innocently.

He said: "Bring it by the house."

I heard: "If I wasn't interested in you. I would have said mail it."

I stepped on the elevator, already planning what I would wear for our "date." As the doors closed, he stood with his back to me, staring at an Alex Colville painting, the one with the horse running head-on into an approaching train.

He had no idea what was about to hit him.

We were both so astounded at getting together that we didn't dare wish for kids. We gave up birth control as a quiet gesture to the gods. Nothing. It seemed proof we'd waited too long.

Then my father had a party for his eightieth birthday. I made him a video. The theme: how my sister and I were witnesses to his life. There wasn't a dry eye in the room. My partner has very little family left, and on the drive home, our mortality hung heavy in the car. He asked the question we'd casually asked on and off for a year.

"Do you want to have kids?"

This time I said definitely, "Yes."

"Yes???" he said.

"Let's just get some help, go as far as we can, so we have no regrets."

At age forty-four, I gave birth to twin boys.

Seven months later, my first book came out.

Careful what you wish for.

. . .

I preface this with: I am truly, truly grateful. But I go in and out of full-blown grief.

I grieve the loss of that completely self-actualized woman climbing the Himalayas solo for a week with a backpack and a Sherpa who disappeared frequently to smoke pot. Who paddled the Zambezi River, a mere mile from Victoria Falls, continuously banging the kayak's hull to ward off hippos and crocs. Who walked across a landslide in China, her left foot shifting gravel into the roaring Yangtze thousands of metres below. This was Life Without Kids. I'd braced myself for the cold, hard upward climb and faced fear squarely. Come to trust myself and my instincts in the Big Bad World. Learned it's a Big Good World that takes care of you if you're paying attention.

All I'm paying attention to now is whether my shit-smearing son has his hand in his diaper again. Which means I'll have to return home weeping from my usually proud walk down the main drag ("oh aren't they cute") because he's painted the inside of his half of the stroller with excrement. Even overalls do not deter. A full-time neck-to-toe onesie, then. If he figures out the zipper, I'm sewing him into it. This is what I spend my time thinking about now.

I won't go into how hard it is. How it's as if I'm waterskiing at top speed, my skis have fallen off ages ago, and the driver hasn't looked back to notice. I won't say how many times a day I go through rage— internal tantrums—only to be tortured nightly by the sleepless tag-team of Thing One and Thing Two. How anciently tired my face feels. How I've almost put our house on the market twice, longing for A Simple Small Town Life. As if a big backyard with a fence could contain the chaos. How my capacity for discord, noise, mess, has grown beyond what I thought possible. How, after a lifetime of learning to take care of myself, I can't. How my partner has started wearing only white shirts, a new style decision that coincided with toddlerhood. He looks smart, you'd think, if you saw him before 9:00 a.m. Before a pasta-sauce handprint, a swiped-at glass of red wine, or a strawberry mouthprint on the left shoulder. An obvious act of denial. I can't blame him. I dream of checking into a hotel and lying starfish on a king-size bed, waiting for this tidal wave to end.

It's really fucking hard. The only people I can say this to are other parents. Twins means double the reason to complain. Double the reason not to complain if I'm talking to people without kids. They hear whining, regret, lack of gratitude. It's the Great Divide. I abandoned my comrades in the No-Kids Camp, shed my Hippie Independent Persona and leaped to The Other Side. And now I have to shut up about it. When I was single, I disliked mothers who disappeared inside their kids, unable to talk about anything else. I find myself downplaying how overwhelming and life-changing this is to women who seem bothered by my new role. I've had whole conversations with friends who never acknowledge the Tasmanian Devils round my feet, who only stop talking to let my kids' screams subside. I understand the need to ignore my passing to The Other Side. Sometimes I wish I could ignore it.

"Just get through the first three months," parents of multiples said. Then: "We lied. It's the first year that's hardest."

But we're on year two, and most days, I still feel I'm just getting through it.

Women with singletons look at me and say, "I can't imagine."

Neither can I.

I can't imagine what it is to take the time to tickle, coo, massage one baby until he signals play is over. I am in constant fight or flight mode; the minute one is content, the other starts. When I approach their cribs in the morning, they both scream, "Poo!" because they've decided that is the key word for being picked up first. The other one grabs at my shirt and holds on for dear life. When I pick him up, the other one hits, scratches, pushes him because he got chosen first. I look at women with singletons, imagine how they raise their child in a lovely bubble, imparting all their values before taking it for a test drive at the first play date. With twins, there is no preciousness.

I have learned to sip my coffee, while one boy pulls a bowl of fruit closer to himself and waits until his brother is reduced to tears. Then with an unmistakable poker face says, "Share." This is the boy who let his brother take every toy from him; right from the beginning, he showed no sense of possession. His gentle nature is now turning to techniques of psychological warfare. "The shy one." "The difficult one." Twins are known for seesawing roles throughout childhood.

I'm on my own seesaw. I find myself feeling a childless woman's shame in a room of moms. Or tearing up when a woman talks about needing a soulmate's hug at the end of the day. Or delighting at a want ad for the perfect bachelor apartment.

Because I am still that woman.

It could have gone either way.

But here I am, fighting green bins on the rainy sidewalk, screaming, "What the fuck?" at a car going too fast, too close to the wide stroller, a heavy guitar balanced on its canopy, late for the Mommy's Group Nursery Rhyme Jam Session. Calling forth bravery daily, in so not exotic locations.

My brain is now biologically hardwired to be afraid. It sees flashes: falls from playground climbers, heads pierced on coffee table edges. Breathing stops when I lose sight of one of the boys in the park. Even watching a stranger take off his glasses, his slightly myopic gaze in the private moment taken to wipe his lenses clear. The few seconds of vulnerability physically hurt. That man is someone's son. When one twin is diagnosed with a benign tumour on his eyelid that pushes his eyes in different directions, I see his whole difficult life ahead and can't stop crying.

This is the absolute worst thing about becoming a parent. The universe has revealed its sad, tragic, scary core. I always suspected I wasn't up for the job, the constant toughening required. I understand why people don't want kids.

The stress of trying to make this all work: the money, the patience, the sleep deprivation, the grandparents too old to babysit, the endless scrubbing down of poo-stained cribs, the eternal Cheerio trail behind bookcase and sofa, the ants and mice that have moved in because of it, the dual tantrums, the days I can't even get out the door.

Then I'm sitting on the floor of the playroom trying to referee a tug of war that includes advanced WWE holds, and suddenly, both boys crawl into my lap. My arms hold them, each teetering on a thigh, as I open their favourite book. A visual dictionary of all the things known. Ball, train, bath, red wagon. They take turns tapping on pictures so that I will say the word and sing a song associated with it. One leans over to kiss the other on the mouth. He giggles and pulls away. Then turns his lips up to mine. We pass the kiss around. I think, there's this. Everything else is to be gotten through. For now. There's this.

Dog Days

DIANA FITZGERALD BRYDEN

Early August. Liam and I are driving Virginia, our old dog, to the farm where she'll board for the rest of the summer. Liam, eleven, has known Virginia all his life. At fourteen, she's getting very near the end of hers; frail, she has a chronic limp and her muzzle and paws have turned white. I know from a close friend that she'll be well cared for here, but I worry she'll think we've abandoned her. I've never been a dog person, but I am now. Nor had I planned to have children, and here's where it gets complicated: this is not actually my dog, and Liam is not my child. And yet they're both mine, too, though it's more accurate to say that I am theirs.

This paradox reminds me of a long-ago encounter outside the Jewish cemetery in Prague. A young man approached me, pamphlets in hand: Miss, are you a Jew? Um...I hesitated, unsure how to explain, and he waved me off dismissively. A Jew always knows, he said, turning away. I found myself bridling defensively at his categorical certainty, as I have since at understandable assumptions about my identity as a childless woman in a common-law marriage. Jewishness; parenthood; wifedom: all of these, in my case—and I can't be the only one—are hard to define with a simple yes or no. It depends who's doing the defining, and how. After we left the dog that summer day,

Liam, who is my sister's youngest son, went away on holiday with his brother and parents; I with my husband. For much of Liam's life so far, I'm the person he's seen most. More than an aunt, different from a nanny, less than a mother: is there a word for what I am, for what my nephews are to me?

From a fairly young age, I resisted the idea that I would marry or have children. (As the daughter of one deeply ambivalent parent and a suicide, I doubted my emotional capacity, despite the loving example of my stepfather.) I was lucky enough to meet a kindred spirit who didn't judge me for my own ambivalence. My husband and I lived separately for at least ten years before we shared a home, and in twenty-two years together we've not felt the need to get legally married, though we live as husband and wife. He was up front about the fact that he didn't want children, in many ways a relief to me. We didn't entirely reject the possibility, but when I found out that I couldn't conceive, it wasn't the blow that it might have been—has been, for some of my friends—or so I've always thought.

When my sister was pregnant with Marcus, her first child, she asked if I'd consider leaving my part-time job to take care of him as a paid nanny when she went back to work. I'd have more time to write, and she and her husband could fulfill their demanding work schedules (as doctor and labour lawyer respectively) with peace of mind, leaving him with me. As well as the baby, there was a puppy: a rambunctious chocolate Lab. Thirteen years, two boys, one ancient dog, and three-and-a-half books later, here I am, in a life that I never imagined.

It soon became obvious that this was not a job in the ordinary sense, and those early days of passionate, unforeseen childcare must have been unsettling for my husband. These weren't our children, after all, whom I talked and thought about non-stop when I came home at the end of each day; some Friday nights my separation from them was so painful I'd wake to find I'd been crying in my sleep. This wasn't the bargain my husband and I had made with each other, and our relationship was tested. Although I tried to balance and distinguish between my two lives, I was as consumed as any parent, and the idea of a self-contained job went up in smoke, much like the notion that I wasn't cut out for long-term commitment. You can't protect yourself from attachment—the hooks go in, and there you are, permanently caught.

The drive to the farm where Virginia will be staying takes us through the Hockley Valley, an intoxicating series of swooping hills that, judging from the signs listing speeding fines and penalties, are irresistible to road racers. Even at our sedate pace, they're exciting. Liam was carsick earlier but is fine now. The faint smell of vomit overlaid with disinfectant plays duelling banjos with the manure that fertilizes the lush fields outside. This summer has been dry, but apart from a few bleached patches of grass, you wouldn't know it. Liam is thrilled by the hawks that cruise above us, over the swaying trees and cornfields.

I've exchanged several e-mails with Anna, the farm-owner, and my impressions are confirmed when we meet. She's both practical and warm, the facilities even better than promised. As we talk about the boarding arrangements, she says, suddenly: I'm confused. Whose dog is Virginia? Well…she's my sister's, but I'm the one who spends most time with her. Liam is nodding. She's sort of Diana's and ours. A family dog, then, Anna says. No description begins to encompass everything Virginia means to me, or what she represents about my bond with my nephews. I start to tear up; I can see that she's anxious we're leaving her. When I kneel to give her a hug, her bones feel light. It's normal to be upset, Anna says, but she'll be fine. She pats my arm when I stand up, steers me away firmly, and there's nothing left for me and Liam to do but go back to the car and drive off. It's a day of mixed emotions, leaving Virginia but spending time alone with Liam, one of my favourite things to do. Listening to him talk, seeing how he examines the world—boys, I've learned, tend to reveal themselves sideways—it's in the quietest, most mundane moments together that I am rewarded by what I can only really think of as glimpses of soul.

I remember the day I left Marcus at daycare for the first time. There'd been a case of chicken pox and my sister, heavily pregnant with Liam, couldn't risk going inside. Marcus sobbed and held his arms out to me with a look on his face—incredulity at this astonishing betrayal—that I still find searing in memory. A daycare worker carried him away from me as he bawled my name. It's better if you go quickly, Yolanda, the administrator, told me afterwards, gently handing me a Kleenex in her office. It actually makes the separation easier for him, and he'll settle very soon once you've gone. I wanted to believe her but was only half-convinced. Don't small children and animals suffer from these temporary abandonments? Or do they help prepare them for worse, more permanent ones? And my raw guilt at leaving him—was that purely selfless? Or did it foreshadow something else: that when he gets older and I'm no longer his daily caregiver, the norms will re-establish themselves and I'll fall back into the role of aunt, not almost-mother. Who will be abandoned, then?

When Marcus was a baby and Virginia a manically exuberant puppy, I took both to the park near my sister's house. It's next to a hospital and a jail and has a steep slope running down to the edge of the Don Valley Parkway. On that day, as hospital workers and jail staff sat on the grass eating lunch, Marcus was strapped to my chest, facing the world from his secure harness. The fine curls on his head lifted themselves in the breeze, and he waggled his feet and hands in the warm air. I let

Virginia off the leash. I was training her with short periods of freedom rewarded by treats, and four times out of five this was enough to bring her back to me. Once in a while though she would cast a wild eye, sniff the air, and take off, sometimes for hours. Too late, I saw that wild-eyed look now.

As I ran after her, Marcus bouncing on my chest, I called out to people watching us, can you grab her? Please, she's completely friendly! Or words to that effect. It seems idiotic now. Why would anyone grab a strange dog on the assurance of a woman whose judgment is so clearly impaired? At some point in the chase, I came to my senses. Dog, baby, dog, baby. Right. The baby is the priority here. I stopped. Marcus hadn't clued in that there was any risk to this entertaining new behaviour, and thank Christ, I didn't trip and crush him beneath me. Eventually, Virginia got bored with the game and came back to us, and we went home safe and sound, but I was haunted by the feeling that a real mother would have handled things more competently.

Parents agonize about their mistakes and near misses. With the responsibility for my sister's children, there's another layer of guilt and remorse. She and her husband have entrusted them to my care, shown faith in my judgment. Look at all those close calls: in a moment of cranky inattention on my part, Marcus, before he can walk, rolls down the stairs, caught only just in time. Another time I shut his fingers in a drawer by mistake, both of us crying at the shock. A shouting match with Liam. I hate you! he screams. I lose my temper and hit Marcus when he almost brains his brother with a heavy object. He hits me back, reinforcing what any fool knows: you can't teach a child that violence is wrong by exercising violence yourself. There have been many nights when my failures repeat themselves in a shameful, unrelenting loop.

One dark winter day about five years ago, Marcus, Liam, and I combed the streets, looking for Virginia. More sedate in her middle age, she'd been seduced into old habits by the siren squeak of an unlatched gate. It was freezing cold and we searched in vain, calling and whistling and combing the alleyways behind her favourite haunts: restaurants and butcher shops and the garbage bins at the nearby jail and hospital. We finally gave up, the boys grumbling at her stupidity. When we got home, cold and depressed, there she was in the backyard, shivering and wagging her tail. A stranger had found and returned her to the address on her collar, shutting the gate properly this time. There was a message on the phone. Wow, Marcus said. That was nice of him, to bring her back to us. The way that "us" includes me is a sip of familiar, bittersweet happiness.

When I held Marcus for the first time in the hours after his birth, his closed eyes shuttling back and forth under scrunched-up lids, a frown between them, I had the feeling that I knew him already, that I recognized him. The depth of my attachment was immediately painful; still is. I was afraid that I might not be able to love my sister's second child as much. Liam, who reminds me so much of her when she was small—the same strong will and infuriating stubbornness, the same glorious capacity for empathy—has embedded himself in me. To say that I love him would be to understate the case. With Liam, most of my shameful moments have to do with struggles of will. I'm stubborn, too, and he has a hot temper of the kind that sometimes blinds you to your own best interest, and a sense of pride to match. He'll voluntarily go to bed without supper, too angry to eat. In a rage, he'll rip up his homework. He is still incapable of the strategic apology, a trait that I both admire and want to help him master, if only to spare him grief down the road. The disadvantage to not living in the same house: conflicts must stay unresolved sometimes. But on those days I won't leave without first telling him I love him, for both our sakes.

In the early years, in particular, the boundaries between all of us were almost too fluid; now that more distance has naturally asserted itself, it can be easy to underestimate the intensity of those days when I sometimes felt as if Liam and Marcus were my sons, too, so entwined were our lives. My brother-in-law often travelled for work, my sister sometimes needed help overnight or on a weekend, and I was already there most of the children's waking hours. A joke Liam made not long after he started to talk is symptomatic. One morning after I'd stayed over, my sister, the boys, and I were all sitting on the bed together. I'd borrowed a pair of my sister's pyjamas, and Liam suddenly pointed to us and said: "Two mummies! Mummy-mummy and Nanny-mummy!" I can't quite identify what I felt then: amusement, joy, and a darker feeling—a kind of deep-water longing.

Risky territory, to be so intensely connected to all aspects of a sibling's life. As children of a mother whose capacity to care for us was blunted by mental health problems and her own childhood neglect, my sister and I were extremely close. Unusual, perhaps, when you consider that while there are only three years between us, we are half-siblings (my birth father committed suicide when I was eleven months old, and my mother married not long afterwards the man who became my father). Because of circumstances my role as the oldest was more parental than sisterly, and that, of course, had its own set of complications. When my sister became ill and our younger brother free-fell into a rocky adolescence—both situations aggravated by our parents' divorce—I wasn't always up to the task. I left home early—let them down, I thought then, and still do sometimes, though it's easier for me to understand at this distance.

My sister's preternatural maturity was enhanced by her illness and recovery, and she has fought to keep our family, small and far-flung as it is, connected. In different ways, so have I. As we confront the usual demands of adulthood—our father's death, our brother's separation from his wife and children, the need to support our increasingly frail mother, marital ups and downs — it's clear that as a family we're committed to raising Liam and Marcus together. My sister often says how good it's been for them, to feel safe with me as well as their parents, to know different ways to live beyond the immediate nuclear circle. Our arrangement couldn't have worked without my husband's generosity and understanding. He says now that he's glad I've had this opportunity, that it was good for us, as well as for my sister and her family, and I believe him, though sometimes the level of my involvement has challenged both of us. I take the boys to their doctors' appointments, volunteer in their classrooms and attend their concerts, help with homework, pick them up from school when one of them has a nosebleed, drive them to camp, stay at their house when their parents go away (sometimes, though not recently, for ten days at a stretch), break up fights before (and sometimes after) they draw blood. Now that they're older, my husband suggests books and films that might interest them, offers a trip to the Grand Canyon to teach them about one of his passions: geology. They're curious about our life at home, and they sometimes stay over and gorge on video games or watch movies with us.

When my sister was contemplating a third child and asked whether I'd be in for the long haul again, I said no. I thought about it hard before I answered. My marriage and my separate life with my husband needed some attention, and I was relishing the freedom of longer writing hours; remembering those early days of constant interruption and blinding love, visceral engagement with the life of an infant as well as the attendant boredom, frustration, and fatigue, I knew I couldn't do it again. I think I would have held to that decision, though in the end it wasn't one I had to make.

As for the dog, she's become primarily my responsibility: vet visits, walks, and clean-up, most things apart from the actual bills. She's such a part of our lives—of my life with the boys—that it's hard to imagine what it will be like when she's gone. There have been near misses: I've rescued her twice from the Don River, and once, Liam and I were on our way to pick up Marcus from kindergarten when I saw Virginia had gashed open her side. A deep flesh wound, it looked ghastly. I ran across Gerrard Street Bridge to the vet with both boys in the double stroller. They were excited by the drama and curious about the vet's office, and while the vet was examining Virginia, we explored the premises, changed a diaper in the washroom upstairs, provoked the talking parrots into a comedy routine. Then, with the dog patched up, we went home at a much calmer pace.

The boys are familiar with the vet's office to the point of boredom now. Virginia has to be lifted up and down stairs, and Marcus is a teenager, Liam a self-possessed eleven-year-old. On snowy days I used to pull them both to daycare on a sled, and now Marcus is taller than I am and Liam can outwit me in an argument without too much difficulty. Our moments of physical affection have become almost unbearably precious. After an August apart, Liam surprises me with a five-minute hug; Marcus, who outweighs me by at least twenty pounds, will still sit on my knee to look at the computer. I know that will end soon, but I won't be the one to say so. Some of the emotion I attach to the dog surely has to do with this: the passage of time, and with it my own aging, the movement from inexperienced nanny to quasi-mother (and then, inevitably, to something closer to a conventional aunt), from fledgling poet to novelist. My nephews' growing up and, of course, away from me.

Marcus was envious when he heard from his brother about the trip to the dog farm. It's so cool, Liam said. And there's a place on the way home where you can buy homemade pies! Can I come with you next time? Marcus asked me. Of course. Fingers crossed that Virginia is OK when we all arrive back—at her age and level of frailty, that's not a given. But probably she'll be fine, for at least a little while longer. Now we go on our separate holidays, my boys and I—they with their parents, I with my husband—and in about a month we'll go together to pick up our dog and bring her home.

Doubleness Clarifies

KERRY CLARE

"Oddly, the epic confusion of my early years was not
caused but rather mitigated by immersion in two
languages: doubleness clarified the world....Every
object, every action, had an echo, an explanation."
— Carol Shields, *Unless*

My second pregnancy was so longed for that it seemed impossible
when it happened, that life could ever be this simple; imagine a person
who simply got what she desired. Except that I couldn't—imagine, that
is. So I imagined the likelihood of miscarriage instead, magnifying the
odds and agonizing about my powerlessness against them. Twenty-five
percent of pregnancies end in miscarriage, I'd learned, and with odds
like that, it seemed unfathomable that anyone gets born.

During my first pregnancy, seven years previously, those odds had
never registered. I was pregnant and didn't want to be, and nobody
trots out statistics then to demonstrate how early pregnancy is
tenuous anyway. No one will advise you to sleep it off, to lie down
for a week or two and let nature take its course. Instead, unwanted
pregnancy is a fate that seems sealed, a destiny threatening to devour
you. Motherhood, when you're pregnant and you don't want to be, is
the horrifying back of an enveloping black hole. Inevitable, except
(and thank goodness) that it isn't.

Everything I know about my abortion, I learned from the pregnancy I wanted. That gestation is dated not from conception, but from a woman's last period, for example, which means that any fetus is actually about two weeks younger than its mother's pregnancy. From poring over *What to Expect When You're Expecting*, I'd learn that the fetus I'd aborted had been little more than a centimetre long, which is a far cry from what pro-life propaganda photos had suggested. There was a heartbeat, yes, but it probably would have been undetectable if I'd looked for it, and the fetus had more in common physically with a tadpole than a human baby.

I learned that for the first twelve weeks, a woman really can be a little bit pregnant. Pregnant enough, of course, that she would be devastated if anything went wrong and if anything did go wrong, no doctor would be able to stop it. She's not pregnant enough to tell the world what she is expecting either, having to keep the news to herself because...and the explanation for this one is always lost on me.

Because it's really so likely that something will go wrong? And because when it does, that pregnancy will have to be a sad secret she carries around inside her forever and always? Isn't it strange and confusing the way that we have determined that early pregnancy is, in these cases, literally unremarkable?

It is only recently, and with a great deal of practise, that I have been able to say "abortion" in conversation without dropping my voice an octave and muttering in order for the word to be nearly inaudible. My aversion to the word has never been from shame but more from fear of offending others' sensibilities. Abortion is such a loaded term that has come to mean freedom to some and murder to others, always accompanied by its inflammatory rhetoric—the language of either/

or, before and after, good and evil—and I just didn't want to have that conversation.

The reality of abortion is nuanced, which won't be news to anybody who is familiar with the experience. The reality of abortion is also that there are a lot of people who are familiar with the experience—one-third of middle-aged women in Canada are reported to have had abortions, which suggests fewer offended sensibilities than I'd anticipated. And among these women, abortion exists on a spectrum of experience consisting of a million degrees.

It is essential for my purposes that you be able to imagine the desperation of being pregnant when you don't want to be, of what it is to be staring into that gaping black hole with everything you've ever worked and longed for lost inside it. I am aware that some people will find themselves more inclined to empathize with the six-week-old fetus in this matter, he or she (still indeterminate) about the size of a lentil, and whether such an inclination represents a terrific failure of imagination or an incredible imaginative leap, I'm still not entirely sure. But I'd like such a person to shake their convictions for just a moment or two.

A single thing can have two realities. A person can hold opposing thoughts in her head at once. A 2008 study showed that 61 percent of American women who terminated pregnancies were mothers already. It is possible that no one more than a mother can truly understand just what it is that a woman who has had an abortion has lost and gained.

During the year after my pregnancy and abortion, the novelist Hilary Mantel published the memoir *Giving Up the Ghost*, in which she addresses the health problems leading to her childlessness. I read her book and found myself struck by the notion of Catriona, named for the novel by Robert Louis Stevenson, the imagined daughter Mantel never had whose existence she would dream of for years and years. She writes, "[Children's] lives start long before birth, long before conception, and if they are aborted or miscarried or simply fail to materialise at all, they become ghosts within our lives."

It was the only script I'd found for processing my experience. I was living in England at the time, and in response to Mantel's Catriona, I took to writing terrible poetry about my own set of tiny ghostly footsteps echoing up and down the cobblestone streets. But I didn't believe a word of it.

My only regret was that I became pregnant in the first place. Of course, there was sadness, a sense that I'd lost something. My relationship had ended, and I wondered if I'd missed my chance to have a family. But then the timing was so wrong, and so were the people. I was also humbled by the experience of having come so close to my whole life going off the rails, and I'd been shattered by the shame and stigma of unplanned pregnancy, shame so profound that abortion had delivered me relief that it was over.

I'd always wanted to be a mother, still suspected I'd become one someday, but this pregnancy had never been about a baby. The fetus inside me was an abstraction, and, yes, my abortion would extinguish its potential personhood, but then potentiality is a theoretical thing and a pregnancy isn't.

I remember lying on the examination table shortly before my procedure, the nurse rubbing jelly on my (relatively) flat belly before waving her wand above me, the ultrasound dismissing my ulcer hypothesis for good. The nurse pointed out the fetus on the monitor, but the image was as abstract as ever, and I couldn't find anything recognizable in the noise of the screen, although all around me, the larger details were entirely familiar—the jelly, the wand, woman on a table. It was a scene I'd watched a thousand times in movies and on TV, but mine was such a lonely inversion of the story, and not the same at all.

With my second pregnancy, from the moment of my positive pregnancy test, everything was different. The fetus growing inside me was never anything but a baby. We'd been quietly dreaming of her for years, imagining the colour of her eyes, her hair, trying out a parade of hypothetical names. Five weeks into my pregnancy, I bought her a book and we started reading to her even though she hadn't yet developed ears. After six weeks, I noted the milestone, that I was more pregnant than I'd ever been, but also noticed that at six weeks' gestation, our baby was remarkably unsubstantial, invisible to the world. So much of my longing and love was already tied up in her being, and yet the fact of her personhood was still just an idea in the minds of her father and me, and to friends and family who loved her already, who were awaiting her arrival, still months away. A single thing can have two realities.

Doubleness clarified. I'd never doubted or regretted my decision to have an abortion, but as (to my great joy) my second pregnancy progressed, I became more sure than I'd ever been that my choice to terminate my pregnancy years before had been the right one. Pregnancy is hard, a complete occupation of one's body, from top (nine months of a runny nose) to bottom (leg cramps that woke me screaming in the night), plus all the more familiar symptoms. It's not something you want to enter into half-heartedly.

And then there is childbirth, the impossible agony of life with a newborn, and motherhood itself, which is an amazing and terrible story without an ending. When, years before, I'd stared into that black hole, I'd had not a clue about the specifics, but in experiencing them, I realized how right I'd been to turn away.

My daughter herself is also a testament to my choice. If I hadn't had an abortion, I would never have had her, this extraordinary creature who is so much more than I ever dreamed, a fierce and fantastic child whose actualness trumps potentiality every time. I would never have had our family either, to have been able to give my child a father who is the love of my life. Not to mention provide her with some financial stability and all its accompanying opportunities, a grown-up mother who was prepared for and wanting to embrace the role and hadn't had to sacrifice or compromise to get there.

When accused of selfishness in the face of all of this, I will plead guilty every time, without compunction. I stand by the dictum of Erica Jong, who wrote in her iconic novel *Fear of Flying*, "You did not have to apologize for wanting to own your own soul."

Undeniably, the fact of my unwanted pregnancy is unjust when one considers how many women struggle to conceive at all, but then justice has never had very much to do with reproduction. Some people would have considered it justice for me to continue with my first pregnancy, to raise a child I didn't want to have as a kind of penance for being a woman who has had sex. These people are ubiquitous, the sort who write things on Internet forums, like "If you open your legs, you slut, you should pay the price," and I really do wonder about anyone who values life so little that they'd invite a human being into the world to serve as someone's punishment.

But, yes, of course, I had other choices, or at least the one. I could have carried a child to term and then surrendered it for adoption, which always sounds like a simple solution to people who have never been pregnant, given birth, or surrendered a baby for adoption. I've been listening carefully, however, and I've discerned that there are few worse advocates for adoption than the birth mother, the trauma of whose experiences so often goes unspoken. In Lynn Coady's novel *Strange Heaven*, the young protagonist who has given up a baby reflects of that option, "Yes, but real human beings shouldn't have to go through that."

I concede, too, that mine was not one of the "good" abortions. I was not a victim of rape or incest, one of those worthy candidates who are always brought up when the abortion debate gets particularly heated. I was just a woman who got in trouble and was unwilling to make two (two!) failed forms of birth control define the rest of my life.

The notion of justice is a hard one to shake, though. I know that much of my anxiety during pregnancy resulted from a fear that justice would be dealt somehow, that I couldn't possibly be allowed to define my life on my terms, to stop one potential life and then go on to create another. Reproductive freedom remains a revolutionary thing for a woman to get away with.

On Mother's Day in 2011, I found myself standing with my husband and daughter outside a storefront around the corner from my house, the site of abortion-rights pioneer Dr. Henry Morgentaler's clinic until its firebombing in 1992. My daughter was just a couple of weeks away from turning two, and I carried her in a backpack. She was too little to understand what was going on but was happy enough to be out in the fresh air and sunshine, a Holly Hobbie silhouette in her giant red hat.

We were taking part in the Pro-Choice Jane's Walk, one of a number of events held around our city that day in honour of urban activist Jane Jacobs. It was an illuminating exercise—I'd walked by 85 Harbord

Street hundreds of times, but I'd never realized its significance, that just ten years before my own abortion, such a terrible act of violence had taken place on my own turf. I hadn't known how wrong I'd been to ever take my access to abortion for granted, which I'd only ever done because it seemed absurd that the decision of whether or not to continue with my pregnancy would have been anyone's to make but mine.

Once again, please imagine the desperation of being pregnant when you don't want to be. Our tour continued on to the University of Toronto Faculty of Law, where we were read testimony by an abortion doctor on the carnage he witnessed in emergency rooms as a medical student in the 1960s, when entire hospital wards were devoted to septic obstetrics. And it occurred to me then that there was nothing I wouldn't have done to end my unwanted pregnancy, that my desperation had been just the same as that of all those women who'd had unsterile elm bark slipped through their cervixes to induce abortion, but that I hadn't had to kill myself in order to relieve it.

Our group wandered through the university campus, underneath the leafy canopy of Queens Park, the very same trees I've walked under on ordinary days. The symbolism wasn't lost on me, the discovery that all my usual routes were lined with pro-choice landmarks and it was appropriate, too, that it would be on Mother's Day that we'd note them. The choice I'd had the freedom to make nine years before had permitted me to become the mother I wanted to be, and it was this freedom that made motherhood worth celebrating in the first place.

If I could, I would give my daughter the gift of immersion in two languages, but English is the only one I have to offer. So instead I take care to pass along English in all its richness, to ensure she understands the wondrous variety afforded by synonyms, that she is a beneficiary of variations between my Canadian-English and her father's British-English speech. We say *tomay-to* and *tomah-to*, though she refuses to eat either. She knows that in England, a cookie is a biscuit, a trunk is a boot, a boot is a wellington, and a sweater is a jumper. Already, she knows well that a single thing can have two realities.

Doubleness clarifies the world, and I want my daughter to know this world in all its complexity. And so one day I will tell her about what happened to me a long time ago, a worthwhile story for any young woman to carry in her arsenal, I think. And my hope is that she will see how the story has nothing to do with her at all, but also the many ways in which it has to do with everything.

Unwed, Not Dead

MYRL COULTER

In the spring of 1967, my boyfriend and I went to the prom. The theme was tropical. I can still see the fake palm trees standing in the corners of our high school gym. I can see them because they're in the background of the picture I still have, my boyfriend in his skinny brown suit, me wearing a very unnatural hairdo and a fuchsia pink gown that my mother made for me. On the left shoulder of my dress, a yellow corsage is pinned to the shiny smooth satin. Other than those recorded details, I don't remember much more about prom night: we went, we stayed up late. We weren't into drugs, though we probably drank beer, maybe even some lemon gin. I vaguely remember that we borrowed a boat and went for a ride on the Red River in the middle of the night.

And then it was summer. The summer of 1967 is often referred to as the summer of love. Against a backdrop of violence across the globe, hippie counterculture in North America flourished. Bead-wearing, flower-bearing, long-haired young people flocked to San Francisco, New York, Toronto, Montreal, Vancouver—any place they could find revolution, alternative living, communal love, creative expression, and sexual freedom.

In Winnipeg, many people were caught up in the excitement of hosting the Pan-American Games. I hardly noticed the games were happening, although I think I did go to one swimming event. I worked my shifts at Safeway, went out with my boyfriend, hung out with my friends, and played my little transistor radio non-stop. "Shakin' All Over" still played regularly on local radio stations. I know all the words by heart even today. My music that summer was all about love: "All You Need is Love" sang my favourite band; "To Love Somebody" sang the Bee Gees; "Light My Fire" sang Jim Morrison and the Doors; "Let's Spend the Night Together" sang the Rolling Stones.

For my friends and me, love was the theme of our summer. The adult community around us left us pretty much alone. As long as we showed up for our part-time jobs and didn't cause any trouble, we could do anything we wanted. So we did. My boyfriend had moved out of his parents' house into a basement apartment he shared with a friend. My memory is somewhat fuzzy here, but I think that's where we finally had sex, on a little bed in that apartment. Afterwards, I do remember being puzzled about what all the fuss was about. I wasn't even certain we really had "gone all the way." If we had, I thought (and kept this thought to myself), this thing called sex was a little disappointing. I know we did it several more times, but I don't really remember how many. I know that I liked lying beside him afterwards, but I don't recall what we said to each other. What I do remember, vividly, is that by the time summer was over, by the time the leaves had started to change colour, by the time I walked across the stage at my high school gymnasium to receive my diploma that fall, I knew I had a problem. I was, to use an often-heard euphemism, a girl "in trouble."

I didn't tell anyone for a while. Then I told my boyfriend. We walked around for a few weeks hoping it wasn't true. When I finally confessed to my mother, she accepted my news with dismay. After a few days of thundering silence, my parents called me into the living room to talk about it. What were they to do? I couldn't stay at home during my pregnancy. They had my brother and sisters to consider. Besides, what would the neighbours think? I already knew that asking to have my baby come into our family was out of the question. By this time, it was obvious to me that my parents were struggling, almost overwhelmed with five children and limited financial resources. My sense was that they were waiting for some of their kids (starting with me) to move out of the house, not to have more move in.

One thing my parents were very clear about was that they didn't want me to get married. They hadn't been too sure how much they liked my new boyfriend before this; they certainly liked him a lot less now. More than that, however, a sudden marriage would have meant public shame. The neighbours wouldn't have to speculate about anything; they would know. A wedding would also have meant that my parents would have to tell my grandparents about my condition, and I don't think either one of them could face that: the furrowed brows, the rigid disapproval, the silent reprimands for failing as parents.

In the midst of all this uncertainty, I did my best not to think about my situation. Mostly I tried not to think about my baby. My youngest sister was only four years old. From the time I had spent looking after her, I knew that I could care for and love a baby, but I was afraid to let myself feel too much love for the one growing inside me. In the days and weeks after our conference in the living room, my parents said little to me. An uneasy silence settled around the household. My mother sighed a lot. My father wasn't home very much. Soon I realized that I was going to have to come up with a solution myself.

Unmarried women did not keep their babies in the sixties. I was to discover during the next year that any young woman in my situation who dared to say that she might keep her baby was immediately discouraged from doing so. Whether from a parent, a doctor, or a social worker, the message was always the same: you have nothing to offer a child; you're not ready to be a mother; you're being selfish; you'll be ruining his or her chances for a good life; you'll have more children when you're ready; you'll forget all about this one.

Underlying these professional words of advice was also the tacit suggestion that an unmarried teenaged girl who was pregnant either lacked good moral character or was psychologically deficient, or both. So, in the absence of encouragement from our families and our communities to keep our babies, those of us who found ourselves pregnant and unwed had three choices. One was to get married. Another was to find someone to perform an illegal abortion. The third choice was to have the baby and surrender it to an adoptive family, a properly married couple whose marriage license gave them instant credibility as parents.

By the end of summer, I had started a job with a bank in downtown Winnipeg. Being young and healthy, my pregnancy didn't show for several months. When my belly began to protrude a little, fashion was on my side. The tent dress was in. My mother had mentored me into a pretty good seamstress, so I made myself a couple of big billowy dresses to wear to my clerking job on Portage Avenue, not far from its windy intersection with Main Street.

Travelling back and forth to work on the bus each day, I would think about my dilemma. While I was somewhat curious about what it would be like to be a married woman, I didn't particularly want to get married. I was only eighteen. When I thought about marriage, I saw my parents' difficult relationship, saw how my father's frequent absences left my mother angry and resentful. I thought about standing in the kitchen drying the dishes after my mother washed them, all the while muttering to herself through clenched teeth: "if it wasn't for you kids…" I thought about my father coming home many nights looking tired, only to be greeted by a horde of clamouring, sometimes cranky, kids and their fuming mother. Marriage, as far as I could see, wasn't much fun for either the husband or the wife.

I didn't think long on the abortion option. Although it would be removed from the Criminal Code in 1969, abortion was still illegal in Canada in 1968. My friends and I had all heard horror stories about botched abortions and internal injuries inflicted with knitting needles. When I imagined searching for a doctor to perform an abortion, I saw a dark alley, a sly exchange of cash, a dirty back room, and an unshaven smelly man wielding menacing tools. As little as I knew about myself at that time, I knew one thing for sure: I was a coward. I didn't want to get an abortion—didn't even like to think about it.

My aversion to abortion was more than just being terrified about the process itself. I also knew that I didn't want to harm the little life growing inside me. I wanted to do everything I could to make sure that my baby was born healthy. I didn't realize at the time that I was already feeling what my society was convinced I couldn't offer my child: maternal love.

Uncomfortable at home, I walked a lot in those days, sometimes by myself, sometimes with a girlfriend, often with my boyfriend. He didn't like coming around our house much anymore, though it wasn't until years later that I learned why. One day, he rang our doorbell. My mother answered, slapped him across the face, and slammed the door shut. For the next few months, he and I would meet somewhere and roam the streets of our neighbourhood, talking about the lives we saw spanning out in front of us, about what we wanted out of them, and sometimes about what we should do about our dilemma.

I remember that we talked around the pregnancy a lot, instead of directly about it. But one night, we did speculate about just taking off and getting married, despite my parents' opposition. At the end of that walk, I thought we'd decided that was what we were going to do. But neither of us ever brought up the subject of marriage again. I suppose if I'd insisted he marry me, he would have, but I wasn't about to trap anyone. I suppose if he'd insisted I marry him, I would have, but he was probably as confused as I was about marriage and what he could offer a child.

There was another option I knew nothing about at the time. Sometime during the first few months of my pregnancy, my boyfriend's parents came to our house to meet with my parents. When they offered to take my baby and raise it themselves, my parents stood up and asked them to leave. I don't know why my parents reacted that way. I hope that my contribution to that conversation, had I been included in it, would have been to point out that I was my baby's mother, that we were a package deal. But I don't know. I might not have been strong enough to say that to a roomful of angry adults. I will never know what went through my parents' minds that night. My father is gone now, and except for one tension-filled conversation years later, my mother has steadfastly refused to talk about that time in our lives.

So I was left with one choice: adoption. In the fifties and the sixties, adoptions were predominantly managed through the closed adoption system, a process premised largely on silence and secrecy. Before World War II, maternity homes and social workers involved in adoption at least made small attempts to work toward keeping single mothers and their babies together by offering young women shelter before and after their babies were born, offering them a place to bond with their babies, offering them time to consider the consequences of their decision.

As cultural paradigms congealed into the rigid model of the ideal middle-class family after the end of World War II, the attitudes of social agencies and maternity homes changed. Girls like me were not young women who needed a helping hand. Instead, we were seen as somehow delinquent and definitely unfit as mothers. The focus of social agencies became one of securing babies for those ideal middle-class couples who were struggling to conform to the modern model of family but couldn't because of infertility. For married couples seeking children they couldn't have, the closed adoption system provided babies along with a guarantee that the biological parents would never be heard from again. For the families of unwed mothers, the closed adoption system provided a way to avoid social stigma. On the surface, the system seemed to offer them a rational solution, a way out of a difficult situation. No one noticed how rooted it was in rigid, even irrational, notions about what families should look like.

I didn't think about these social and cultural contexts at the time. Caught in an untenable situation, in a bed of my own making as my mother reminded me the few times she actually spoke to me about it, I didn't know I could insist on different options, that I could insist on my rights as a mother-to-be, that I should expect support instead of silent condemnation from both my family and my community at large. Those things never crossed my mind. So, on a crisp winter day, having quietly resigned my job at the bank, my tent dresses no longer hiding my condition, I slipped into one of those mid-century relics, a maternity home.

To call these places maternity homes is highly ironic: maternity homes were not homes nor did they function to promote maternity. They were institutions to house and hide those deemed maternally inappropriate. Also known as homes for unwed mothers, they were busy places in those days. Winnipeg, a small city, had three. I didn't know their exact locations, but I knew they were out there somewhere. Teenage pregnancies were a bit of an epidemic at the time. Much unofficial information about these mysterious foreboding places floated around my circle of friends.

The one I served my time in was not dingy and dank, but clinically clean and tolerable, with a cool, no-nonsense atmosphere. I'd been expecting a brooding old place, something creepy, dark, and gothic. Instead, I found myself in a fairly new building, low and sleek in mid-century modern style. Located on a secondary highway on the outskirts of Winnipeg, safely on the opposite side of the city from my neighbourhood, it was secluded, the building set well back from the main road on a small plot of land surrounded by trees.

Sparsely furnished throughout, the main wing had a common room with a number of sitting areas, a dining area with several big round tables, and a spacious kitchen where we all pitched in to prepare the meals. The bedroom wing featured rooms with two single beds and a big common washroom at the end of the hall. A roster sheet was posted on a bulletin board assigning domestic chores to each girl, more rigorous ones like vacuuming and cleaning bathrooms to the newer arrivals, lighter ones like dusting to those further along in their pregnancies.

Although I certainly felt lonely, once I settled in, I also felt relief. I was able to relax there somewhat, to recover from the stress of hiding my growing belly, of avoiding friends and family. During the four months I spent at the maternity home, my outings were few. My boyfriend worked a lot of hours because he was paying for my room and board. But he came to visit me about once a week, borrowing his best friend's car to take me out for a drive after dark. Occasionally we went to a drive-in movie.

One day I received a parcel in the mail. It was from my boyfriend's mother. She sent me a pretty nightgown and a few other small items. Included was a short note hoping that I was doing well. I was pleased with this unexpected gift from the outside world. I hope I sent her a thank-you note. I never was very good at writing those, despite my mother's efforts to train me.

During my four-month residency at the home, I rarely saw my parents. They drove out one Sunday afternoon to see me, but they wouldn't come inside the building — even though it had a large comfortable room for such visits. They sat in the car while I stood wrapped in a big borrowed coat and talked to them through the window. One of my sisters thinks that she and all my other siblings were in the back seat, but she's not certain and I don't remember. It's entirely possible that they were all out for the family's customary Sunday afternoon drive.

My parents were not cold and unfeeling. I know that they felt my situation deeply. The way they dealt with it was deft avoidance. They told any family and friends who noticed my absence that I was away on a trip and just hoped no one would ask too many questions.

For the most part, the maternity home staff (to us, they were "den mothers") were distantly pleasant to the inmates, as we jokingly referred to ourselves. One exception was a part-time den mother who lived nearby and often invited the girls to come to her house for coffee and games. Sympathetic to our plight, she was at ease with us, non-judgmental in both her words and her actions. We liked the nights when she was on duty.

Although the home discouraged too much familiarity among its residents, most of us became instant friends. We laughed a lot. The prevailing public image of an unwed mother was of a bad girl who should hang her head low, acknowledge her shame, and adopt an attitude of atonement for her lapse in character. I never felt that image had anything to do with me, and I don't think the other girls did either. As far as we were concerned, in a rigid social order filled with inequities, double standards, and conflicting messages, we were just the ones who got caught.

As we served our time banished from our communities, we created moments of fun, playing pranks on one another, forming strong alliances. We took long walks down the rural highway nearby, preferring to think of ourselves as exiles, not prisoners. To wile away the evenings, we sat together in the front room. As we chatted, we kept our hands busy by knitting, making crazy-long scarves for our friends, instead of booties and bonnets for our babies. I remember some of us sitting in that room one evening when the den mother on duty scolded a girl she had caught in a passionate embrace with her boyfriend at the front door. The girl responded with a fiery "I'm unwed, not dead," and stomped off down the hall. We all turned away to hide our grins and that phrase became our shared mantra.

We shared our stories and our fears with each other. Very few of us knew much about what was going to happen to us during labour and delivery. The home provided some instruction—in the form of pictures in medical books about the birthing process. The staff told us to direct any questions we had to the home's doctor, a man who made weekly visits to see us so that we didn't have to expose ourselves to public scrutiny going to his office. Although he was a kind man who said we could ask him anything, most of us were either too uncomfortable to give voice to any questions we did have or didn't know what questions we should be asking. As a result, anything we learned about what was going to happen to our bodies usually came from each other.

Despite my relative comfort, the months dragged by. It felt as if winter was reluctant to give in to spring that year. My due date came and went. No baby. One week passed. I paced up and down the hall day and night. Another week passed. Still no baby. I began to think pregnancy was to become my permanent condition.

When I finally went into labour late one night early in May, only one den mother was on duty at the home so she sent me to the hospital in a taxi by myself. Once admitted to the maternity ward, I spent my time in the labour room alone. At first, the contractions were quite mild and I was fairly calm. Nurses, busy and officious, came in to check on me. Eventually, the pains became more intense, closer together, and then pounded right on top of each other. Suddenly, a host of nurses appeared in my room, focused intently on my body but somehow not on me.

When they wheeled me to the delivery room, I grew frightened and began to cry. Very quickly, my crying turned into screams of panic. The nurses tried to calm me down. Then the doctor arrived, a man I had never seen before. He didn't speak to me but did ask the nurses what all the fuss was about. One nurse replied that I was "one of those unwed mothers from the home." "Well," he said, "just put her out and let's get on with it." (As strange as it seems now, back in the sixties, most North American women gave birth while under a general anesthetic.)

When I woke up, all was calm and I was on a stretcher. The doctor was nowhere in sight, but several nurses still bustled around me. "What happened?" I asked. "You had a little boy," they said. "Is he all right?" I asked. "Yes, he's fine," they said. "Can I see him?" I asked. "No, that's not wise," they said.

The next day, I wandered the halls until I found the nursery. I looked in all the nursery windows until I saw my name written on the end of a bassinet, a beautiful baby boy sleeping peacefully inside it.

I wasn't supposed to hold my baby, much less feed him. Every day, when the nurses brought hungry babies to the three other mothers in my room, I left and went down the hall to stand at the nursery window. For the next five days—a routine postpartum hospital stay in the sixties—this was what I did.

The day before I left the hospital, a nurse came to me and said that I had to give my son a name. They needed it for their paperwork. But every time I thought about naming my baby, my mind shut down. Finally faced with the moment, I stalled for a few minutes. I asked the nurse why I had to name him when he wasn't going to be mine. She gave me a stern look that I can still see. I don't know whether she actually said these words but in my memory I hear them: "You don't even want to give him a name?"

I did want to name my son. Even though I knew the family who adopted him would change it, I wanted to give him a good name, a name from me that boded well for him. During my pregnancy, I hadn't let myself think about names. I hadn't let myself think of a he or a she; I didn't want any little girl or little boy faces coming into my mind. So I called my baby "Bump." When I patted my belly, I patted "Bump." Sometimes when I lay awake in bed late at night, I talked quietly to "Bump"; sometimes "Bump" would respond with a kick.

But the nurse standing in front of me with a paper form dangling from her hand was not going to accept "Bump" as a name. I had only a few minutes to come up with something good enough for a baby I would never see again, a baby who would probably never know what names I chose for him. Looking down at the hospital bands around my wrist, I noticed the delivery room doctor's last name. I asked the nurse if she knew what that doctor's first name was. She did. So I named my baby after the two doctors who had tended to me: the kindly doctor who came to visit me in the maternity home and the doctor who delivered my baby. As the nurse walked away with the completed paperwork, I said my baby's new name out loud to myself. I liked the way it sounded, dignified but friendly, the name a little boy who might grow up to be a doctor would have.

If I'd kept him, I would have given him a different name. Had we been raising our son, my boyfriend and I likely would have had fun deciding what to name him. I'd have made an argument for the boy name I liked the best at that time of my life: Stéven. My boyfriend would have thrown his favourite boy name into the mix. I have no idea what that might have been, because we never talked about it. I think we would have come up with something that honoured both our families and our son's individuality. I had a healthy list of names to choose from, names from my family's multiple histories, names that held a host of stories about the family that he should have been part of.

The day I was released from the hospital, I returned to the maternity home. Over the next twenty-four hours, I gave away all my tent-shaped clothes, packed my little white suitcase, and said goodbye to friends I would never see again. Once our babies were born, maternity-home friendships usually dissipated for good. As unobtrusively as I had slipped inside its walls, I slipped out and returned to my family.

Almost without comment, I fell back into the familiar daily routine of our household. I think my sisters and brother were happy to see me, but it was clear that they'd been told to ask no questions about my absence. In turn, I offered no explanations. I complied with the directive I'd received from my mother back in the hospital, that my father expected silence from me on the topic of my pregnancy. Decades would pass before I dared to talk to my sisters about this episode in my life.

In the sixties, the birth of a child was not the highly documented family event it is today, eagerly attended by fathers, birthing coaches, grandparents, and digital cameras. Back then, happy parents usually waited until the day mother and baby were released from the hospital to record images of the new arrival. At the same time, most hospitals did have professional photographers on staff so that proud new moms could order their babies' first official portraits. While I was still in the hospital, a photographer visited all the mothers offering to take baby pictures. The day he came to our ward, he somehow knew not to stop at my bed. In an unusually assertive moment, I followed him down the hall and convinced him to take a picture of my baby. I gave him all the money I had—I think it was about $1.25—and my home address.

I knew that my parents would not have wanted me to have such a painful reminder of this period in my life, so I remained on watch for the postman after I returned home. The day it arrived, I was at home babysitting my little sister and got to the mail before anyone else. The picture is a beautiful photo of my infant son with his eyes wide open. After staring at it for a very long time, I put it and the two identification bracelets I'd worn in the hospital—one for me, one for him—in the envelope the picture came in and placed it in my night-table drawer. As I write this, it's still there, in a different night table, but the same small envelope, somewhat yellowed by now, my old Winnipeg address handwritten in a casual scrawl across the centre, a cancelled pink four-cent stamp in the top right-hand corner.

No one in my extended family inquired about my "trip"; in fact, not many people inquired about my absence at all, so explaining it was not necessary. It was as if my first pregnancy had not happened; I could simply pretend it away. Except for the small black-and-white picture of a wide-eyed infant tucked deep into my night-table drawer, the stretch marks on my breasts, and a strange emptiness that hovered uneasily in and around my thoughts, I could wrap up the entire experience, stow it somewhere deep in my psyche, and hope that time would dull my memory.

The world outside Winnipeg hadn't calmed down in my absence. In Canada, one month before my baby's birth, Canada's justice minister,

Pierre Trudeau, approved amendments to the criminal code that legalized, among other things, abortion and contraception. The state, he famously said, had no business in the bedrooms of the nation. A few years earlier, I wouldn't have known what he meant. Now I did.

In the United States, one month before my baby was born, Martin Luther King had been assassinated in Memphis. One month after my baby was born, Robert Kennedy was assassinated in Los Angeles. Two days later, James Earl Ray was arrested in London for the murder of Dr. King. A few weeks later, newly promoted to prime minister of Canada, Mr. Trudeau called an election, launching a summer of Trudeaumania. Although I followed these events, I felt detached from everything going on in the world around me.

My parents sent me on a short trip to Montreal to visit my grandparents. Shielded from knowledge of my pregnancy, they were proud of me and introduced me to their friends and their friends' grandchildren. We went on several drives to see the sights of Old Montreal. They sat in the back of their chauffeured car while I walked up the steps of St. Joseph's Oratory. They took me to their favourite Montreal restaurants and proudly introduced me to maître d's who obviously knew them well. They lamented the fact that they didn't know anyone my age they could invite to dinner. One night, my grandfather asked how I liked my job at the bank. He was mildly perplexed when I said I'd quit during the winter, but he didn't ask for details and said he was certain I'd find something else soon.

Back in Winnipeg, on a hot July day, I was tanning in our backyard when the beautiful St. Boniface Cathedral caught fire while under renovation. I didn't see the fire itself, but the smoke smell lingered in the city for days. I could smell it as I rubbed baby oil over my legs and arms. On my radio, The Guess Who had a new hit with "These Eyes." It is a beautiful ballad, a song that I think I would normally have taken to immediately, but I was strangely untouched by its emotion. I was calm inside, too calm. I missed feeling my baby inside me, moving, but other than that I didn't feel much of anything at all. It was as if some part of me, my feeling self, had been amputated or gone numb. It'll pass, I thought. I remembered what the den mothers at the home and the social worker had told me: it'll be like it never happened, you'll have other children, you'll forget about this one. I didn't yet recognize the lie. Birth mothers never forget.

A year went by. On the radio, it was "The Age of Aquarius"; The Fifth Dimension urged everyone to "let the sun shine in." Sometime shortly after his first birthday, I must have signed the final adoption papers. For years afterwards, I wouldn't be able to remember that moment at all. On the subject of my baby and the adoption, I'd held to my promise of silence. In fact, I held to it so well that I even silenced myself to myself.

By this time, my life had adjusted to new routines. I was back in school, taking a two-year program in X-ray technology. In my mind, I was no longer an "unwed mother." I was me again. But nothing was ever the same. I saw and heard the world around me differently than before. When I was at home, I stayed in my room. On the radio, Aretha Franklin sang "Chain of Fools." I felt taunted. I was a fool, a weak link, a missing weak link in a life I'd created.

If I didn't like what was on the radio, I pulled out the small portable record player from my closet and my modest collection of albums. Over and over again, I played Simon and Garfunkel's "I Am a Rock." I sang along with Paul and Art, feeling like a rock and an island. In September that year, the radio airwaves were full of a new single by Diana Ross and the Supremes: "Love Child." I could hardly stand to listen to it.

To me, it seemed as if 1967's summer of love had been replaced by a less naive, more sombre tone. Everything felt so turbulent. Or maybe it was just me. I didn't know, so I put my head down and did what my social environment conditioned me to do: buried my feelings and carried on with my life.

—from *The House with the Broken Two: A Birthmother Remembers* (Anvil Press, 2011). Used with permission of the publisher.

These Are My Children

CHRISTA COUTURE

"You have two children?" she asks. We'd only just met. Our mutual friend, the connection between us, sits next to me, and I feel her discomfort immediately. I know in that moment that the woman asking has read my bio online, the bit about "after a two-year hiatus to have her second child..." and I feel my friend glancing nervously between us, the woman starting to feel awkward, unsure. The friend decides to answer for me.

"Noooo," she draws it out. A firm line, a tone to change the subject. I understand she wants to protect me, but I can answer for myself.

"Yes," I reply. "I have two children."

A long time ago, a midwife described to me that before a woman ever gives birth, her cervix's opening, the os, whose two-lettered name I find sweetly and appropriately small, appears as a dot. After vaginal birth, the os looks like a line, "more slit-like and gaping," according to Wikipedia, forever changed. I liked this idea of an internal record, that my cervix would hold proof of my child's passage through me.

That was before I knew about the other physical records my body would bear — a stretch-marked belly, almost quilted by the many criss-crossing lines, a belly button I can turn inside out, smaller post-lactation breasts — and it was before I thought I would want, or need, those reminders, that evidence.

Now I am glad for this map drawn on my stomach, for these signs pointing "you were here, here, and here," and grateful also, because it's easier to consult this external confirmation than look to that dot-turned-line to affirm the children I bore, for proof that I am a mother. Their mother.

There are photographs, too, of course, but they can seem like a dream. The woman holding children in the photographs looks much like me, but I feel a dark doubt at the digital image, the glossy print. The photos are either unconvincing or too much a part of the past. In search of a tangible present, I'll instead lift my shirt and run my fingers across my still-round and sometimes mistaken for still-pregnant belly — stretch marks, inside-out belly button, yes. They were here.

Sometimes I answer differently. At a music festival backstage, a woman is describing her children to me, the circus of getting them on the road with her, the adventures of camping on-site with them. She pauses to ask, like most people with children do, "Do you have children?" Her invitation to swap parenting anecdotes.

"No," I say.

I don't have children I've had to wrangle into long road trips, or whom I need to shortly rustle up dinner for, and I think that's what she's asking. But I always feel a little hurt by the lie when I tell it, even when I use the lie to protect myself.

I'm also instantly distracted by it — I start to wonder where the conversation would turn if I answered "yes." I feel guilty at the exclusion. *I'm not forgetting you, little ones.*

I couldn't guess how many times I've been asked if I have children or the similar, related question, "Do you have other children?" Each time I'm asked, I twitch, or wince, and I've yet to feel prepared for it. And each time, I make a decision on how to answer, trying to gauge what the following questions would be, how the person I'm talking to might respond. I'm often making a quick judgment call on a person I barely know, guessing what their spiritual leaning might be, their openness to sorrow, where they land on the hug-it-out to suck-it-up spectrum. Whether saying "yes" feels like the right or wrong choice depends on how my own beliefs, openness, and axis aligns or collides with theirs.

In a support group for bereaved parents at Canuck Place Children's Hospice in Vancouver, the problem of how to answer these questions comes up often. The facilitator, who for fifteen years has engaged in conversations with parents of dead or dying children, shares a story, as he often does, from a past member of this club no one wants to be in.

When asked whether she has children, the woman in his story replies, "That seems like it should be a straightforward question, but for me it's not." The person asking the question can then leave it at that or ask for clarification. The woman feels like she's finally found an answer that feels honest, in that it acknowledges that the answer depends on perspective, including her own frequently shifting perspective, and as well challenges the assumption that the answer to that question should be a simple "yes" or "no."

Though no parent who has lost a child has ever felt that "no" is an honest answer, "yes" can feel unnecessarily complicated.

Another woman shares that she always answers "yes," regardless of who asks or the context of the question. Should the inevitable questions follow —"How many?" and "How old?"— she answers, "One child, who would be five if she were still living." She doesn't waver. Yes.

I'm not always as strong.

But do I have children?

Yes.

How many?

Two.

How old are they?

Emmett would be seven and Ford would be four were they both still alive.

"Do you have children?"

"No."

I feel a pang of guilt and quickly assure myself that in the interest of self-preservation it's okay to lie to some people, in some situations. Saying "no" can be an awful feeling—the denying of what's important to me, the quick revision of how I truly see myself in this world. That edit can protect me, though, from questions I'm not ready to answer, from feedback I don't want to hear.

It can be exhausting, I find, to say "yes," to say more.

Saying "yes" can lead to having to console the person who asks, in their sudden discomfort and regret, and I resent this. Why do I feel compelled to make others feel better? I notice my automatic impulse to be polite in an attempt to alleviate their worry around their feeling impolite.

Sometimes I have revelled in the other's discomfort—*yes, feel terrible that you asked, feel terrible that my children have died, I certainly do.* Bitter. Angry. Hurt.

I'll reply bluntly, indelicately, "Yes, but they're dead," and then watch them fumble.

"No, I don't," can come out heavy, dismissive, frustrated, and similar to the above, to the same effect.

I haven't, in seven years, found a suitable reply to the question. I admit, considering the human variables, it is probably impossible to find a consistent staple response.

At a table with a group of people, cellphones are out and people are proudly showing photos of their children. I wear a locket around my neck with a photo of each of my boys and I open it, beaming, too, over my own beautiful children, but hesitant also, vulnerable to feeling alienated, or alienating.

This is Emmett. This is Ford.

I want to leave it at that. I want to be connected by this understanding of what it is to love and celebrate your children. In both photos, my kids are intubated (the placement of a plastic tube into the trachea to maintain an open airway — most colloquially known as a "breathing machine") and clearly hospitalized, and that gives many people pause. Most people see the paraphernalia first and the babies second.

I see Emmett, and I see Ford.

To then reveal that both of my children have died puts a damper on the mood, though I wish it didn't. Often it distances me from the common ground. But I love my children. I'm proud of them, as much as I would be if they were alive, and I want to share that.

Looking back at their photos, I don't see the tubes that kept my babies alive while they lived. I see Emmett, my dark-haired first baby, his big (almost-11-pounds-at-birth) body in my arms. I see his long-awaited arrival. I see my changed heart. I see Ford's fluffy, strawberry-blond hair and his wide, laughing smile. I see that he was happy. I see that he was in pain. I see how we were all waiting and hoping. I see his strength in his pure, unknowing babyness.

"Was it genetic?" people will ask. It is, for many, hard to believe that in this western world, a family could lose two children without something being "wrong." I find I get defensive over this question, feel I'm being accused of fault. I've practiced saying, "They died at different times, for different reasons," and sometimes I emphasize the randomness of these events by saying, "Different *unrelated* reasons," but it's unnecessary, I suppose, to clarify.

It's not my fault, I'm thinking as they puzzle over what could have caused such similar tragedies, piling sandbags against my own puzzling.

Indeed it is the unlikeness of losing two children that for so long fuelled my belief that Ford would live, despite his congenital heart disease. From those around me, that belief was affirmed from the time I was pregnant, that "nothing like the last time could happen again," meaning death. (And I darkly assure those people now, in imagined conversations, that they were right. My second child's death wasn't like the last time.)

Looking back to the group introducing their offspring via cell-phone picture albums, I can feel that these people see me differently now. They don't want to be like me, and I can tell who is so afraid of losing their own child that they can't even engage with me further on the subject. I get it. Others don't think I could be like them, don't think that I could relate to parents of living children. I sense some people are hesitant to continue the conversation now. I imagine others are possibly resentful of that hesitation. Some might consider my sharing morbid. Others are moved by sadness at the thought of ever losing their own. I try to look for only those empathetic few and resist my defensiveness to the discomfort I might have caused in the others.

My mind gets noisy with my defenses and sad at my feeling of not belonging.

I want to tell them: but I am like you, a parent too. My relationship with either of my children did not end with their deaths. My daily thoughts are full of them—with joy and gratitude for them, on some days, and with grief and longing on others. Children who are no longer here still take up time and space in a parent's life.

I am not unlike you, I think as I close the locket and hold it close to my chest.

Little ones, I don't come here to your grave enough. I do often look for places to rent nearby though, thinking if I could walk or ride my bike here, my visits would be more frequent. However, if that proved wrong, I think it would only be my guilt that would increase.

I'm trying to write an essay about you, about us. On what it is to mother and to be a mother when your children are not with you. It's been hard. The feelings are complicated and my thoughts, as I try to articulate them, are contradictory.

I've realized my defenses are high, that bitterness and isolation run through them. I've realized that I am quick to stab a flag into the ground and assert my title of Mother—to dare anyone to try to take it from me. It's a fierce impulse and my breath quickens, ready to fight off the naysayers.

The most nagging naysayer, it turns out, predictably perhaps, is my own voice of doubt. My tightening grip on the title of Mother, and the volume I proclaim it with, fights most diligently against the questioning in my own self, my own attempts at reconciling what I would imagine a Mother to be with what I am.

Sure, there are details of parenting I haven't known—details that most would consider common—and yes, my babies, both of you and I had experiences that were rare. One in one hundred. One in eight thousand. There became so many statistics over the years that they have lost meaning. We were those ones; it's moot to consider how many were not, most of the time.

So I rattle off, "Sure, there are differences," and get back to affirming, "but I'm still a Mom, like the rest of them." But the thing is, these differences are drastic, and vast.

I want to be like the rest of them, desperately.

More desperately, I want you back.

How do I mother you now? I come to your grave. I cry for you daily. I try to stay in the centre of being in love with you for as long as possible, that centre where I feel only gratitude and joy at your coming into my life, before my thoughts tip into being reminded of your absence and of what I'm missing, before I feel anger and helplessness.

If I follow my anger, it always leads me to longing. I miss you. Is that what my mothering is, this missing?

I think about you, Ford, more than I think about you, Emmett, and I feel terrible about it. I consider how parents balance their relationships with their different children, when they have more than one, and I wonder if it feels like this.

Emmett, I feel you and I lost all our potential—you never even opened your eyes. Losing ever knowing what colour they might be is only the beginning of what we both had to discover about each other, and did not get to.

Ford, I lost your blue eyes. I lost our locking gazes and knowing exactly what that's like. There is a year's worth of specifics that I can point to, and know what I'm missing.

But Emmett, you were my first and because I knew you almost entirely only in utero, the memories of your kicking echo more strongly within me than your brother's.

While he was living, I would tell Ford about his older brother. I imagined how we would celebrate your birthday every year, and how he would look at photos of you. I imagined him pointing and saying your name, not able to enunciate the t's in his early years. I imagined him drawing a family tree in school and the branch he would extend for you. I imagined he wouldn't struggle to say, "Yes, I have a brother," when asked if he had siblings. He would grow up knowing you, like this. A name, a few photographs, stories.

We would trace the lines on my belly, and he would know you both grew there.

I trace your names on your gravestone, brothers, interred together behind one cement block.

I don't come here often enough, but I think of you always.

I felt it most significantly after Ford was born—in Emmett's one day of life, in the chaos of the events that surrounded it, the feeling didn't have time to be articulated, this radar in my belly, this feeling that I'm a lighthouse that searches and beckons.

I could find Ford in the dark. He slept, for most of his life, in a building blocks from my home, under the watch of the ICU, but no matter his whereabouts, I could, I know I could, walk miles, eyes closed, to find him, guided by this invisible tether between us. As long as he was living, I felt the blip on the radar, the assurance of his whereabouts, his safety on the sea.

I feel my son's physical absence in this world like a phantom limb, yet truly knowing he is not here has not deterred my momma-radar from searching. I easily tune into that search for a response, and I deeply feel the ache of no reply. It is, at times, the most crippling pain of my loss—the acute physical awareness that he is gone. "He's not here," I try to reason with that animal instinct that searches constantly for him, for them, but there is no changing this innate behaviour.

At their grave, this searching slows its pace as I feel the nearness of their physical remains. My hand to the gravestone, I reach for this additional reminder of their place in my life. Like when I run my fingers over a stretch-marked belly, I now lean close to their ashes that sit behind the stone and breathe out toward them. "It's not enough, I know," I tell the mother in me, "but it's as close as we can get."

It came up that I had lost a child—this was before I had lost a second—and the eyes of the woman I was talking to lit up. "I have a prince of skies," she said. She had lost a boy, her baby, late in pregnancy. It was a premature labour with complications. She described us as special and I was taken aback. Special had never occurred to me. "We know something very few people know."

I do feel witness to exceptional events.

I never could have imagined the love I felt when my first son was born—how my heart grew, how a part of my being was illuminated that I never knew was hiding within me. Similarly, there was no way to predict the change his death in my arms would make, the privilege of holding him through his beginnings in this world to his end.

There is, of course, a shift in perspective when we experience loss, and for me, the loss of a child has deepened my compassion for others, expanded understanding, inspired a letting go of little things and a deeper feeling for what matters.

People matter. Children matter. The importance of life's other obstacles and triumphs shifts. Nothing could make my children's deaths seem worth it, but I can also feel gratitude for some of the changes. It's a duality that's hard to accept.

I might argue that ignorance is bliss, and I would have been content to complain my days away on more trivial challenges. I didn't want this insight.

But I can agree, we are a special few and sometimes the separateness I feel from parents of living children is rooted calmly in this knowing.

"You sure get a sense of time passing when you see how your friend's kids have changed," he says, marvelling that our mutual friend's daughter is already five years old. Others present agree, nodding and groaning at their advancing years.

I have to leave the room with tears ready to fall and a knot in my throat. *My kids don't change.* Time has stopped, and I cannot use their lives as a reference to track my own. *This time two years ago, this time three years ago,* I count backwards, thinking of what I was doing then as a way to differentiate what I am doing now.

Sometimes I feel my mothering is finite, or plays on a loop. I can replay both of my children's lives to their conclusions in my mind, rewind, and play them again. There is no wondering what they will become.

The memories kick in my womb as ghosts, my stretch-marked belly carrying the shadowy recollections safely within me and the line drawn by Ford's Caesarean birth emphasizing their shapes above it.

These are my children, echoes and scars.

I Taught My Kids to Talk

NANCY JO CULLEN

About birth control, my mom used to say: "Which of you wouldn't be here now?" My parents planned only two of their seven children and I, the second, undetected twin of my mother's final pregnancy (in the days before Doppler fetal monitors), was the biggest surprise of all. Of course, my mother's question made no sense, because really, if we had never been born, how would we complain about not being here? I sometimes find myself pondering a similar, ridiculous idea with respect to my own children: if I had remained childless, wouldn't life have been easier? Happier? In fact, the idea of life without my children, now that they are here, is unspeakable. But some mornings as I harangue two teenagers to get a move on, I wish my mother had asked about having children: "If everybody was jumping off a cliff, would you?"

My parents, devout Roman Catholics, raised us in the Church. Each Christmas when I was a little girl, Santa brought me a cherished baby doll. I became an aunt for the first time at the age of eleven. I just assumed I would be a mommy when I grew up. In my case, becoming a mother could arguably be as much about indoctrination as it was about choice. Not that anyone told me I had to have children; there was a just lot of baby making going down all around me and having kids seemed as ordinary as eating breakfast.

My mom also used to say: "Don't wait until you're ready to be a mother; you'll never be ready." My former partner, Josette, died eight years ago. She was struggling with addiction and serious mental-health issues. We were separated at the time, so I was already ten months into my life as a single parent and, like most single parents, overwhelmed. And some days, regardless of the fact that I've been at it for sixteen years now, it still feels like I'm not ready for motherhood. There is no manual, no test for preparedness; you get knocked up, and—even if it was no accident and you planned and paid, or asked a friend—you're off to the races.

I am a fifty-one-year-old single mom of sorts. I am in love and have found great support in my new partner. But she lives in another city, so we are managing a long-distance relationship and maintaining two homes until both kids finish high school. My son is sixteen, and my daughter is fourteen. I have a constant sense of foreboding that I'm not doing my job right. I should never have given my kids sugar or juice. Why don't they eat like French kids? Why don't they want to volunteer at the museum or a hospital? I never should have let them watch *The 40-Year-Old Virgin*. I should have taught them to snow camp or build an organic square-foot garden, but the only thing I've taught my kids to do is talk, and now I'm paying for that one in spades.

I was cool before I had kids, and you might be too, but after kids—even if you're a dyke or a vegan, or even if some people still think you're cool—you're going to be a damn sight more conventional. And even if you manage to remain unconventional and you can still stay up late enough to attend events that prove it, nothing will stop you from, one day, being totally embarrassing. It is the natural order of things.

"Hush, Nancy," my kids are inclined to say whenever I broach such subjects as adequate sleep, healthy diet, booze, sex, or weed. There is also, "Mom. Don't." These special words are used in shopping malls and coffee shops, and mean, more specifically, stop talking this instant. There is also the ever annoying, "Yeah, yeah." Roughly translated, this means: why are you such a bitch, Nancy?

Somewhere, about the halfway point of grade seven, both of my kids experienced a seismic shift, one away from me and toward their peers. I am now required to walk demurely, either ahead of or behind my children. No dancing on the sidewalks, no public displays of interest in anything that might embarrass them (that's everything, in case you're wondering). I should not have conversations with their friends, aside from "Hello." And, if they're talking to their friends in Calgary on Skype and I can hear the deep boom of male adolescent voices, I should not call out in greeting. I am allowed to taxi them, but in the car I should shut the eff up, for I have become TOTALLY embarrassing.

It was a slow decline toward totally embarrassing. When we brought Luke home, we stuck him in the window to rid him of bilirubin and sat and shook at the wonder of our bundle of joy and whatever the hell it was we'd gotten ourselves into. But we were up and running pretty smoothly within a month, and Luke never ceased to be a delight. He was such a smart baby, speaking in full sentences at eighteen months. No, he wasn't just smart; he was brilliant.

He was so brilliant he wouldn't nap (a certain indicator of brilliance, my friend Joni told me), but he was asleep at 7:00 each night. Of course, he was in our bed by midnight, sleeping like a starfish so that we were left to sleep on the outer quadrants of a queen-sized bed, but at least he was sleeping through the night. He weaned himself, he fed himself, and he could imitate the sound of crows. He preferred Emperor Zurg to Buzz Lightyear, and his playschool teacher said he was a friend to everyone, that he was one of the most well-balanced kids she'd ever taught.

My second pregnancy was considerably different from the first, which any seasoned mother could have told me would be the case had I asked. But when our daughter, Claire, arrived it was just more of the same, only different. Claire napped and slept through the night, but it wouldn't have been fair to leave her out of the bed. She didn't talk as much, but she was very effective at making her wishes known. She was solid and physical. She occupied herself and preferred having one friend to having twenty. She was hilarious and wide-eyed and prone to biting when she felt great affection. In kindergarten, we met with her teacher to work out a strategy to help her say "no" in a manner that was kinder than her current method. After that meeting, I said to Josette, "I think it's better to have a son who is kind and sensitive and a girl who doesn't care so much if people like her. Don't you?"

When Claire was six months old, we moved from a small two-bedroom, inner-city house to the far northwest corner of Calgary. We managed to parlay our inner-city cottage into a 1,800-foot suburban castle. We had a big yard, three large bedrooms, two full baths upstairs, a half bath on the main floor, and a fully developed basement. Our new street was swarming with children, and our kids made friends they still have today. Our neighbours had no concern that lesbians had moved in. They cared that we mowed our lawn and shovelled our sidewalks. We drank beer and ate hot dogs with them. We commiserated on potty training and sleep schedules. Our kids, easily occupied by other children, ran in and out of each other's houses, which made long days with preschoolers considerably more tolerable. Despite the decline in cool that moving to the suburbs brought, we were happy.

When our kids were little, they thought we were as excellent as Pop Rocks. My son liked to sit with his little preschool hand just inside the top of my shirt; my daughter liked to rub my earlobe. They held my hand while walking down the street, and they wanted to cuddle while they fell asleep. They wanted to be in the same room with us, whether it was the kitchen or the toilet.

We were the centre of their universes, and they wanted to watch movies with us, shop with us, eat with us, sleep with us, and travel to the wilderness with us (with no thought to private showers or technology). We were important and comforting, and when Josette googled my name for Claire, and it came up, trust me: I. Was. Cool.

Sure, I periodically ate Cheerios off my kids' backs and was no longer able to keep my eyes open past ten at night, but my six-year-old daughter thought I was awesome, and so was her other mom, who had showed her how to use Google.

When Josette and I separated, it was a complete shock to our kids. They were too young to understand how serious her mental-health issues were and we had kept her addictions well hidden from them. We did our level best to keep all friction out of their experience of our separation, but it was a terrible period and its outcome was devastating. When my children were in grades one and three, they lost a mom who had, despite her mess of problems, provided an anchor in their lives. We spread her ashes in one of our favourite spots in Kananaskis Provincial Park so that we could have a place to return to. Josette remains perpetually awesome, enshrined in their minds as the person she was before they could get a better look at her. They have now had a better look at me, and it seems they saw all at once where my faults lie. One day, my daughter will have Josette's name tattooed above her heart; my son thinks he might have a fleur-de-lis tattooed on his arm, in memory of Josette, who was French Canadian.

Despite the heartbreaking turn of events in our lives, my kids still held me in pretty high esteem. They were still happy to be seen with me in public. They both crawled into my bed, more nights than not, perhaps out of habit, perhaps because we were grieving. When it came time to keep them out of my bed the solution was remarkably easy: I simply told them I would be sleeping naked. At ages eight and ten, they had started to practise their adolescent vision of me. While I wasn't quite totally embarrassing, the spectre of my naked body was enough to keep them from wandering into my bed in the middle of the night. The bloom, it seemed, was coming off the rose.

We moved to Toronto when my kids were nine and eleven. At those ages, both of them were still willing to hang with me in the house. Our first year in Toronto, we watched the complete series of *Buffy the Vampire Slayer* together. My daughter was still willing to hug/kiss me in public, although my son preferred at this point that we behave like strangers to one another. "Don't your other friends have mothers?" I asked him. "Yes," he said. But just because everyone had a mother didn't mean he had to take his out and trot her around. Now, when my kids are home, they confine themselves to their private spaces; my son in his room in the basement, my daughter in her room on the second floor. They are connected to their friends via the wonder of the Internet. I see them when they wander into the kitchen for a snack or join me at the table for supper.

Another thing my mom was heard to say was: "You make your bed; you lie in it." That's how this stage of mothering feels to me. I still have the ongoing irritation of their clutter (dirty socks on my favourite chair, Q-tips scattered across the bathroom floor); their sometimes distressing affinity for loud, cussy hip-hop and hyper-sexualized former Disney stars; and of course, I have their disdain, the benchmark, in this house at least, that a child has arrived at adolescence.

For instance, when my son realized I was writing this essay, he offered the following gem, "Say your son smokes weed and your daughter is a crack addict." To which my daughter added, "Tell them I've succumbed to feminism." (Like it was a disease.)

"No, seriously," my son said, "No one reads those magazines—"

"It's not a magazine; it's a book," I said.

"Oh really? That's worse," he said. "The only people who read those are really weird strict parents, or new parents." Then they laughed and headed back to their separate spaces. Sometimes I think people pester their children for grandchildren just so their own kids can also experience the derision of teenagers. But my darlings are doing exactly what they should; they are creating distance between them and me. They have a vast private life I'm not likely to ever share again, and if that's not bad enough, now my babies go out, after dark, on their own.

When your child is a toddler, you worry about her tearing down the sidewalk at too great a distance from you; when she's preschooler, you worry she'll fall off the monkey bars. It turns out this is nothing to letting your teenaged kid go out with his friends to return home in the middle of the night. It's nothing to having your kid progress from a birthday party sugar rush to a mishap with cheap brandy, the kind of mishap that involves your child resting on the cold tile of the bathroom floor, lifting his head only to puke in the toilet bowl. It's nothing compared to your child learning how to drive, or getting in the car with some other teenaged driver whose brain isn't going to finish developing for approximately eight more years.

Risk-taking behaviour takes on a whole new meaning once your kids are out there on their own. And it's not like I *let* them go, it's just that I can't stop them. They are bursting with their own power. Now, it all comes down to trust. I have to trust that I have equipped my kids with the tools to manage adolescence and that they can use their experiences as stepping stones into their adult lives. I am not the only one lying in the bed of my own making. Now my kids, too, are making decisions (decisions I am sometimes aware of, but more often not) and are living with the consequences of their actions, from failing a class, to losing a friend, or making themselves sick on drink.

It's not the law that you have to let them do this shit, but if you don't, they'll never learn to leave home, and I'm a big proponent of kids leaving home. My plans for the future don't involve parenting my adult children, not like those two moronic parents in the laundry commercial who are folding their adult sons' clothes while rejoicing that they can save money using cold-water wash. Let me just say now, if my adult kids return home, they're doing their own damn laundry. I shot out of the house when I was eighteen, like all of my siblings—except for the ones who left earlier. I don't expect my kids to do quite the same, but I hope I'm training them to do something along those lines.

In the end, that is the long task of parenting: we are training our children to leave us. The little baby who I held in awe on my chest while he slept, is leaving me, and his sister is not far behind. They are leaving me by inches and with the curl of a lip or a toss of the hair. They no longer think I know much. I mean, they know I know things, but they think I don't know how it feels to be them now. Kids, I say, I grew up in the seventies. I know how it feels.

Some days parenting adolescents truly sucks; all that teenaged hubris can be exhausting. But when it doesn't suck, it's bloody brilliant. They're on the verge of so much potential, good and bad. And I don't mind the leaving, really. By the time they both go, I'm pretty sure I'm going to be ready to send them off. The twenty-plus years it takes to set a child loose on the world are long ones, and my needs have (rightfully) been second to my children's and will continue to be until my kids leave home. Then, I imagine, things are going to change, despite my mom's other ominous little bit of wisdom: You never stop being a mother.

But I suppose most of us realize that the moment we bring our baby home.

Never mind. I look forward to the adult relationship I'll have with my kids. I predict it's the big reward for the Sisyphean task of raising them.

What Can't Be Packed Away

MARITA DACHSEL

We are moving again, the second time in as many years. Last time it was from Edmonton to Vancouver, and I was seven months pregnant. This time it will be from Vancouver to Victoria, with two little boys and a nine-month-old girl.

My boys are upstairs playing a game that includes Lego, dinosaurs, motorcycles, and pirates. My daughter is napping in the hammock in the kitchen. I look around the house and don't know how to say goodbye. Two of my children were born in this home, my youngest this past year when we were officially tenants, and my middle child four years previously when we were staying in the basement suite for two months while my husband was in town directing a show. I always imagined that the home would stay in our circle, but the owners, close friends of ours, have decided to sell. This is a beautiful old home full of quirks and character, but it is Vancouver, which means there is a good chance that whoever buys will tear it down.

My husband has a great new job which brings us to the Island. The employers are paying for our move, so the movers will be packing, too. The relief in having someone else do this work is more than remembering how difficult our last move was. I consider the weight of my surroundings and am thankful not to have to wrestle with that desk, those toys, these books, but I know that once the movers leave, I will still have the heaviness of what can't be packed away—what remains, the invisible.

How can loss be so heavy? How can fear?

I don't believe a person can be blessed. You're lucky in life or you're not, and the luck has nothing to do with talismans or being a good person or praying to a particular deity. But I admit that when people say that I'm blessed, I don't argue. I have a loving husband, three wonderful children, and we are healthy, vibrant, and alive.

That said, I am superstitious. As I wrote the above sentence, I made sure I touched wood, even knocked on it for good measure. I was not smug-pregnant. I knew the risks and was duly superstitious. I knew many pregnancies ended far before birth and that, even if the pregnancy made it to full-term, babies died.

Babies die. Babies died. My brother Dean died of SIDS on Halloween when he was two days shy of turning two months old. I was one day away from turning twenty-five months old. I have no memory of him, but my sister (who was born twenty months after Dean died, with a miscarriage and a vasectomy reversal between them) and I have always known about our brother. Infant deaths are often kept quiet in families, or are revealed much later. He was never a secret within the family and for that I am thankful. He has always been a part of my life despite being here for such a short time.

When I was pregnant with my first son, I thought of Dean more often. I carried an edge of fear and uncertainty. I refused to have a baby shower because the only baby shower my mother had was for Dean. Because the true cause of SIDS is still unknown, I was afraid that perhaps there was a hereditary link. The days leading up to when

Atticus turned the same age Dean was when he died, I was obsessive. I couldn't stop thinking about Dean's death and was overcome with fear that Atticus would die at the same age. My fear was so heavy, I couldn't even voice it. My husband was able to soothe my fears out of me, gently rationalizing them away.

With my second pregnancy, I was much more relaxed. I had a feeling I was having another boy, so I asked my mother if we could use Dean as a middle name. Soon after our conversation, I had a pang of fear that the name was somehow cursed or that, because he was the second born, we were tempting fate, but I simply acknowledged the fear, the superstition, and let it go.

Foolishly, I once believed that if my children survived their first year, then I could relax. They were safe and all would be good. But there is always a new calamity. Tragedy is lusty and gluttonous.

My father has been diagnosed with a terminal neurological condition. He is seventy-six. I know I should feel sadder than I do, but I can't help but think: yes, this is how it should be. We hate to use the term "old," but yes, he is old. He is elderly. Of course, we would like another ten or twenty years with him, but I can't help but whisper gratitude to the universe for choosing him over one of my children. This is how my superstition works.

Beside the stairwell in this house, at least a decade's worth of names and heights are scrawled, from twenty-six inches to six-and-a-half-feet. I recognize all the names—friends and family. When the house cleaners come, I will tell them to leave it. I don't know if our friends, the owners, will want to leave it there, but I imagine they'll want to see it one last time. I know I would. I've taken photos.

The names of our friends who own the house are there, as are the names of their daughter, and their niece and nephew who lived five doors down. The kids' names appear several times, representing their weedy growth from young children to towering teenagers. We added our children, too, though we haven't lived here long enough for there to be more than two entries for each.

Even before we became parents, my husband and I spoke of the childhood of our young friend and her cousins as the ideal, something we wanted for our future children—close family, creative and physical opportunities and outlets, freedom to roam and play live creatively. They, along with three other cousins, congregated at a family property with a few cabins every summer, where they had the freedom to be children.

When I was young, my family spent every summer at the same campground. I belonged to a small gang of kids, all close in age. The boys had motorcycles and would take the girls out on long rides along logging roads. We'd spot deer and bears, eat berries, go fishing, run along logging booms, and swim and swim and swim.

For two months, we'd have breakfast and not return until dinner and then again not until bedtime. We lived and we played. For me, this is summer, this is childhood: freedom to explore, to play, to be.

Three summers ago, days after our friends' daughter turned fourteen, she and her cousins who lived down the street died in a cabin fire on their family property. Their deaths shook our world, and we are still learning to live with its aftershocks.

The movers arrive and we escape to the relative quiet of a park. The boys play a made-up game called Lava Lake with a pair of girls, and I push my daughter on a swing. The man beside me pushes a little girl who I think is his granddaughter but later learn is his daughter.

We talk about the old days, days we didn't share but both of us can remember. We talk about being kids allowed to roam, to explore. The man's seven cousins grew up in a 1,200-square-foot house only blocks away from the one we are leaving. He was raised by a single mother in a small apartment at the busy intersection of Broadway and Clark and spent a lot of time with his cousins when his mom was at work. He tells of his aunt kicking them all out of the house after breakfast and of getting into trouble if they returned before the next meal. We are both nostalgic for the freedom we had as kids, the ability to wander, to explore, to simply be on our own away from what felt like watchful, oppressive adult eyes.

I've had many conversations like this since becoming a parent. We cite the same studies on how overwhelming attention from parents is changing how kids think, how their brains work. I've heard news reports about parents coddling to such a degree that they help set up their adult child's work cubicle on the first day of a new job. The media keeps telling us we're a generation of helicopter parents who are repressing our children's development so that they will never grow up and will become a generation of privileged brats who can't do anything or think for themselves. And all of this in the name of safety.

The man I am speaking with identifies a specific date when childhood freedom stopped: May 25, 1979, when six-year-old Etan Patz was allowed to walk to his school bus stop two blocks from his home in New York City and never made it. In my mind, the switch flipped in 1991, when four-year-old Michael Dunahee went missing from a playground in Victoria, steps away from where his mother was in football practice and his father watched while caring for Michael's baby sister. My sister, four years younger than I am, is still haunted by his photo—those blue, blue eyes staring out.

My husband has argued that in Canada it all changed with Clifford Olsen. His father worked with a parent of one of Olsen's victims. And yet my husband remembers having a lot of free rein, much more so than what we'd be allowed to give our children today. I wonder if there was never a single moment when everything changed, that we each connect with a story when we lost our own innocence, and these stories collectively have created the shift in society's view of safety.

Usually when I have this conversation with other parents, we lament the diminished freedom and wonder what we can do to help swing the pendulum back. We offer small choices we've made with our own kids—how far they're allowed to roam, play in the backyard unsupervised, et cetera—and then blame society and not ourselves for the imposed limits. If the other parent doesn't beat me to it, I like to bring up a story I heard on *As It Happens* a couple of years ago, about a mother who let her ten-year-old son walk a mile alone to soccer practice one night. She was arrested for neglect.

But the man at the swings veers off script before I have a chance to cite my favourite CBC story. When I mention the pendulum, he says that, sure, the odds of something terrible happening to your child are really small, but so is winning the lottery and that happens to people every week or so. He says, "Unless I could be 100 percent sure, with a money-back guarantee, the risk, as minuscule as it is, is simply not worth it."

I shouldn't be surprised by this, but I am. I expected a father who grew up with freedom even I couldn't imagine would understand the value of freedom in childhood. Could he not see the futility of trying to hold on too tight?

Here's the thing—I don't want anything to happen to my children. Does such an obvious statement need to be made? I think so (and as I write, I knock on wood).

. . .

When writing this essay, I looked up Etan Patz and Michael Dunahee to get the spelling of their names correct, the details precise, and my heart lurched. Their stories could so easily transfer to someone I know, to me. Etan was six, my eldest's age. I can see Atticus begging to walk to school or to the corner store by himself, convincing me that he could do it. He could do it, I know, but the question is, should he?

Michael Dunahee was four when he went missing. I can see Avner, my four-year-old, asking to play at a playground while I run the adjacent track—not always in my line of sight but close enough that it would feel safe.

But what is safe? The answer feels like: nothing. Nothing is safe.

At the memorial for our young friend and her cousins, one thing that came up over and over again was how much they lived. They were fourteen, fourteen, and eleven, and their lives were so rich with experience and love and creativity. They had travelled, they had created, they'd had adventures, they had performed, they'd had freedom, and they had lived.

I keep thinking about the man at the swings and how, of course, *of course*, we don't want bad things to happen to our children; we don't want them to die. But they do, don't they? Even when they are close by and sheltered and cared for, some get cancer, some are shot in public places, some are killed by "acts of God." As tight as we hold on, sometimes, it simply won't be tight enough. And do we want that tightness to smother? Because I think it can.

. . .

My youngest was born in our young friend's bedroom, which had been transformed into a library/spare bedroom when we moved in. Although it took us twelve days to name Harriet, we knew even before she was born that we would give her a middle name to honour our friend—her first name if our child was a girl, our friend's middle name if Harriet had been a boy. I can confidently say, even without touching wood or throwing salt over my shoulder, that I have no superstitions about her name. That said, I can't predict whether or not the superstitions will creep up on me when my children turn fourteen. I hope not. I am ready to box away my superstitions, hide them in the crawl space, and abandon them with the move.

It's not easy finding a path between societal pressures and what I want to give my children. I hope to model my friends' example of parenting, their love and openness, their pattern of exploration, creativity, and freedom. I hope to be able to give my children every opportunity to truly enjoy this one short life we each have and to do it as fully and beautifully as they can. This is what I hope, but I struggle with its execution. Yes, I let them play outside, out of my sight-line, almost daily, but that seems so paltry. I worry my heart isn't big enough to give them what they need, what they deserve, that my love for them doesn't have the room to be at peace with possibility of letting go, doesn't have the room to face their deaths. You need a whole hell of a lot of love to be open to that, and I simply don't have enough of it.

Weeks later in our new home, I hear the boys in the backyard playing with neighbours, their shouts and laughter easily reaching our second-floor suite. Harriet naps and I grab a moment to unpack a little more. We are mostly moved in now, except for our books and art. I open a box of framed photographs to sort and pull out the picture of the mandala composed of flowers and rocks, made by the hundreds who attended our friends' outdoor memorial. Tears, as always, rise swift and full. More than a physical symbol of manifested grief and loss, the mandala was a coming together of a community bound by love and hope. At once it is the past, the present, and two futures—the one that is, and the one that could have been. It is legacy, it is potential, and it is sacred.

I am holding the picture, contemplating where it should live, when I hear Harriet stir. As I rise, I place it on the desk, knowing it won't be returned to the box. Eventually, it will share the stairwell with other photographs of family and friends. I pick up Harriet, her cheeks flushed from sleep, breathe in the fleeting sweetness that is the back of her neck, and try not to squeeze too tight.

Babies in a Dangerous Time: On Choosing to be Child-Free

NICOLE DIXON

To breed or not to breed is not simply one question a woman asks herself at some point in her life—it's *the* question. Being or not being a mother—no matter what millennium it is, no matter how many university degrees we have, no matter how many books we've published or career ladders we've climbed—is what defines us. If it didn't, then writers wouldn't add pregnancy plotlines to TV shows and movie comedies wouldn't end with the births of babies. We obsess over celebrity baby bumps; we post weekly updates of our own growing bellies and quote the things our precocious toddlers say on Facebook. We like babies—their pictures make us smile, those quotes make us laugh, and hell, when the world is too much with us, when we start growing tired of getting and spending, these babies, they are ours and we give our hearts to them.

But for a woman who chooses not to have kids, each Facebook friend's ultrasound and baby bump and tiny knitted sweater and "iPood" onesie and first-day-of-school picture is yet another version of the same old questions: When are *you* having a kid? Don't you *want* a baby?

Actually, no.

In an ideal world, you could just say no and be done with it. You could go write another short story, go to work, come home, have an after-work beer, make a locally sourced meal with your partner, go to bed, have some great sex, read, sleep, and do the same tomorrow. But we don't exist in that ideal world. Sometimes it's January, and you can't get local lettuce. Sometimes you're too tired to have sex. Sometimes — a lot of the time — you can't write because you have to go to work, and sometimes — most of the time — you have to explain to people why you don't want to have kids because people are never happy with the simple answer, "No, I don't want kids." They look at you. They raise their eyebrows. They call you anti-kid or assume you're barren. They tell you, actually say to you, as if they know your mind better than you do, "Oh, some day? Don't you worry. *You'll change your mind.*"

I don't need anyone to tell me I'll change my mind. I'm a writer: all I do is conceive of every possible scenario for every situation. Deciding not to have kids has not been my hardest decision — it's been my longest. Hookups, breakups, accepting or quitting jobs: these are decisions I've made in a weekend or even a minute. Choosing not to have children is one I've weighed monthly, even daily. I am always asking myself, "Am I sure?"

Am I sure? Yes, I am. I'm 90 percent sure. Why not 100 percent? Well, if living almost forty years has taught me anything, it's that nothing is ever 100 percent guaranteed: relationships end, jobs get cut, and women who don't want kids get pregnant. Nothing is permanent and everything, anything, can change.

A few years ago, I wrote an essay for *Canadian Notes & Queries* about the disappearance of feminism from Canadian literature. I asked why women in Canadian novels had become passive. I wondered where the child-free—by choice—characters were. I worried that the prevalence of these passive female characters indicated a coming change in women's rights. In Canada and the US, a woman's ability to make choices is being taken away: our federal government has cut funding to Status of Women Canada, the wage gap between men and women is increasing, the national childcare program was scrapped, and Canada rejected a UN call to review violence against Aboriginal women. Down in Texas, Senator Wendy Davis held an eleven-hour, pink-sneakered filibuster to block a new anti-abortion law. "I've said it before, straight folks, and I'll say it again," American sex advice columnist Dan Savage has written, "the right-wingers and the fundies and the sex-phobes don't just have it in for the queers. They're coming for your asses too."

During and after writing the *CNQ* essay, I was angry. I got sick of explaining why I didn't want kids and fed up with our pro-baby society. I picked fights. I told people I was proudly anti-kid. I defriended or unfollowed almost all of my kid-having Facebook friends. I wrote pages and pages of child-free fiction. My then-partner bought me Corinne Maier's *No Kids: 40 Good Reasons Not to Have Children*, and we drank wine and read it to each other and laughed like cartoon villains: Mwa-ha-ha! Not us! We are *happier* and *better* than those *breeders! Look at us!* Our choices are *better* than theirs!

Eventually, I realized I was being a jerk. There's a meanness to Maier's book which begat a meanness in me. I didn't like who I'd become. I'm not anti-kid. Children—childhood—delights me. I was a teacher for ten years. Sure, we can all think of teachers who don't like kids, but I was never one of them. To this day, I fondly remember the poems my students wrote, the days we'd devote to learning songs and dancing, yard duty on crisp autumn mornings, the sound of children in the playground. I still write about being a teacher. I don't miss teaching, but when I look at the picture books on my bookshelf and see them gathering dust, I miss kids. I miss reading and discussing those books with them, miss being in their presence—but not enough to have a child of my own.

When my relationship ended, I had to stop and think. Was I choosing not to have kids because *he* didn't want kids? Was it his decision, ours, or mine? Now I know. The utter relief I feel each time I get my period? My love of silence and solitude? My tiny 1.5 bedroom house with a room of my own? I love my child-free life.

After my *CNQ* essay was published, women thanked me for writing it. Privately. Whispers in hallways, back-channel messages, e-mails. Several women admitted that they, too, had never been interested in having kids. "It would break my parents' hearts if they found out," one woman told me. A fifty-something mother admitted, "If it'd been another time, if I could go back and do it over again, I would have chosen not to have kids." Another thanked me for putting into words what she'd thought for years. "I was just afraid to admit it," she said.

No woman should be ashamed of any reasonable choice she makes. Yes, we make choices that aren't always the best, but that's exactly what being human is all about—making choices, succeeding or failing, then learning and growing and becoming better. If we're ashamed of our choices, pretty soon we stop making choices, and instead of doing, we have things done to us, and we have our rights taken away.

Something else has happened since my *CNQ* essay was published. The child-free are getting a bit more attention. Journalism fads come and go, and articles about being child-free tend to be those debased us-versus-them articles that get people arguing instead of talking. Nonetheless, it's exciting to see "The Childfree Life"—hooray! not child*less!*—on the cover of *Time* magazine. CBC's *Maritime Noon* call-in show (the realm of eighty-year-old gardeners and home renovators) recently devoted an episode to choosing to be child-free. Childless-by-choice websites and blogs and articles proliferate. Child-free characters appear in movies and books. Maybe attitudes are (slowly) changing. Maybe, in the future, when a woman says she's choosing not to have kids, she won't be questioned. She won't be told she'll change her mind. Maybe the woman she's met will say happily, proudly, loudly: Me too!

Before that can happen, the dialogue has to change. We can't follow the example of popular journalism: it's not us versus them; it's just us. We can't hate someone else's choices simply because they are not *our* choices. We can't fight each other. The bigger fight—the more important fight—is the fight to continue to *make* our choices. I'm not just talking about the choices that women face: the choice to have or not have a baby, or the choice to work or stay home. I'm talking about the choices that ensure a better future for our children and our planet. *Those* will be our most important choices, and those are the choices we cannot lose.

There's an assumption that choosing not to have kids is a selfish decision, that the child-free look inward instead of out, that we're not nurturing or caring enough to raise a child. I've never felt this. I contribute daily to my community and world—through my art, as a librarian and teacher, as a gardener and homeowner and supporter of local businesses. Calling someone selfish for having or not having a kid is ridiculous. Yes, this decision is self-involved. It's the most personal decision we'll make. In fact, my decision to write instead of parent was made with children completely in mind. I would never want to resent my kid(s). I know there are many writers who make it work, who can be mothers *and* be writers. I know I can't.

In the end, the most important reason I have for not breeding is this: our planet is dying. More and more people are competing for fewer and fewer jobs and resources. Choosing to have kids now means bringing a child into a very difficult future world. Humans are a hopeful species; having children is evidence of that hope. Babies are a legacy, a connection from one generation to the next, an easy way to leave a bit of us on this planet after we die. But humans are also incredibly destructive, and the irony is that we harm our planet by having babies. The hope we put into our own children can and does eliminate the hope of other children around the world.

If I had a baby, I'd add thousands of diapers to landfills, I'd have to buy furniture and clothes and toys and most likely a bigger house, all of which require more oil. I'd probably be fine with my little Toyota, but I'd soon burn more gas driving my kid to school, to piano lessons, and to soccer practise. In essence, I'd be helping to make our planet hotter. A recent UN report states that it is 95 percent likely that humans are behind climate change. Temperatures are expected to get hotter in just thirty years. As sea levels rise and droughts and floods intensify, as Canada continues to rip up more and more of the earth's crust to satiate our increasing demand for oil, as farmland and wetlands are replaced by suburbs, my deciding to procreate now would be, quite simply, denying that the air we breathe, the water we drink, the food we eat, the flora and fauna that make up our forests and oceans, and even the human species itself is endangered.

The only humans I want to create do not, in essence, exist. As a writer, I spend a lot of time inside my head, creating worlds and characters to inhabit them. I lie awake at night mulling over not only work conflicts, day-to-day conversations, and food choices, but also the actions and personalities of these made-up characters. As I said before, I've spent years weighing the decision to have or not have kids. Stay at home or daycare? Home-school or public school? No TV or TV as a reward? I can think about these things, but then, because I've decided not to have kids, I can stop thinking about them. No child of mine will ever beg me for an iPhone and scream at me when I say no. I don't have to worry that the neighbourhood kids are a bad influence on my child. Though these are all excellent conflicts to explore in my fiction, once the story is written, I can put those characters aside and worry about something else.

That something else is our planet, which is why we have to stop fighting each other. We have a bigger fight ahead of us. Our government cares little about green energy, transportation, and conservation, about our parks, water, air, and people. This us-versus-them mentality only distracts us. Just as the feminists before us knew that women's rights could not be won if women fought men or other women, our rights to clean air and drinking water will also be taken away if our anger is misdirected.

"Think of the children!" is a common refrain. "We have to make the world better for our children." Absolutely we have to, but we can't lose sight of the present. As well as making the world better for future generations, we need to make the world better for us now. I'm afraid that by having children, I'll stop thinking globally, and my nurturing, mothering side will focus solely on my kids. I don't want everything in my life to be only about my children. I want everything in my life to be about everything, and everyone else; to nurture not just one life, but all life.

. . .

A year ago, when I was once again considering kids, I asked a friend how she balanced her academic work with raising two sons. She admitted it was harder to find the time to work, but she also said that her kids inspired her to get stuff done. One of the most incredible things about having children, she said, is seeing them experience the world for the first time. The connections they make, their wonder at the planet, make it possible for her to see the world afresh, to look at our planet from a new perspective.

It's something I've heard many parents claim. These connections and realizations—that an autumn leaf looks like an old woman's hand, that foxes seem more like cats than dogs, that sometimes the ocean looks like the sky and the sky looks like the ocean, and aren't we all just upside down?—are what parents love to quote on Facebook. As adults, we don't have to stop looking at the planet with wonder. It's not that we need to look at the world with the eyes of a child; it's that we should never lose sight of how everything on this planet is interconnected. The world is fascinating and beautiful and deserves so much more respect than we're giving it.

People often think that saying no to having kids means saying no to life. My choice not to have kids, however, is a choice made from love. I've realized that the legacy I want to leave on the earth after I'm gone is as small a mark, as tiny a footprint, as possible. My writing is enough of a legacy to leave behind. Shouldn't we all strive to prepare our kids, together, for a compromised future? With love and intention, all of us can teach our children to garden, to visit farmers' markets, to buy local, to go for walks instead of watching TV, to read and love books, to ride a bike, to reduce and reuse, to live with less, to share instead of wanting and having it all. My choice not to have kids does not close me off from my community or my planet. Instead, it allows me to nurture my own life and to mother everyone's mother, Earth.

Primipara

ARIEL GORDON

When I was in the last month of my pregnancy, I looked like a turkey crammed full of stuffing. Even my obstetrician thought so, the one time she looked at me.

"You're huge!" she exclaimed. And booked me for a follow-up ultrasound.

I wanted to say, "I was this size last week." And, "It's all right there in the file…"

But I refrained, since she was scheduled to have her hands inside my vagina/uterus in a few weeks' time.

The scan proved I didn't have gestational diabetes. I just had lots of baby inside me, so much baby that my belly was a ledge my breasts rested on.

For the first time in my life, I had heartburn. It felt like death. But attempting to drink down a thick glass of Metamucil was also dreadful in that my gag reflex, heightened somehow by the pregnancy, was having none of it.

My partner, M, stood next to me at the sink, urging me to drink down the mucusy beverage, while I dry-heaved and hiccupped and blinked rapidly.

"Come *on*," he urged. "It's not that bad."

"I'm tryyyyyyying," I replied. Eventually, I gave up. By then, he was so frustrated he nearly cried.

Only wanting one child was also an involuntary reaction.

After the girl was born, whenever we were out in the world and I saw a sleepy-looking mother with a newborn in a bucket car seat and a rampaging two-year-old, I felt sorry for her. With one child, you can sometimes pretend that nothing has changed. Write all afternoon. Go to a restaurant. Sleep in. But with two or more, you have to give yourself over, admit that parenting and householding will take up the bulk of your time and energy.

Now, I know that some women don't view those full-up years when children are small with dismay. That they are, in fact, able to do other things besides parenting. That they welcome the transformation that mothering brings to their lives. And that parenting, in addition to all the other things they do, is what makes them feel fulfilled.

But I never had the certainty that some women seem to have: "I will have children." And its corollary, "I will have at least two children."

My only given as I approached adulthood was that I thought I should try to be happy.

I knew I wanted to be a writer when I was thirteen. But I also knew that I needed some way to make money because I understood early on that very few people make enough from writing to make their living from it.

My much-vaunted plan didn't include children, necessarily. Neither did it include a long-term relationship. It wasn't that I didn't like children or was opposed to commitment per se, but I just wasn't sure that I had the temperament or the tools for either path.

I hadn't always liked the hubbub of our medium-to-large family. I hadn't especially enjoyed my parents' separation and later divorce. And I'd noticed that my scientist mother's ambition wasn't always satisfied by — or relevant to — the life of our family.

So I foresaw a bookish existence in an apartment somewhere. And that was about it, in terms of my long-term planning.

⊙

My first book came out in 2010, four years after my daughter was born.

Hump was two-thirds poems on pregnancy and mothering, preceded by twenty urban/nature/love poems that set the stage for the transformation that is having a child.

I never would have guessed that my first book would be so tightly themed. But I'd been involved in a poem-a-day project toward the end of my pregnancy, when the only thing I could think to write about was being heavily pregnant. And then, after the girl was born, the public health nurse assigned to my bad old neighbourhood wanted me to chart the girl's "output" for two weeks. I found it immensely reassuring to look at the filled-up pages of the chart. Here was my incomprehensible baby, my incomprehensible life, on paper. Here was what I was doing. So I kept it up for four months, until I relaxed a bit. And because the chart was usually next to me when I breastfed, and because I was breast-feeding a lot of the time those first few months, it became my notebook. So I started writing tiny poems at the bottom of the pages, because tiny poems were all I could manage.

I don't believe in languid muses or that the poems just "come" and I'm just the one who holds the golden pen. I also don't think becoming a mother somehow improved my writing. But I will say that I had never felt so *compelled* to write poems on a particular subject before I got knocked up. Pregnancy and mothering and gender roles and the uncontrollable body and transformation and family. Sex and intimacy and sadness.

I wrote like stink in the years after the girl was born.

But when I was preparing the manuscript, I started to worry that people would want to talk about breast-feeding instead of the poems I'd written on breast-feeding. I was worried that my book — and, by extension, all the years I'd put into the poems, before and after baby — would be dismissed as "women's writing," which is sometimes code for writing that is based on experience instead of craft, writing that is emotionally baggy, even blowsy. Writing that is of interest only to women.

And I wanted what I had always wanted as a writer: to have my poetry read by a wide range of people, parent and non-parent, male and female. So I worried.

Three years later, people mostly ask me when my next book is coming out instead of when my next child is due. It's a relief to have the poetry and the parenting separate again, though really they're not separate at all.

My choice to have only one child came, in part, from a desire to protect my writing. Most of the choices I've made in my adult life have been about protecting my writing, actually. Where I lived, where I worked, how I spent the off hours — all chosen based on how much or how little they impacted my writing time.

But this was a decision of a different magnitude.

When it came right down to it, I didn't think I could be a working writer with more than one child. And I was unwilling to take a break when my writing and my writing life — the time I spent in the company of other writers at readings and conferences and retreats — were finally starting to gel.

⊙

My scientist mother was one of five children. My accountant father one of three. I have two full sisters, a half-sister, and a stepsister.

The house where I grew up was loud. Sitting around the dinner table, we could talk about anything. And we liked talking about our anything at the top of our voices.

Now that we're all grown up with children of our own, arranging for everyone to sit down at the dinner table takes several go-rounds via e-mail. And the assembly itself usually overflows the dinner table and the card table dragged up from the basement, with people sitting on the couch with plates of food in their laps.

There's never just one conversation at these dinners. And conversations are frequently interrupted by children wanting something. So any dialogue that requires all of us means paring away spouses and children or activating our *particular* version of the telephone tree.

Ours is not an emergency response system in the usual sense. Basically, when someone's feelings get hurt, whoever *isn't* involved will get a series of phone calls. If my sisters fight, for instance, I'll get phone calls from each of them and, also, usually, from my mother—each one pleading her case, each wanting someone that understands to hear her out.

I mostly just listen and try not to make it worse. And I tell each party that I've heard from the other party too, just so there aren't any crossed wires. And that's usually enough. The interested parties feel consoled. And if the argument isn't specifically resolved via these conversations, then a couple of weeks with limited contact in the midst of our busy lives usually does the trick.

My partner will sit and listen to this flurry of phone calls for a while. Then he'll leave the room, muttering, "You're all nuts."

He's an only child. I had to teach him how to fight and have it not mean anything. What he didn't understand then is that, for my family, fighting was a form of exercise, a game with lots of shouting. What he doesn't understand now is that this argument is my mum and my sisters and I trying to figure out how to be close to each other, despite our differences, despite the demands of our lives. We're trying to make sure that no one has to be alone.

For M, having one kid was *enough*. And that was as complicated as it got for him.

For me, it's a different story. I sometimes wonder how our daughter will feel about being an only child. Will she regret not having siblings? Will that deficit be part of the story she tells about our family?

"I'm an only child," she'll say, tipsy, looking longingly at the big family at the next table. "Because my mother was too *selfish*. Writing *poems* was more important to her than having babies."

⊙

My partner and I were together for seven years, from our late twenties until our mid-thirties, before we got knocked up.

Early on, I told him that if I got pregnant accidentally, I would probably abort. Because I was ambitious, just like my mother before me, and I wasn't ready. He agreed. We'd both had friends who had had condom failures and had gone for the morning-after pill or who'd had abortions.

So when two pregnancy tests confirmed that I was pregnant, he looked me in the eyes, his face neutral, and asked me what I wanted to do.

I loved him for that. But without having to think about it, I knew I couldn't abort. Because we were no longer in our twenties. We had a house and a car and had settled into some version of the careers we each wanted. And there was a delicious warmth, suddenly, around having a child together.

And that was that. Our next family planning conversation, which took place a few weeks after our daughter was born, was just as brief:

"Do you want to have any more?"

"No."

"Me neither."

Now that I'm forty and my reproductive window is about to slam shut, I sometimes regret that my daughter won't know what it's like to have nieces and nephews. That she won't be able to lean on her siblings the way that my sisters and I sometimes lean on each other.

I regret, too, that the girl won't know the burnt caramel of loving and hating a sibling.

Sometimes I wish that I'd had another child so that she would focus on that sibling sometimes instead of always on me. That I wasn't able to set up an us/them, parent/child dynamic in our house. For her, it's always "us," so she doesn't understand, for instance, why her father and I get to share a bed and she has to sleep in a different room all by herself. There's no good argument to counter that, or at least one that a young child would understand. In her mind, she's being excluded from our group for no reason. And that makes her enormously sad.

So we got a king-sized bed.

⊙

By the time the girl was three, I was working two days a week at a used bookstore, writing one day, and taking care of her the other four.

A co-worker who was about the same age had two kids. One day he announced that he and his wife were having another. "Yay!" "Congrats!" chimed my co-workers. I smiled and well-wished him too.

Three weeks before his wife was due, he disclosed that they had just discovered that she was carrying twins.

"What?" we all exclaimed. "How?"

He leered at that. "Yes, yes," we said, rolling our eyes. "You know what we mean!"

Having hoped to reuse the crib/car seat/clothing they'd used for their previous children, they soon realized they'd need an extra set of *everything*. As I read his jolly/panicked e-mail, asking if any of the parents of his acquaintance had cribs/car seats/clothing they could spare, I felt the familiar tickle that meant there was a poem somewhere in all of this. And then I went home and wrote this:

Primipara

A woman who is pregnant for the first time or who has borne just one child. — Webster's New World Dictionary

If I had had twins, I would have eaten one.

If I had had twins, I would have cracked
a beatific smile. *Thanks,*
but no. And primly given it/them back.

If I had had twins, I would have tucked
them under my arms like footballs or small perfect
hand-grenades aimed at my breasts: *fuck.*

If I had had twins, I would have kept mum.

I more or less finished the poem a few months after the twins—fraternal girls—were born. And I couldn't help myself: I gave my co-worker a copy of the poem to share with his wife.

◉

My daughter understands that I'm a writer. She's come to a few readings of mine and even told me when she didn't like particular poems. ("You know that poem about Granny? I didn't like that poem. *Why* did you write that poem?")

But she's only six and she doesn't really like it when I'm away from home. So I limit my retreats and workshops to fourteen days. Any more than that and it's too hard for both M and the girl.

So this spring, when I was packing up to leave on a two-week retreat to a farmhouse in the woods all by myself, I wasn't entirely surprised to have my daughter sidle up and tell me she didn't want me to go. And sniffle a bit.

I explained that she and writing were tied for my favourite things in the ENTIRE world. And that I *needed* to go write for a few weeks to be happy.

She looked at me and then suspiciously asked where tea was on my favourites list. (When I was home with her, I used to tell her, "Don't knock over my tea or I'll cry.") She also wanted to know where her father ranked.

The girl was pleased when I told her that tea was No. 2 and that M was No. 4 or 5.

My daughter is young. She likes things to be black or white. But I understand, and M understands, all the subtle shifts in our life together, all the negotiation it has taken so that I could have both an all-consuming daughter and an all-consuming craft.

And so, even though the girl won't have siblings to lean on when I'm old and impossible, when I'm dying, when I'm dead, I'm hoping that she can lean on the texts I've left behind.

That she'll be able to see me, to see our family, through them the way she might have through the eyes of a sibling.

A Natural Woman

AMY LAVENDER HARRIS

We are reading the anatomy book, my daughter and I, looking at hearts, neurons, and the digestive system, when she asks to see "babies being born."

This is her favourite part of the anatomy book. In richly illustrated detail, it describes reproductive anatomy and fetal development, from the structure of the ovaries and fallopian tubes to the development of the fetus in the uterus. It's my favourite part of the anatomy book, too, and we have spent long moments considering its mechanics and meanings before bedtime.

"This is what you looked like growing inside my body; inside my uterus," I tell her each time. It is a story she loves to hear — the story of her own becoming — and with her small fingers she traces the shape of the fetus, a plankton-turned-tadpole, deformed, then doll-like, a shifting cipher representing the stages of evolution.

It's when we get to the being born part that we run into trouble. We look at drawings of women in labour, at images of babies sliding through the slipstream of the birth canal, the placenta following like a fleshy parachute. A newborn, still glistening with amniotic fluid, lies at its mother's breast.

The trouble is that Katherine already knows she wasn't born this way. Like Macduff, she was "untimely ripped," wrenched from my body by Caesarean section at thirty-five weeks. She spent no glistening moments on my chest but was removed instead to an Isolette, electrodes taped to her chest, a feeding tube protruding from her nose. She spent no time in my arms until she was thirty hours old.

Images in the anatomy book of babies suckling at their mothers' breasts are equally unhelpful. Katherine enjoys poking at the springy texture of my breasts, and she thinks nipples are hilarious—but having drunk pumped breast milk for her entire first year, a legacy of the need to measure her food intake to the millilitre, breasts have no comforting associations, and drawings of milk ducts are as abstract to Katherine as river deltas on Mars.

For the moment, we have glossed over the mechanics of sexual reproduction, including the currently unmentionable details about how all those sperm end up floating in the fallopian tubes—details that are proscribed not because of the usual prudery about describing sexual reproduction to a four-year-old, but because I don't yet have the language to tell my daughter that her conception had little in common with drawings of a doe-eyed couple lying down together, and everything to do with the sterile, harshly lit environment of a fertility clinic.

A female infant is born with a million eggs—the store of her entire reproductive capacity. By puberty, their mass is reduced to about four hundred thousand—and, of that number, fewer than four hundred follicles will ever mature. The rest are absorbed into the dark matter of her body. And of the follicles that erupt from the surface of the ovary and begin their long journey through the fallopian tubes, very few will ever be fertilized, and even fewer will produce a viable embryo.

The production of follicles is governed by a delicate series of hormonal interactions, and if any of those chemicals are out of balance — or if something else is awry in her body's universe — they will never grow robust enough to be released into the fallopian tube. Each failed follicle is like a dead star.

In my lifetime I have ovulated — perhaps — a dozen times. My ovaries are an orbit of dead stars, ringed with follicles that never achieved sufficient mass to be released. This is because I have Polycystic Ovarian Syndrome, known colloquially as PCOS, a common cause of infertility affecting as many as 10 percent of fertile-aged women.

PCOS has a complicated etiology and a wide range of effects, of which infertility is not the only or perhaps even the most disconcerting one. Most women with PCOS do not menstruate often or regularly because they do not usually ovulate, putting them at increased risk of developing uterine cancer due to irregularities in the lining. Insulin resistance — a disruption in the body's ability to regulate and use insulin — means many are hypoglycemic, obese, and at risk of developing diabetes and heart disease. Because PCOS is an endocrine disorder, the body's entire hormonal regime is disrupted: some women show symptoms of androgen excess and grow unwanted body hair, develop male pattern baldness and battle persistent acne; in other women, an excess of estrogen unopposed by progesterone produces persistent weight gain and exaggerated PMS symptoms.

In me, PCOS has manifested as a parody of femininity. I have had large and buoyant breasts since my teens, appendages I thought of for years as udders and concealed under bulky sweaters. My hair is long and lush, my skin soft and pliant, and my body, when I am not overweight, matches that magical waist-to-hip ratio heterosexual men reportedly associate subliminally with optimal fertility. I Am Woman — in every way but the one that counts.

. . .

A fertility clinic is a perverse place. Behind the well-appointed waiting room and the richly upholstered office of the chief clinician is a stainless steel shrine to the age of mechanical reproduction. In tiny rooms, men, encouraged for once to check out the porn, ejaculate anxiously into tiny cups. Down the hall, their wives are penetrated by ultrasound probes measuring the size and number of follicles produced, in most cases, with the aid of powerful drugs. In every corner, fallopian tubes are flushed, sperm is centrifuged, embryos are transferred to waiting uteri. Actual infants—the desired product of this process—are never seen in the clinic, but the promise of them is everywhere in the form of snapshots, supplied by grateful parents and stapled to bulletin boards or arranged behind glass. In one montage among hundreds is a set of triplets, captioned with the scribbled warning: "Oops!"

When the results of our initial fertility workup came in, the chief clinician practically slapped my husband on the back, congratulating him heartily on the excellent quality and quantity of his sperm. More muted was praise for my reproductive potential which, clear fallopian tubes and plentiful ovarian reserve aside, was marred by my apparent inability to produce ripe follicles even with drug stimulation.

On fertility drugs notorious for their hormonal side effects, I felt . . . nothing. Not even a twinge. When we got into the big guns—the injectables used primarily in in-vitro fertilization—my ovaries condescended to produce a few tiny follicles, none large enough to be released. It was only when our doctor agreed, in violation of clinic policy, to double the dose in mid-cycle that we saw action. Four or five lovely follicles, one noticeably larger than the rest, grew luminous on the ultrasound screen like stars, at long last, achieving sufficient mass for fusion.

Scheduled the next morning to return to the fertility factory for a "trigger shot" meant to push ovulation, after which my husband's centrifuged sperm would then have been injected directly into my uterus, our plans were derailed by a December snowstorm. Unable to reach the clinic, we were instructed instead to attempt procreation in the traditional manner. And so we did. While the wind roared and snow whirled around the house, we lay down together. And by the time we returned to the clinic, I knew already that I had successfully ovulated, and a week later, when I felt something travel from the furthest reaches of the cosmos to crash-land on the surface of my uterus, I knew I was pregnant.

It's a myth, of course, that motherhood cures infertility. Apart from needing to repeat the entire emotionally exhausting, financially draining process with any subsequent attempt to conceive, infertility complicates not only your identity as a mother but your worth as a woman.

In this post-feminist era of "natural" mothering, in which "fertility awareness" conception planning, drug-free vaginal delivery, extended breast-feeding, co-sleeping, and attachment parenting have become what amount to a new morality, women who resort to technological means to conceive and carry a pregnancy are deeply suspect.

We are judged, too, against a social stigma in which infertile women are denigrated as selfish bitches for having "waited too long" to conceive, instructed to "just adopt," accused of financially draining the public health care system, and—perhaps worst of all—told our infertility means we are biologically unfit to reproduce.

This stigma persists despite the reality that infertility affects up to 20 percent of couples hoping to conceive; that men are as likely to be infertile as women; that the average age of women referred for fertility treatment is just above thirty-five; that adoption is often more expensive and can take longer (and has as low a likelihood of success) as fertility treatments; that few fertility treatments are covered by the public health care system, let alone private insurance plans; and that most women who do conceive via fertility treatments go on to have healthy pregnancies and bear children who thrive.

One product of this stigma is a kind of "don't ask, don't tell" approach to infertility. When we were trying to conceive our daughter, I told no one, not even close friends and family members, because almost as bad as the judgment and incomprehension would have been instructions to "just relax," followed by the incessant "aren't you pregnant *yet*?" Even when we did finally conceive, after a year of trying and six very intense cycles of fertility treatments, I didn't tell people I was knocked up until months into the pregnancy, and even after that I referred resolutely to my daughter as "the fetus" (or "the parasite") as an emotional hedge against further disaster. I read online blogs, mainly anonymous, maintained by other infertile women who tended to adopt similar practices for self-protection.

Since my daughter was born, I have been quite open about my infertility. In some ways, I can afford to be. I was thirty-five when I conceived and thirty-six when I gave birth—too young to be saddled with the "geriatric mother" label. My ovarian reserve was excellent for my age. My reproductive parts were properly formed. My problem amounted to a hormonal missed cue, treatable with the right combination of drugs. My daughter's premature birth, the result of her amniotic sac rupturing spontaneously, was completely unrelated to my infertility. And let me not even start on the medical expediency of a C-section that healed so quickly I was back on my bike ten days later, or the wonderful efficiency of a breast pump that filled our freezer with so much extra milk we made fabulous hand-churned ice cream with the surplus.

In "A Cyborg Manifesto," biologist and feminist social theorist Donna Haraway argues famously against both patriarchal and feminist perspectives that essentialize women's bodies, holding instead that technology has profoundly altered what we may think of as "natural." Haraway's manifesto has been understood primarily as a call to rethink cultural metaphors about gender and science, but in an era defined by intelligent prosthetics, artificial hearts, deep brain stimulation, and (perhaps most pointedly) reproductive technologies, we need urgently to reconsider the ways we embody our tools—and the way our tools embody us.

Technological alarmists, religious fundamentalists, and some feminists assail assisted reproductive technologies for tampering with the God-given order of things, for commodifying fertility, and for producing "designer babies" whose characteristics are pre-selected in a petri dish. They fixate on forty-something celebrities pushing their $100,000 babies around in $10,000 strollers, on sex selection and selective reduction, and on Bengali women serving as surrogates to wealthy North Americans for the price of a motorcycle and a few chickens.

The reality, however, is that most infertile women hoping to conceive aren't looking to replicate *Gattaca* or design the perfect brown- or blue-eyed baby boy or girl. We are simply hoping to accomplish the one thing that seems most natural to most women: to conceive and carry a child, to share our love and experience with a creature we have helped create, and to seed something of ourselves into the expanding cosmos.

. . .

We named our daughter Katherine Aurora because she is made of pure light. Like a star spiralling from a distant supernova, she travelled from the farthest reaches of the cosmos to belong to us and be our girl.

She is our golden child: glorious, effervescent, and vividly alive. She is so lovely that I weep: to be so fortunate as to share this world with her, to have come so close to not having her at all.

At school, she shows us her drawings, the colours scribbled only loosely within the lines. She is proud of her work and we take pleasure in her pride. This child, created out of nothing more than a few cells and the dust of distant stars, counts to twenty, recites the alphabet, builds elaborate structures with wooden blocks: she is all potential, and the universe opens itself for her.

At home, she plays serious, experimental compositions on an inexpensive electronic keyboard, then asks me to help her strap a baby carrier and hideous doll to her chest, and puts on a silly hat and dances to the theme from *Peter Pan*. Yes, child: you can certainly fly.

There is something vitally redemptive about watching a child—especially a daughter—unfurl. Motherhood, for me at least, is a time for second chances. Like all parents honest enough to admit it, I live vicariously, at least a little, through my daughter. What else can explain the sheer pleasure—the delight—I feel in buying her lovely little clothes and in washing and hanging them to dry? In coming across new plastic ponies to add to her prodigious collection? In watching her twirl, climb, swim, and ride a bike: the ease with which she moves her luminous limbs is restorative to me.

She is all girl: a lover of dolls and kittens and unicorns, a snail shell collector, an amateur ornithologist, a dancer, and an aspiring paleontologist. She is a storyteller, a memory artist, and a confident negotiator. She is gentle; she is strong; she is as smart as a whip. She is all these things and more—and the effortlessness of her embodiment has taught me something I never learned as a child: how to be utterly comfortable in my own skin.

To hell with the anatomy book, I have come to think. To hell with tidy drawings that cannot begin to describe the tragedy—and wonder —of inhabiting bodies that accomplish so many things even as they betray us. To hell with biological determinism, "natural" motherhood, binary feminisms, and gender dualisms. Because, as Donna Haraway suggests, we are all cyborgs, made of mitochondria and bits of metal, elements absorbed from the atmosphere and the cells of every child we have ever carried. We are hybrid beings as women, regardless of whether we were born that way, how we perform our gender, when and how and even whether we are mothers. We are all these things and more, and the universe opens itself for us.

A few weeks after we bought our daughter a telescope so she could look at the constellations and planets, she woke us up weeping, she said, because she was afraid the stars would disappear before she could look at them again. Oh, they'll wait for you, my child, I thought. They'll wait for you because they'll always recognize one of their own.

The Best Interests of the Child

FIONA TINWEI LAM

In late August 2011, I had lunch with a cousin from England who was visiting for a family wedding. During the course of the meal, we chatted about the upcoming nuptials and about everyone's travels and activities. At one point, I inquired about the news reports of mobs of young men engaged in rioting, looting, and arson in London and other towns in England earlier that month. As my cousin was a London resident, I thought he would have an insider's perspective on issues of poverty and social alienation there.

"Why is this happening now? What do you think the root cause of the riots is?" I asked.

He paused to look me directly in the eye. "Single mothers," he replied.

I nearly coughed out my salad. My cousin knew very well I had been a single mother for almost nine years.

That night, I brooded over his words. They seemed to crystallize all the unspoken judgments made about me by my extended family and by strangers unfamiliar with my background. I thought back to the moment I emerged from the doctor's office having just received confirmation of my pregnancy. I was in a state of shock.

"What do you want to do now?" asked a close friend who'd accompanied me.

I considered this for a moment, and then said, "Celebrate!"

I'd yearned for but not expected my child. That he came to me was a great blessing. It also set me on a difficult, heart-opening journey into the most profound and meaningful transition of my life.

As my pregnancy progressed, however, I felt like a teenaged mother having to break the news to my elders, even though I was in my thirties. My paternal grandmother in Hong Kong and other conservative relatives made me feel as if I were shaming and dishonouring my family. My grandmother was so horrified at the news of my pregnancy that she refused to inform other relatives about it. After I sent out birth announcements, she avoided the subject. Even my mother, in the intermediate stage of dementia, exclaimed to my sister, aghast, "She must have had *sex* with that man!" after it finally sunk in that I was eight months' pregnant.

When I thought about my cousin blaming single mothers for the London riots, I wondered once again about the origins of those old-fashioned and paternalistic attitudes toward single mothers, and how they have persisted into modern times. In the spring of 2012, *The National Post* published a series of articles exposing the systemic practice by social workers, medical practitioners, and church-run maternity homes of coercing thousands of single mothers across the country to give up their infants for adoption from the 1940s through 1980s. A class-action lawsuit was launched in March 2012, accusing the BC government of abduction, fraud, and coercion in relation to the adoption of infants of unmarried women during that period, with more class-action lawsuits to be filed in other provinces later this year.

At the time, unmarried and pregnant girls and women were considered "loose" and too "feeble-minded" to care for their babies.

Some young women were told their infants had died during birth. Others were tied down and covered with sheets to prevent them from seeing or touching their infants as they were being born. Shortly after giving birth, when they were still reeling from the after-effects of medication, many were compelled to sign surrender documents without being advised of their legal rights to revoke the adoption, to request temporary wardship, or to obtain social assistance.

Both sexism and society's judgmental, sanctimonious, and hypocritical attitudes about sex outside of marriage were at the basis of attitudes that separated mothers and fathers from their children, causing untold social and psychological damage. Vestiges of those attitudes still exist in North America today and flourish in conservative religious and cultural communities, despite the significant rise in the number of women who are single mothers by choice. In 2010, 281 single women registered with the Genesis Fertility Clinic in Vancouver out of a total of 2,081 patients, and there are likely many more who are single mothers by choice who have conceived through natural means.[2]

Before my pregnancy, when I was mulling over my future and whether to have children, two family members suggested I should babysit someone else's kids before I considered adopting or having a child on my own, as if this could even come close to replicating the experience of parenthood. They assumed that I was deluded or naive about the difficulties of raising a child on my own. I knew that if I did not have a child I would deeply regret it for the rest of my life. This yearning wasn't about wanting to be a wife or to have a perfect family, or to have a new experience or adventure that would provide me with companionship and future support. Rather, it had to do with a profound sense of who and what I was meant to be, of my life purpose. There was absolutely no substitute.

A lineage of single moms

I grew up in a family headed by a single parent. When alive, our father had been a distant figure orbiting us. He was present at meals and someone to defer to, but he rarely interacted directly with us except to engage in an occasional awkward conversation about school. After he died of cancer at forty-two, my mother raised the three of us single-handedly. I was eleven, my sister eight, and my brother only three. Everything became harder. My mother was always exhausted and stressed. She had a difficult return to the practice of medicine after an eight-year absence, taking over my father's office, and taking on locums, house calls, and night deliveries. We all coped as best we could. Our mother was used to not having a father around the home, having been raised by a single mother herself after my grandfather died during the Japanese invasion of Hong Kong during World War II when she was only eight years old. Because of the war, my grandfather's large household, composed of his four concurrent wives together with two dozen children and various servants, had been broken up. My grandmother, the fourth and youngest wife, was left with her nine children to raise. Somehow the family survived the war and the challenging years afterwards.

"I need a wife!" my mother declared one day after work as she came through the back door, exhausted, knowing she had to make dinner, clear the sink of dirty dishes, and deal with the three kids clamouring for her attention. She needed someone to support her — someone who would cook, clean, take care of the house, do the paperwork, register us for after-school and summer activities, chauffeur us to those activities, do the laundry, and shop for our clothes. Although she repeated this declaration a few times over the years, she never once said, "I need a husband." Our mother also never talked to us about the need to pull together, to do more to help her out. We eventually just figured it out. As a twelve-year-old, I learned to make dinner so she could rest. When we went out to eat, it wasn't unusual for her to lay her head down on the table to nap after our orders were taken, so that she could catch a few moments of sleep. Sometimes the stress became too much and she would lash out at the staff. Mortified and critical, I didn't understand until much later the kind of pressures she was facing.

When my father was alive, I'd witnessed my mother struggle within the institution of marriage, her ambitions and independence compromised by my father and his family, who had refused to let her work as a physician, who even suggested she become my father's receptionist, despite her having diplomas from the UK in obstetrics and gynaecology. She was meant to be a doctor not a traditional wife, let alone someone's personal assistant.

Her frequent admonitions to me about never becoming dependent on a man financially, her rants about my father's family preventing her from working as a doctor, plus the memories of the tension between my parents made marriage seem highly unappealing, even threatening. I didn't date until my twenties, and even then rarely. But after falling in love with a classmate in law school, I decided to give marriage a try. During the six following years, I increasingly chafed against being a "wife," just as my mother had. When faced with having to relinquish a career of my own and move to another country to immerse myself fully in the role, I panicked. This was exactly the loss of identity, status, independence, and selfhood that my mother had experienced and railed against, and I was not willing to risk these things for a man who no longer desired me and whom I no longer desired either.

Not wanting to be married didn't mean I didn't want to have a child. This desire to be a mother and not a wife did not seem contradictory to me, given how I'd grown up. But no one else I knew at the time seemed to feel the same way. I'd seen how difficult single motherhood had been for my mother, yet I thought I could somehow manage it with just one child. I even thought I might do better than she did by giving my child the nurturing that I hadn't experienced myself growing up. When I mentioned to a counsellor that I was considering having a child on my own, she admonished me, "A child needs both a mother and father."

Professor Margaret Somerville, founding director of the Centre for Medicine, Ethics and Law at McGill University, said essentially the same thing in 2005 before a parliamentary committee deliberating the legalization of gay marriage. She was castigated for this in the media and by gay rights groups across the country. Although her arguments were focused on the issue of gay marriage, she also used them later in criticizing adoption, assisted reproductive technologies, single women seeking donor sperm, or anything that would "unlink child-parent biological bonds." She described how adults conceived through donor sperm experience "powerful feelings of loss of identity through not knowing one or both of their biological parents and their wider biological families." She has also stated that "knowing who our close biological relatives are and relating to them is central to how we form our human identity, relate to others and the world, and find meaning in life."

I pondered this position for a long time. The pendulum has swung back and forth about the importance of heredity and biology, but was it right to privilege biological links over other significant factors in raising a child? Innumerable examples past and present of incest and physical and emotional abuse demonstrate that some biological parents can be harmful to their offspring. I thought about some of my friends and acquaintances who had been adopted. Two had absolutely no interest in discovering their biological parentage. Another who contacted her biological parents faced disappointment upon discovering the truth about her birthmother, and did not wish to maintain contact. I wondered about the offspring of sperm donors who might have untold numbers of unknown half-siblings throughout the world. I'd also read about the cultural dislocation caused by international adoptions and the murky ethics surrounding the procurement of children for adoption in some countries. I considered my own situation: my father had been absent for the majority of my life, and barely present when alive. Had I needed him? Was a father necessary, even relevant? I thought of that popular quote by Gloria Steinem, that "a woman needs a man like a fish needs a bicycle." Was this true?

I'd missed having a relationship with my father. I felt a deep ache and sense of loss from not having known him or spent more time with him. My siblings and I had grown up to be healthy, educated, productive citizens. But for much of my life, I had felt there was a chasm—a missing piece, a mystery. People told me I looked like him, that I had his forehead, hands, and eyes. I wondered about my father, his life, his feelings. I ultimately decided that I didn't want to risk my child experiencing the feeling that something fundamental to his identity was lacking in his life. If it were possible, I wanted my child to have a strong relationship with the person who was 50 percent responsible for his existence and creation, and to have a sense of his roots from both directions.

The realities of single motherhood

When I became unexpectedly pregnant, I was surprised at how ambivalent I felt, given that I'd longed to have a child for years. I'd fallen deeply in love with a man who was recently separated and was unready to commit to another serious long-term relationship. It wasn't clear at the time how much involvement he would have in our child's life. I was frightened and apprehensive of the reality of becoming a single parent but felt compelled to continue the journey into motherhood. The child I'd wished for was about to arrive, irrespective of my personal circumstances or situation. I'd have to "gird my loins" and prepare myself as best I could for what lay ahead.

The first night home from the hospital after my son's birth, I had dinner with my family. For twenty minutes, I sat at the table, very hungry but unable to cut the meat on my plate with the baby on my lap. No one noticed, and so eventually I asked for help. This was one of the more important if elementary lessons I would learn as a new mother. In the past, I had avoided asking people for help, afraid of feeling obligated to another person or being perceived as weak. Now I would have no choice. For my child's sake and my own, not only would I need to learn to recognize when I needed help and how to ask for it, but I would also need to learn how to accept and receive help graciously when it was offered. I had to unclench myself from the private, guarded stance I'd developed since childhood as a self-sufficient introvert, and open myself up to the possibility of networks of support around me that I could create or participate in.

Those first four years were challenging. From the start, my son had difficulty napping and falling asleep. He didn't sleep through the night consistently until he was four-and-a-half years old. The years of sleep deprivation took a severe toll. Also, I felt trapped and isolated at home and so would try to escape with him to the park or community centre, which would often lead to him catching a cold. I, in turn, would get sick, making sleep even more difficult for both of us. I didn't know many other new moms, let alone single ones, and often felt profoundly alone.

I gradually recognized how powerful the ties of family were, especially as my mother's dementia progressed and she became increasingly child-like and dependent. My sister and brother, although consumed with my mother's care, rallied around me. When it was difficult for me to visit my mother in her care home, we organized weekly potluck dinners at my home so that we could all be together. My sister attended prenatal classes, midwife appointments, and the hospital birth with me, and was right by my side in the operating room. She has been a devoted aunt, supplying piles of toys and clothes over the years, and was always available to babysit if asked when I needed to see the dentist or get a haircut.

I also came to realize how supportive so many of my deeply trusted friends truly were, from the close friend who came with me to that first doctor's appointment, to a neighbour who brought over a few homemade casseroles when my son was a newborn, to another who came over to hold him one time so I could take a shower in peace, and others who gladly offered to babysit. In those early months, my son's father occasionally granted me a few extra hours of precious sleep in the early mornings by taking him for a walk up to a neighbourhood coffee shop. As our son grew older, his father became much more involved as a parent.

It is a cliché to say that I came to understand my own mother better when I became a mother myself, but it is very true. There was a sudden, searingly lucid moment when I understood my mother's hardships as a single parent. One morning after another long night alone, of little sleep interrupted by frequent bouts of getting up to nurse, I was groggily making pancake batter in the kitchen in my bare feet, when my elbow tipped over a full litre bottle of maple syrup on the counter. It smashed on the tile floor, spraying shards of glass, cornering me against the stove. A large sticky puddle of syrup expanded to cover half the floor.

My toddler came running over from his room. Terrified that he'd step on the broken glass, I ordered him to stop. He paused, confused, but tottered forward again. I shouted and finally screamed at him to stand back, but this only made him cry harder and move forward, reaching out for me. Certain he would get hurt, exasperated that he would not obey me, I gingerly ran through the glass. Brain burning, I grabbed him and yelled at him while he stared at me in shock. As if from far away, I heard my mother's own irrational rage channelled through my own voice. So much for trying to be the perfect mother, the kind who taught her baby sign language, recited nursery rhymes, made organic homemade purées, bought organic cotton clothing and educational toys, did mom-and-baby yoga, played classical music during and after pregnancy, tried to speak phrases in three languages at every opportunity, breast-fed for over two years. Instead, I had become my mother, the woman who I had harshly judged decades before—as blind, impatient, exasperated, and deeply flawed as she had been. It was a moment of karmic comeuppance.

The majority of single mothers I know have had a much harder time than I have. Some single mothers are financially secure and others face ongoing, serious financial challenges. There's a considerable range in how much financial or logistical assistance single mothers might receive (or not receive) from the fathers of their children or other family members and friends. Some fathers are involved in their children's lives, perhaps seeing them regularly on weekends or holidays, while others see them rarely or not at all.

At one time, I lived near another single mom who had left her abusive spouse and had a son the same age as mine. The father provided no support and only rarely saw his son. To make enough money for rent, she worked the night shift doing data entry work. She'd arranged childcare but it fell through, so for a while she had to bring her son with her to the office at night. She'd bring her laptop so he could watch a movie, as well as a sleeping bag and pillow so he could sleep while she worked. In the wee hours, she'd carry him to the car with all her gear.

A friend who was a teacher adopted a six-month-old baby girl from the US. After several months, she had to wear splints on both her arms due to tendonitis caused by lifting and carrying her child. Her lease ran out, and the home she had purchased and was renovating wasn't ready for habitation, so she stayed with her baby on a friend's couch for a few months. When she had to return to teaching, she needed me at the store to hold her baby while she tried on clothes she desperately needed for work. She told me that she had been trying to repair the kitchen herself after moving into their new home, but that the baby would start to cry as soon as she was put down. My friend could only hammer a nail every fifteen minutes. Their stories are similar to those of married women who must raise children single-handedly because their partners are chronically ill or working long hours or living far from home.

I've learnt that whether you are a single or a married mother, perfection is unattainable and raising a child can be an exhausting and lonely experience. The economically, socially, and culturally diverse single mothers I've come across as friends or participants in the writing workshops I've conducted for YWCA Single Mother Support groups, whether single by choice or by circumstance, are trying their utmost to raise loved, stable, balanced, happy children at great personal cost. If anything, it's greater family and community support they deserve and require, not criticism and skepticism. Yet, like others, I've had to deal with assumptions that single mothers must lack some essential ingredient that all married mothers must possess just because they have husbands, as if having a husband were a stamp of social and moral acceptability and a guarantee of future stability. We seem to be under more scrutiny, more subject to the misguided assumptions and moral judgments of others. One of my son's teachers presumed that my son must be a product of a traumatic divorce simply because he lives in two separate homes. A mother, whose son my child had just befriended, interrogated me about divorce proceedings, property division, and custody arrangements, not knowing that none of those legal steps were necessary in my case. My son's father and I always had a relationship of mutual respect and could resolve any disagreements ourselves without need to seek recourse through the legal system. Also, we never fit the definition of cohabiting spouses under the law. It was always clear that I would be the primary caregiver and that I was capable of financially supporting my son.

Shifting definitions

In May 2011, BC Supreme Court Judge Elaine Adair sided with Olivia Pratten, who had discovered that her mother's doctor had destroyed records with information about the identity of her biological father. Echoing Dr. Margaret Somerville's position, the judge agreed that Pratten and other children conceived by sperm donation "who are deprived of their genetic backgrounds suffer psychological harm." This attitude about the "best interests of the child" represents a complete *volte-face* from the official position not so long ago when so-called illegitimate children were taken from their young single mothers, let alone when First Nations children were forcibly placed in church-based residential schools. The concept of a child's "best interests" is not neutral but has clearly shifted, reflecting the norms and prejudices of a particular time.

In our case, my child has been extremely fortunate: he has always had a strong relationship with both me and his father, as well as both our families. Knowing how much I missed having an emotional connection with my own father, I've always fostered the bond my son has with his father. My son's life has been full of family, rich with exploration and activity both athletic and artistic, and most importantly steeped in love from every side from day one. It's appalling that some people still harbour conscious or unconscious prejudices and stereotypes about single mothers when such a diversity of parenting styles and structures exists in today's world—and in reality, have existed in other cultures and other eras where older siblings, grandparents, aunts, uncles, and other extended family work together in tightly knit communities to provide strong support networks for each growing child.

I'd occasionally joked that my mother, who never remarried (and never wished to), could have been happily married to a carpenter, someone whose profession was completely different from hers. She had superb mechanical and artistic skills: she could take apart a radio and put it back together again, sew, perform surgery, birth babies, sculpt soapstone, paint watercolours —and admired mechanical and artistic skills in others. I imagined her happy with someone practical and creative, someone whose career wouldn't interfere with hers, who would admire and support her, yet be self-sufficient, not requiring the secretary/cook/nanny/housecleaner/decorator/hostess/nurse that many professional men seemed to expect from their spouses in exchange for financial and emotional support—a constellation of servants rolled into one rather than a true equal.

After many years alone, I'm the one who has ended up with a carpenter, a cabinet-maker to be exact—a combination of companion, lover, and best friend who doesn't expect me to play the role of a wife, just as I don't expect him to play the role of a husband. He is a much better housekeeper than I am. He has a warm and playful relationship with my son, leaving the parenting to me and his father. Most importantly, he fully accepts and encourages me as both a writer and a mother.

I look back on the past ten years with amazement—both at the child who has shot up to the level of my nose and who now reads as fast as I can, and at the personal journey that has transformed me from the person I was into who I continue to become. Having witnessed various dysfunctional family dynamics between married people, I know not to make easy assumptions about what kind of family is best. All kinds of unexpected challenges can arise in any type of family—personality clashes, conflicting philosophies, let alone different economic, logistical, and emotional stresses and strains. What constitutes the ideal is more complex than merely having a biological mother and a biological father living together in one household parenting their biological children. To establish a strong foundation of true stability and connectedness requires fostering a deep sense of rootedness in family and community and providing consistent nourishment and shelter for the body, heart, mind, and spirit. There are as many possible ways to establish that strong foundation as there are kinds of people and kinds of families. The one-size-fits-all rigid, simplistic equation for family happiness ignores our human diversity, adaptability, and complexity.

The Girl on the Subway

DEANNA McFADDEN

"How warm and lovely it was to hold a child in one's lap, and the soft little arms, the unconscious cheeky little legs." — D.H. Lawrence, *Lady Chatterley's Lover*

On my way home from work on the days that I don't pick up my son from daycare, I often see a man on the subway. He rides home with his daughter, who looks to be about three, just a touch older than my son. The dad reads to her from a much-loved Slavic-language picture book, its edges frayed with use, and he carries a banana in one of those plastic protectors that I find slightly ridiculous. The little girl eats her banana slowly and pays close attention to each page. When she finishes, her father takes the peel back and places it with equal care in its plastic case. The story always ends just as they get to their stop.

They are calm. The little girl is attentive and doesn't fuss. I hear her ask questions, and also listen carefully to her father's answers. Tired, angry people surround them, people who are hot, frustrated, and confined by an enforced patience that doesn't come naturally to those of us crammed into a metal box as it hurtles down a track. The little one notices none of this — she's not openly fascinated with the subway like other kids, nor does she pay much attention to the people around her. Happily encased in her daddy's arms, she's safe on his lap, and when their stop comes along, he swoops her up and carts her off with ease. The tenderness of the everyday catches me up each time. It's not something I ever would have noticed before I had a baby.

No, I'm lying.

Before I had a baby, I would have watched them together and felt a deep, almost indescribable longing for my own child. I couldn't admit to the ache out loud; it would get me nowhere. There was nothing to be done about it—the decision was made. We weren't having children. Our lives were moving in a different direction. And, on the whole, I was okay with that. I had plans. Places to go. Words to write.

Before I had a baby, this perfect scene of a father and daughter was how I imagined parenting was for most people. Well-behaved children, quaint scenes of reading books while commuting—that's what I pictured: a pretty little girl on my lap, attentively listening to the same stories I read when I was a child. Oh, how foolish.

My kid, a source of raw energy that could power a small nation, never sits still on public transit. Trapped, he kicks and bucks, colt-like and half-crazed. I've got about four stops, during which he's preoccupied by a snack, but after which he's writhing in his stroller, shrieking and attempting to pull everyone's knapsacks open. Unleashing him turns out to be even more of a mistake. Once he slid down me before I could get a good hold on him, and within seconds, he was under the filthy seat, pawing at something disgusting. And then he climbed up me to get to the top of the seat, half on top of the person sitting next to us, just to get to the window. I spent the whole ride apologizing. Of course, this is a pretty typical subway ride with an almost-toddler. It's not his fault. The world remains wide open to him, every bit of him humming toward an adventure, every sense on high alert, an unstoppable force.

Then one day we took the car to daycare. Soon after, I gave up my dream of being a *green* mom who proudly totes her kid back and forth on public transit. Those days during the week when he's in daycare, I'm in full-on suburban mom mode—I am as my mother was. We grew up in Mississauga and we drove everywhere, my brother and I rolling around the backseat of our lemon-yellow Chevrolet. I feel guilty every time I buckle my son into his seat, contributing to the carbon crisis. The car's packed with musical entertainment, and my bag is full of anything else that might allow us to get from point A to B without suffering a complete baby meltdown. I feel revolted every time I shell out fourteen dollars for parking and look longingly at the cyclists beside us as we spew toxins into the air. But it's easier. Sometimes I can't forgive myself for making it so, as if I've given up in a way, being so far off from what I imagined, from the kind of good parent I think I recognize in the father of the little girl from the subway.

No, my boy isn't a quiet, attentive easy-going subway rider, and that's okay. I have a different dream now. On the best days, one of us (him) will become utterly enthralled by the sight of a street filled with construction vehicles. What route has the most roadwork? Yes, that's the way we'll go—traffic and timing be damned—to see diggers, excavators, cranes, bulldozers. That makes him happy.

This is my life *After*.

On the three days he's home with his father while I go to work, I go back to *Before*. I walk to the bus stop with an open book in my hand. I'm surrounded by space on the commute, and it feels strange to not have a child attached to some part of my body. The people around me are the same tired sort populating the transit every day, and from the outside, I am one of them. But on the inside, I feel distinct. The familiar faces on the bus in the morning, I'm sure, do not notice that I took a year off to stay home with my son. They can't tell how much has changed in my life now—if anyone notices at all, I'm just the same bookish girl as I was before I had my son: a person who sometimes gets a seat or who sometimes doesn't, but one who never takes her eyes from the page.

But everything, everything is different on the inside. I'm discombobulated by not having slept enough. It's earlier than I imagined being awake was possible. Before, I'd have to drag myself out of bed, snooze button well worn, always late, always dreading the morning. Now our alarm clock sits bedside, dusty, because our boy wakes up so, so, so early. I used to rail against the time I'd have to spend getting to and from work—the stops and starts when a train's delayed, the crowds, impolite people. Now I savour my commute because the half-hour that I spend in transit to and from work five days a week is just about the only time I have to myself these days. And I'm often too tired, too overwhelmed, and too broken to actively savour it. Sometimes it's impossible not to romanticize how easy life was before I had a child. Even though I have always wanted him, I wasn't at all prepared for how he, that sweet, sweet boy, would blow my life up like a bomb.

Before, I had come to terms with not having kids. That, I think, is the right way to put it. My husband and I had made *plans*. Big changes. A move overseas. Something fresh, different. "Do it while we're still young enough to enjoy it." He had never wanted kids, anyway. I always wanted children, but my complicated health situation (I have a rare autoimmune disease called Wegener's granulomatosis) meant it wasn't realistic. In my husband's words, why would he risk losing me for some kid he's never met? He had his music; his band has done well. I wrote in my spare time. We watched movies all weekend. Went to rock shows. Travelled. It wasn't perfect. We were both relatively miserable in our jobs. Neither of us had ever lived anywhere other than Toronto and its surrounding suburbs.

And then, on the happiest weekend he had had in a long, long time, when a wonderful, creative project he was involved in came to fruition, I dropped the news that I was pregnant —and sort of ruined everything. What's that awful saying? There's nothing like life to come along and crash into your plans? Indeed.

Pregnancy, for the most part, was a breeze. Or it was until the end when my disease exploded, and I almost died. Modern medicine worked wonders. Great doctors, great nurses: they saved my life. Here should have been a clue to how much everything in my life would change once our boy was here: the blood doctor—who was trying to stop the hemoptysis in my lungs—told me that the baby was going to be fine. According to the hematologist, babies are, for the most part, parasites, sucking whatever they need and leaving behind the mother's body as a shell. In my case, the plasma-exchange therapy was a desperate measure—they needed to stop the bleeding in my lungs. My body was taking away my life just as intensely as it was giving it to this new human being. At thirty-four weeks, the baby was perfect, cocooned in my belly while the disease pummelled my kidneys, my lungs, and my blood counts. I have never been so scared or so sick in my entire life.

Yet in the moments during the day when they'd wrap my belly in the tensor bandage that hooked me up to the fetal monitor, I would hear that heartbeat thrumming along, and it was all I could do not to reach inside and hold onto that baby for dear life. I *wanted* him. I needed him to be okay. I worried so much about him while he was growing inside, and it was beyond irrational. In the end, I should have spent more time worrying about myself, because when he emerged, he was just fine.

So he was born in a whirlwind, and we were unprepared for his arrival—they induced at thirty-six weeks, judging that the disease would only progress as long as he stayed inside. The day they decided to reach in and pull him out, my husband was at home having carpet installed. Our house was in disarray. When I called to tell him that they were wheeling me into the maternity ward for sure, he said no, we couldn't have the baby now, we needed that extra month, the house was a mess. I needed to tell them to hold on.

Our friends and family came together in amazing ways to help us get ready. They did laundry. Organized the things we'd need. Pitched in. Nothing prepares you for having a baby. It never turns out like television or the movies. But I've always thought that if you can set up a crib, you might begin to understand what's coming at you. We were so unprepared that we didn't even have a camera (it was packed away; see carpet situation above). The nurse took some pictures and then kindly printed them off before she went off shift. The baby had arrived safely. I was alive. These were good things. These were the good things we held onto for the first few weeks because so much had gone so very wrong, and I was still so very sick. The disease, the medicine, the side effects: it was all so outside of how I thought I would be spending the first few months with the only baby I would ever have.

Shell-shocked and disease-riddled, we muddled through a month, two months. The baby gained weight. I really enjoyed breast-feeding. I was used to not sleeping. I managed to worry too much and read in abundance. We went to the emergency room once, and to the doctor's more than once. It's almost embarrassing to admit how very little you understand instinctively, at first, with a newborn. All your schooling, many degrees, so many books, and still it's a wonder our children survive. Despite a period of about six weeks of intense fussiness, my son was an incredibly easy baby. On the whole, I was happy and thankful to have him. Calling him our "miracle" baby didn't feel disingenuous.

Days, weeks, months: a period of mat leave blurs in my mind into going back to work, which blurs again into the patterns of the days as they are now: scheduled, busy, full, and demanding. Our *Before* selves have evaporated like water left in a glass—the particles of our previous life floating around above us, disappearing where they may never be retrieved.

All those years I longed to have a baby, I completely took for granted the sheer bliss that comes with a life heavily weighted with free time. We had worked hard to find a balance between the tedium of responsibility and the need to make our lives, well, ours. Sure, we had jobs to ensure the bills get paid, and our weekends were often crammed with chores—but we also did as much with the moments of freedom as we possibly could. We built up our creative selves. We travelled. We saw, we conquered, we fought, we fell into a delicious pattern of a happily married life. And what I've come to know is that the time that I spent outside of what I *had* to do—whether it was reading, or writing, or spending an afternoon as an extra on a friend's film —defined who I was, and without that time, I feel trapped, angry, and not unlike someone caught on a subway stuck between stops, on my way to being myself but never truly getting there. And here is the mockery of motherhood: even when you get a moment to yourself, a nap time, an early bedtime, you're either too tired or too overwhelmed to properly enjoy it.

Still, the love I have for my boy crashes into my better judgment. With work taking up so much of my days, all I want to do is spend the rest of my time with him. Weekends are crammed full of cooking, playing, walking, playing, talking, playing, and then even more of me disappears into a whirlwind of chores and preparations for the next day, the next week, and all of a sudden, I realize that I haven't read a book in ages, written a blog post in a month, and have abandoned any hope of a freelance career.

For the longest time, my son, my boy, would look into a mirror and say, "Mummy!" Not knowing there's a difference between the two of us, I provide context for him, and he can't define himself without me. I work hard every day to ensure he's happy, well taken care of, beloved, but the frustration I feel is in having to admit that the only way for motherhood to work for me is to leapfrog completely over the person I was *Before.*

Joan Didion says that when we talk about mortality, we are talking about our children. The very simple progression of someone coming after you. To give your things to. To build a life for. Now I'm obsessed with Wikipedia, spending hours, while my husband watches *Coronation Street*, looking up family histories on the Internet. Did Mary Shelley have children who survived? What happened to them? Did you know that Diana Spencer has nieces and nephews who continue a line of Spencers that go back five hundred years? I'm exhausted, bored, and then even more tired, and yet I still feel the need to do *something*, anything. And so I google in the space that's left by complete and utter exhaustion. I have never been so tired. I have never been so actively played out in my everyday life. Fumbling through work, mumbling through evenings, dropping down into bed at an hour where *Before* I would be just considering leaving the house and seeing a rock show.

With my boy in my life, I am no longer completely just *myself*. It's hard to put into words how that makes me feel. How I wonder what my grandmother felt like, my mother, when I continued them. My son might continue me, but for the moment, I'd be happy if he was less a part of me, and I could at least eat breakfast without almond milk spilled all down my nightgown and cereal in my hair.

My mother-in-law, who adores my husband in a way that made me finally understand what family means, consistently tells us that a life with kids is a better life. I couldn't use those same qualifiers. No, really, it's not a better life; it's a different life, a different choice. Because, as I have come to appreciate, my life was pretty terrific *Before*, too. And I've been preaching this to so many of my friends. Women, like me, who waited to have kids and who are now facing the very real possibility that science may not overcome the issues that come with their bodies falling into middle age. We don't look old. But we are not young inside.

What I always say—and it's so pretentious, arrogant even—is that you have to be okay with either way—you have to be as okay with not having kids as you are with having kids. You have to fill up your life and make it rich and pile it up with people and places and books and movies and experiences and anything that can mitigate the sheer, unrelenting fact that your life will never, ever turn out as you want or expect. This is not a bad thing.

And so I'm defining and redefining and coping and not coping and crying and laughing and sliding in and out of a person who had completely come to terms with having space to herself—and turning into one who finds herself crammed into the corners of her own life. Corners that are crooked and far too crowded already. But if I only have moments, I have to find a way to keep them to myself. I have to find a way to balance the immortal me, the mother, the one who will ever be defined by something I have biologically produced, with the other me who wants to produce so many other things that have nothing to do with him.

. . .

None of this has anything to do with love. I love my family. I do not know what I would do without them. But everybody says that. Everybody feels that, even if they don't know how to express it. But what I never realized, what never even entered into my mind, was how deeply having my son would hurt me. I was flippant with my health, flabbergasted when the disease decided to have its merry ways with me and have been utterly defeated by the side effects, the churning ordeal of the disease's treatment over the last two years. It's not just the pure act of mothering him that forces the *Before* into thin air, but the toll of bringing him to life, and the obliteration of my hard-won health. I was the healthiest I had ever been before I got pregnant —and the disease had been solidly in remission. Now I'm sunk deeply into a post-partum situation where my body has not recovered and has been irrevocably damaged from pregnancy.

I hold all of this anger inside and then unleash it on my husband. He's the only person in the world I am openly angry with—I feel bad for him most days, my temper, ancient and god-like in its wrath, barrelling him over when he's as exhausted as I am. So yes, I love, I love, I love my son—desperately, wholly—so much so that I wonder on an almost daily basis how I ever made something so amazing. But where is the space where I can resent him a little bit for plowing me over just by coming into this world? It's not practical; I don't resent him, I don't even dislike him, I revel in him, but it's not enough—it's not enough, this being a mother. This being only a mother in the time I have outside of work. Every minute of the day, my time is accounted for, and I miss the wide open space that used to define my days.

We go on, watching for trucks out the window, eating half-brown bananas, falling down, bruising ourselves, hugging, holding, aching, and squeezing, and I am almost willing to give into the happiness here, almost willing to be redefined. Maybe I don't need to be that me that was. Maybe I can be someone different, a suburbanesque, momish character with a bad dye job and a few extra pounds who bikes to work sometimes. Who tries so very hard to be that patient parent who plans enough ahead to remember the banana protector. Maybe I can become her; maybe I already have.

Junior

MARIA MEINDL

Surgeon to acupuncturist: "It's an inert lump of flesh. For twelve years, it's been inside her, doing nothing but grow. Now, it's blocking her kidneys. It's got to come out!"

Acupuncturist to surgeon: "Show some respect! It may not be a child; it may not even be any species you recognize, but it's a being in its own right, the only thing her womb will ever produce."

That was a dream. They were at the top of a hill, silhouetted against an orange sky, my Asian-born surgeon and Western-born acupuncturist. It was 2009, the night after I had scheduled surgery to remove a fibroid tumour and my uterus along with it. I also like to think of it as the night Junior was conceived.

In the middle of dinner about a week later, I felt like my throat was closing up. I could not swallow and could barely breathe. My husband rushed around the table and crouched by my side, just as I began sobbing. I blurted out my fears of dying, of becoming paralyzed, incontinent, of being left alone. I said, "Years were taken from me!" and, "The years! The years!"

When I was quiet again, he asked, "What can I do?"

"Make a doll, the most disgusting doll you can imagine. Make it freakish and hairy, and make it the size of a newborn."

My husband likes making things. He said, "I can do that."

Nineteen ninety-two: another dream. I open my closet to find my sister tearing up my favourite blue dress with her teeth. She says, "You'll never have babies. All the babies will be mine."

I was in my early thirties when I had that dream. My heart had just been broken and was about to be broken again. My sister, who is five years younger than me, moved in with her boyfriend that year and, soon afterwards, gave birth to her son. She wrote me a letter saying that since she had a partner and a singing career, since she had a child, now it would fall to me to care for our chronically ill mother. I was angry, of course. It was an obnoxious thing to say, not to mention mean. On the other hand, I knew she was right.

I would like to find a scene that illustrates the start of my mother's illness, but I can't. It was just there, for as long as I can remember, even though the diagnosis was not handed down until I was a teenager. Lupus, so named because it can take the form of a facial rash which resembles the markings of a wolf. Like a wolf, the disease moves from place to place, searching for prey. The T-cells, whose job it is to attack infection, turn against the sufferer's own flesh. Sometimes the skin is affected; sometimes it's the muscles or connective tissue; sometimes it's the organs. With my mother, it was all of these. Her doctor told me she had never seen anyone that sick with the disease. She also told me she had never seen anyone that sick stay alive for so long.

Before I knew of anything called "lupus," I knew there were times when I wanted to stay away from my mother. Times when she smelled funny, when she lay in bed all day or paced the floor all night. She blamed her joint pain on eating grapefruit, her sleeplessness on tomatoes. The rash must have come from new soap or from the carbon paper at work. But, to me, it seemed clear that the illness had to do with who my mother *was*, more than anything she had done. She was someone who waited by the telephone, who swore and cried and smoked too much. Someone who loved, without being loved in return.

My father often stayed out late or didn't come home at all. He went on trips for weeks at a time, his letters home addressed to all of us "girls" and not to my mother alone. Even, some years later, when he was living with his then-girlfriend and her daughter, my mother hoped he would change his mind and take us back. He didn't. Later still, he wrote a letter professing friendship, which made my mother fall in love with him all over again. But she could not have him. The letter that raised her hopes ended with a blow. His girlfriend had become his wife. The reason, my mother concluded: "I'm not all there."

But wait!

Here's a photograph, dated June 8, 1963, my fourth birthday party. It is taken in the dappled shade of a garden. My mother squats in the foreground, her spike heels dug into the gravel. A white dress hugs her shapely hips. She often designed her own clothes and had them made by a dressmaker. Scooped low in the back, the dress shows off what she considers her best feature, her long, straight back, brown from the sun. She's cutting the cake, about to bring her thumb to her mouth to lick the icing.

My mother was beautiful. She loved cake.

I still remember the dress I wore to that party. Instead of the smocked bodice that was popular in those days it had a boxy cut which complemented the checkered fabric, a Marimekko pattern in beige and brown. My mother searched a long time for it, and it cost a fortune. "I am so goddamned sick of pink," she said, presenting me triumphantly with the box.

I know there was more to my mother than just illness. But it takes a photograph to remind me.

Easter weekend, 1989. On my way out to dinner with a friend, I called my mother. She'd been acting—well—crazy. She'd been forgetting conversations and was subject to bouts of rage when anyone challenged her. She complained about "foreigners" buying up all the houses in Toronto. She barely ate, and her skin had taken on a greyish pallor. Her hair was falling out. The problem had been creeping up over the last few years. My sister and I exchanged stories of the strange things she had done. We urged her to go to a doctor. She didn't.

Now, her speech was disjointed, her voice weak. I stopped in to see her after dinner, and never made it home. It was the flu, she insisted. This is why she felt sick to her stomach, why her body felt heavy, why she could hardly breathe. She promised she'd be better in the morning. I lay down and tried to get some sleep, but my mother kept calling me. She used my childhood nickname, Marija, shortened when in a hurry to:

"M'rij!"

"Yes."

"Are you awake?"

"I'm right here."

She would be quiet for a minute or two, then begin again.

Three days later, I walked out of the elevators and into the lobby of Women's College Hospital. My mother was in intensive care, being treated for congestive heart failure. I carried her clothes in a plastic bag and wore her rings on my own finger: my grandmother's engagement ring with its three large diamonds, my mother's wedding ring, which she still wore on her left hand.

I leaned against a pillar, trying to gather the strength for one final task. My mother's cats, I realized, had not been fed since I finally convinced her to go to Emergency the day before. There we had waited twenty-four hours for her to be admitted. No one knew what department she should be in, which of the many things wrong with her should be addressed first.

I saw a couple come along the hall, the man pushing the woman in a wheelchair, a bundle in her arms. A group of people jumped up to greet her. They passed the bundle amongst themselves, spoke to the baby in sweet voices. They kissed it, admired its tiny hands. There were no other children. Maybe this was the couple's first baby. I watched as they left the cocoon of the hospital and started their life together as parents. The rings rattled, loose on my finger; I had to close my fist to stop them from slipping off. I realized I had not had a meal since dinner with my friend. I felt a gush of moisture: my period.

Didn't I just finish one, though?

It was two weeks early, at the time when I would normally ovulate.

The weekend my mother was admitted to hospital, my sister's back went into spasm and she couldn't go out. I called her from a pay phone in Emergency whenever I got the chance. As she wept on the other end of the line, I mustered a calm voice to give her progress reports. My sister was in her early twenties and had just left home. It felt good to protect her, to take charge. It helped me organize the welter of information that was coming at me, and it helped me set aside my own feelings so that I could function. A few days later, when I could not muster the energy to get to the hospital, my sister was able to go in.

My mother was hospitalized for three months that spring. Whenever my work schedule permitted, I sat in her cubicle in intensive care, watching the laboured rise and fall of her chest, watching the machines that monitored her heart rate and oxygen. I rejoiced when she took a few bites of food, a sign the anti-inflammatory drugs had kicked in. When I was at home, she would often phone to tell me she needed a Kleenex or a glass of water. I would take a cab to the hospital, even though the nursing station was right at the end of her bed. I had always had a prickly relationship with my mother; now, I was terrified of losing her.

"Give us a cuddle!" My mother's cockney accent returned when she called her children into her arms. My sister seemed to know how to do it. All of it. To nestle against my mother, to laugh and cry at the right times. I was solitary, complicated, angular. The very word "cuddle" made me feel panicky, as if I had just been called to go on stage, unprepared. Now, as we realized how much care my mother was going to need, I appreciated my sister's expressiveness. Her operatic hissy fits could produce a bedpan, a doctor's attention, a change of rooms. I was good at waiting in line and playing by the rules. We fought about our mother as we had about everything else, but, between us, we managed to look after her. Then my sister had a child.

"There's something in there!"

Most fibroids are asymptomatic and are discovered in the course of a routine pelvic exam.

How could my body do this without my noticing? I didn't notice a lot in the mid-1990s. It had been going on for seven years, the full-on, perpetual emergency that was looking after a person with lupus in the beleaguered Ontario medical system. Even at the start, it had taken a woman on the brink of death twenty-four hours to get admitted to hospital, and it only got worse from there. I was trying to earn a living, trying to·see my friends sometimes, sometimes write. Occasionally there was a love affair: brief and painful, because I knew it could not last. I didn't leave any of the men; they left me. Being left felt inevitable, as if I had chosen it myself. The little flurry of romance had been nothing more than a distraction. I welcomed any distraction. Pain did the job well.

As I lay back for what was to be the first of dozens of ultrasound tests, I glowed with happiness. Happiness? At being able to lie down and close my eyes for a few minutes. Yes, I was that tired. And having this part of me, the reproductive part, be the centre of attention. At *feeling* my uterus. Knowing it could make something. Anything.

Here's an excerpt from my journal from that time:

October 12, 1996
To spend time in [my mother's] presence is to make the
decision time and again to swallow rage. She's not responsible
for what she's saying. She's sick and can't be confronted.
Standing up for myself becomes an attack on her. Yet from her
hospital bed she displays verbal and emotional violence. I feel
it's my failure to meet her needs that puts her in this position.
If I would provide a home for her, if I had listened to her
signals that she needed more care, she might not have broken
her hip. Her suffering is my fault.

What prompted this soul searching, other than my mother's usual ongoing illness? She had a stroke in 1996, and a few months later, the day I started graduate school, she fell and broke her hip. Now I had to make time for classes and a new part-time job. She was deeply unsettled by the change in my usual routine of calling and visiting. I asked her to manage her anxieties just for a week or two while I got a handle on my schedule, to rely on a friend, a nurse, a social worker as her anchor. She was in hospital; help was a call-button away. But I was the one she needed.

That year, I sublet an apartment in an expensive neighbourhood. The busy artery of Queen Street dwindles, at its eastern end, to a smattering of quaint shops and low-rise apartments. At the end of my tree-lined street was the boardwalk, and beyond that, the lake. The move stretched my budget, but I thought the water would calm me down, bring me into balance again. Water was natural. Natural was good.

But I was not natural.

Daily, I trudged the length of the boardwalk before catching the streetcar downtown to classes or to the hospital or to work. The fibroid was starting to weigh down my belly. My limbs were leaden with fatigue. With each step, tears flowed from my eyes, sometimes freezing in the wind that came off the lake.I was grieving for children.

Not having them?

Not wanting them.

I knew only too well what it was to be needed. After seven years of caring for my mother, all our visits carried an undercurrent of resentment, and I had learned—out of self-preservation—to harden myself against her suffering. Every day, I faced the reality that love has limits. And that I had nothing left to give.

The doctor resembled a Giacometti sculpture, with curly hair rising up from her forehead, adding to her height and a general sense of verticality. She had narrow shoulders, and a pencil skirt stretched from one gaunt hipbone to the other, creating a flat plane. She spent a long time looking through my file while I fidgeted in my seat.

"Shall I get changed?"

"I don't need to look down there. The films are good."

She drew a diagram of the female reproductive organs on the paper which covered the unused examination table. In the middle of the uterus, she made a black dot.

"This kind of fibroid causes next to no problems, but it's going to get big. Really, the best way to get it out is by hysterectomy."

"Hysterectomy!"

"You're thirty-nine. Your fertility is of no concern to us."

"Is it doing any harm?"

"Not really, but..." she paused. "You have a very nice figure."

"Thanks."

"You don't need to dress like that."

I was silent. I had put on my best outfit for a job interview that day.

"You must be about...what, a size five?"

"I guess."

"You could be wearing a three."

"Thank you very much, Doctor. I have to go now."

"You'll be back."

"I don't think so."

"You have no idea how big those things can get."

· · ·

In books and articles suggesting alternatives to surgery, I found information on herbal supplements and exercise. There was often a sidebar titled "Energy Medicine" or "Body/Mind/Spirit."

Here, I read that fibroids arise from second chakra issues, and here, under Second Chakra Issues, was my life, mercilessly described. I had, it was clear, "boundary issues," for I could not say "no" to my mother's needs enough to care for myself. Nurturing felt like it had been forced on me and was being given not to the next generation but to the one before. I was creatively frustrated. I had gone back to school because I knew it would force me to keep writing, but in my state of caregiver's hyper-vigilance, imagination had deserted me. I had set aside writing a novel with more pain than my saddest love affair. And I was poor. Too poor to afford the forms of bodywork that would, in the words of one book, "release the emotional and cellular memories that are obstructing the flow of energy in the uterus." I had suffered, as another author put it, "blows to the feminine ego," in the form of repeated rejections by men, several of whom went on to have children with others. All this left me feeling frozen, stunted. Unborn.

And I was angry about it. Anger that I could not express to a sick woman. Anger that was building up inside me, taking solid, monstrous form.

"...illness is not a metaphor, and the most truthful way of regarding illness—and the healthiest way of being ill—is one most purified of, most resistant to, metaphoric thinking."

With these words by Susan Sontag, I felt myself emerging, like a drowning woman, into the air. I gulped *Illness as Metaphor* in one sitting. Then I read it again, following Sontag's exquisite line of reasoning. She deconstructs the metaphors we use to talk about illness, pointing out how various psychologists have seen repression of impulses as the cause of disease. In the past, the sexual urge was blamed; more recently, the culprit has been anger. The disturbing implication: anger must be expressed for the good of our own health. And this becomes a justification for immoral behaviour.

The book saved my life.

I moved to a co-op on Church Street, where rainbow flags hung from nearby businesses, and gender and family stereotypes were being overhauled everywhere I looked. I switched my major to philosophy, honed my critical faculties like a blade. I set up a routine of daily walks and pursued cognitive therapy to change my habits of negative thinking. I made a radio documentary about caregiving, politicizing what is too often thought of as personal. Among the experts I interviewed was sociologist Pat Armstrong, who framed the issues in terms of choice. We may claim to champion reproductive choice in this country, yet when it comes to the other end of the lifespan, women are increasingly "conscripted" into care. I marched in demonstrations to protest cuts to hospitals. My mother, recovering from a second broken hip, came down in her wheelchair to the lobby of the rehabilitation hospital, a few blocks from the legislative building. We waved to each other.

My sister and her family moved to Europe. My anger was not gone, but I stopped believing it was dangerous to me. My ups and downs of emotion didn't matter. I was doing this because my mother was a woman, the woman who had brought me into the world and she deserved the care, even if she herself didn't believe it. And because it was right.

I kept at it, clumsily, grouchily, and with moments of grace, until the end. Sitting by my mother's deathbed, I thought, "We made it!" I was proud of both of us.

. . .

But wait! Here's another journal entry, from the time I was making that politicized documentary, from the time when I was scathingly critiquing the narcissism of New Age theories on health:

> *July 21, 2001*
> *...This lump in my uterus makes me feel dirty, guilty, as if*
> *I'd done something wrong...A lump of useless white stuff.*
> *Anger which I have pushed deep down into my own belly.*
> *And now it's there, a hard, white lump. And my needing to*
> *get it removed is almost a demonstration of my failure, my*
> *weakness.*

These were the thoughts I confessed in my early morning writing. Then promptly forgot. They did not fit the rationalistic outlook that got me through each day. A lump in the belly as unexpressed anger. Illness as sin. A metaphor is a weed, a virus, a double-edged sword, a two-way street. You can't argue with a metaphor. It must be met in its own territory, on its own terms.

Three months after my mother's death, I got married. When "the kid thing" came up in conversation, my soon-to-be-husband looked at me with the same baffled expression that came over his face when I constructed elegant arguments for why our relationship would not work. Eventually, I accepted that he just wanted to be with me.

For our fifth anniversary, he told me his idea for a present. "It doesn't make a difference, since we're married and anyway, we aren't going to get divorced, but how would you like it if I put your name on the deed of the house?"

"I'd like that." I said. "Thank you," and thought, *Now I can have the operation.*

"Do you have any questions?" The surgeon asked.

I had studied anatomy books in preparation for this interview. "Where do you cut the *Rectus Abdominus*?"

She leaned forward with a conspiratorial wink. "I don't cut any muscles." She wriggled her fingers in the air, advancing them as if probing through some material she loved to touch. "I separate them!" Sitting back with a grin, she asked, "Anything else?"

"How soon can we get rid of this thing?"

Junior, I decided, would be my fibroid's name. This, and a prospective birthdate, was all Junior needed. My belly "popped."

I enjoyed my solid gait, the difficulty bending over, the internal tug and shift when I turned to one side. I even enjoyed the indigestion. Junior was filling me up. I patted Junior, turned all angles in the mirror to observe my roundness. Gleefully, I accepted seats on the bus.

At my last ultrasound, I asked for a picture, the kind new parents get.

"Excuse me?"

"I want a picture of the large uterine fibroid that I'm here to have checked."

"I can't do that."

"It says here I can have a picture."

"I need to ask the doctor."

"Why are you whispering? This young lady is getting a picture. What makes my ultrasound any different?"

I ended up paying extra. My 4-by-4-inch picture set me back thirty dollars, where the same money would buy a pregnant woman twenty prints for family and friends. It was slipped to me in a plain white envelope, with a shaking head and a look shared with a fellow receptionist. The ultrasound showed Junior had surpassed "sizeable" and "large" and was now described as "huge." Twenty-four centimetres. The size of a six-month pregnancy. The size of a baby that could live outside my body.

"How are you feeling?" I opened my eyes to see my surgeon striding into the room with a smile.

"Okay."

"I came to tell you it went extremely well."

"Good."

"Nausea?"

"Not really."

She approached the bed, glancing at the door. She lowered her voice. "I couldn't resist. Afterwards, I had to..." She mimed making a precise cut. "Incredible! There was blood everywhere. It was like a hollow sack, full of blood."

I imagined stunned gasps from the doctors, a blood-spattered operating theatre which would take hours to clean. Huge. Incredible. That was my Junior.

These days, babies come to us in lots of different ways. Some are conceived in test tubes, some gestated by surrogates, some adopted from halfway across the world. Junior was created in my husband's workshop in the basement of our house and laid in my arms when I returned from Women's College Hospital, November 8, 2009. Most of Junior's limbs are made from socks, but one arm is taken from a faux-fur hat we got at a rummage sale the first holiday we spent together. The same fur gives Junior a healthy thatch of hair. The ears, one black, one red, stick out at different angles. Junior's body is plaid, with a neon-pink plastic umbilical cord. One eye is an embroidered X, the other, bloodshot and bulging, recycled from a Halloween mask. Junior is the product of my husband's ingenuity and devotion, and of my subversiveness, a legacy from my mother, Hetty Ventura, born January 5, 1930, died December 30, 2002. She would have loved her grandchild.

Bananagrams

SALEEMA NAWAZ

Buffalo buffalo, step turn step! Buffalo buffalo, step turn step!
Shuffle hop step, shuffle hop step, shuffle hop step, shuffle hop
  step!

I'm falling behind the music when it comes to calling out the moves. For some of the tap steps, I can hardly remember their proper names. But though I am no dance instructor, not by any means, she is following what my feet are doing. More and more, her feet are doing the same.

She is tired but excited, and I can tell that she is summoning new resources of adult maturity to push herself through this rehearsal. We have only been at it for thirty minutes, but then again, she is only ten years old.

This little girl I will call Blythe. She has occupied the better part of my thoughts for the past year and a half, and I have given more consideration to our particular relationship than I have to possibly any other relationship in my life.

When I suggested the performance—after watching her endlessly clop around the apartment after her dance recital, and reminded, too, of my own tap shoes gathering dust at home—I was attentive to any sign of reluctance. I was excited by my idea, and I suspected she would be thrilled, but I was wary at the same time. If she wanted to do it, I would put aside my concerns about the whole thing seeming too precious, or too cute, or too designed to send a particular message about the way that things were going between us. If she really wanted to do it, I wouldn't care what anybody else said or thought. It would be fun.

"What do you think?" I did my best to keep my own voice close to neutral.

Breathless with anticipation, she almost whispered her response. "*Yes.*"

The first time I met her, I changed my clothes four times. My mind raced through a dozen possible scenarios of how it might go. I was hyper and nervous, and I wasn't ruling out anything. It was the end of December, and I eyed some chocolate coins in gold foil left over from Christmas. Maybe I should pocket them—delight her with some uncharacteristic (and, given my lack of magical training, improbable) sleight of hand? Or maybe I would pull out my change purse to buy her a bagel and she would notice the shiny, oversize loonies mixed in among the regular change, seizing upon them with a child's unerring candy radar. Magnanimously, I would let her have them. Her inevitable conclusion: who *was* this bewildering and fantastic new girlfriend?

Although her father, Derek, and I had only been dating for a few weeks, I felt sure I was about to meet my future stepdaughter. For all I knew, this might be the only child whose life would intertwine with mine at all. The occasion was momentous. I put on makeup, but not too much. I left my hair down. At last, I settled on a typical outfit:

jeans and a top and my red jacket. I didn't want to seem like I was trying too hard.

I had strategized with Derek that the visit should be short, just five minutes. I had already read everything I could find on the topic. *Keep it brief. Give her time.* As in my relationship with her father, whom I already loved more than I could have imagined possible, I wanted to do everything right.

Before the buzzer rang, I came to my senses about the chocolate. I left it behind and ran down to greet them, but we ended up meeting halfway, on the stairs. Blythe was small, very small. According to her dad, she had just turned nine, but to my eyes, she looked about six. On our way downstairs, her father held her hand and smiled at me over her head.

We went next door to buy bagels — the official pretext for the visit — passing in front of a driveway with an idling car, and I found myself hurrying to move between its bumper and the little girl. I took it as an encouraging sign and hoped Derek noticed. There were, I was relieved to discover, at least latent parental instincts lurking somewhere within me.

Derek bought a dozen sesame bagels and a blueberry one for Blythe, at her request. We chatted about *Tron*, a movie they had just gone to see. As Blythe bent her head over her bagel, Derek kissed me swiftly. In a minute, they were saying goodbye.

As they crossed the street to their car, I could hear Blythe talking animatedly to her father, though I couldn't make out the words. Later, he told me what she said:

"I thought she would look different."

"Different how?"

"I thought she would look like Mommy."

. . .

At first, Derek's general advice counselled adopting a more outgoing approach.

"Jump up and down on her bed with her," he said. "Pin her down and tickle her."

"But I can only be myself," I said, getting weepy. Every visit, I tried to stretch out of my comfort zone, but sometimes when I was alone, I found myself crying again about the future. I imagined an adolescent rebellion, her utter rejection of me. Even if we achieved an equilibrium, which I didn't doubt that we would, there was a lifetime ahead in which I might always be the interloper, the scapegoat.

But thinking along these lines was paralyzing. Instead, I went back to strategizing, combining an excess of Internet research with my own intuitions about children. I felt I had an advantage in being essentially immature. I vividly remembered being a child. Indeed, besides an inevitable accumulation of knowledge, I did not, in essence, feel very different from one.

"Please tell her ahead of time when I'm coming over," I asked. "The day before, so she can get used to the idea." This was partly because I thought it was the right thing to do and partly because I didn't want to risk seeing her face fall in disappointment.

I tried to keep our visits short but regular. I canvassed my own memories of age ten. The things I thought about. The stories I wrote. Though we shared many interests, Blythe and I were not very much alike. She was outgoing where I was reserved, bold where I was cautious. But she was whip smart, an avid reader, and chatty. She was also polite, good-natured, and essentially curious. It was a combination that worked in our favour.

I began a list entitled "Things Blythe Likes": dancing, chocolate, Archie comics, old movies. A smaller list enumerated dislikes: oatmeal (in cookies), Brussels sprouts.

I was happy the day she included me in an e-mail she sent to her three best friends, her mother, her grandmother, and Derek, though I made a mental note after reading it to debunk the notion of bad luck associated with not forwarding chain letters.

The next morning, I awoke to three new e-mails in my inbox, all from the same person. Derek had spoken of his acrimonious divorce and the ongoing problems with his ex, who was bipolar. Most of his concerns revolved around Blythe and the damage that might be accruing from witnessing her mother's rage and erratic behaviour. When we met, Derek had been divorced for a year — a process that had taken almost four years after he moved out.

He had described his ex-wife to me as someone who had transformed since they first met in grad school. "She was a flower," he said, "who bloomed in a very dark way."

It appeared that the dark flower had wasted no time in noting my e-mail address.

You are no mother, began the first one. *You know nothing at all.*

The Blythe lists grew longer and I brought them along with me on our vacation. A summer trip to a country cottage near Derek's parents' place, it was scheduled to last over three weeks — the longest amount of time the three of us had ever spent together. I could tell Blythe was apprehensive that the trip marked a change that was about to become permanent, and my heart ached for how much she had already had to cope with in her young life. Blythe was aware of her mother's mental illness and repeated suicide attempts. Her mother was also moving away, a fact that made me relieved given her dangerous behaviours. But Blythe's mother, a former ballet dancer known for her beauty, was the bright star on her daughter's horizon, and her daughter was grieving.

In the country, Blythe talked about her mother a great deal. Sometimes a mention of her mother would have an edge to it—a pointed flag of allegiance to her old life, or maybe a test to see if I would lose my temper—but more often it didn't. She missed her mother and worried about her, and she needed to find a way to keep her present. I tried to listen with interest and patience. I didn't want to be false, so I pretended the woman she was talking about was different from the one still sending me dozens of hateful e-mails. I had only written to Blythe's mother once, asking her to stop. Instead, my request had provoked another torrent of words.

Sometimes working her mother into the conversation proved to be a stretch. One night, as we were settling down to watch a movie, Blythe remarked, "You should really thank my mother that we get to watch *Star Wars* because she's the one who got me these DVDs."

"Oh, really?" I was discovering that the elastic edge of my patience could grow brittle. Blythe, at least, could not detect my sarcasm. "Well, tell her thank you for me."

Her eyes opened in alarm. "I don't think that's a good idea. My mother's not a big fan of you."

It was hard to keep the dryness out of my voice. "You're kidding."

"No, she's really not." Blythe couldn't help drawing out the *really*. It would almost have been funny if it weren't so awful.

"So I've heard."

We'd brought the banana-shaped zippered bag of tiles out to the country because it was a game we'd enjoyed playing together in the city, and we were all good at it. A little bit like Scrabble, Bananagrams is a game played using lettered tiles. You arrange an initial set of tiles into a crossword formation, but every new letter you pick up must be incorporated into your existing set of words. It is a rapid, constantly shifting game. Like life, it is improvisational and always changing. You have to work with what you get and make it fit the best way you can. Everybody plays all at once.

It had been a long day, a good day. We had gone to the water park. We had ice cream cones for dessert. Derek and Blythe had some time alone, just the two of them, before we dumped out all the tiles to start a game.

We each won a round. It was fun. We were all people who cared about words and letters. Then Derek teamed up with Blythe for certain victory in the last round.

But when the game finished there was a lull. Nothing had happened, really, besides a possible drop in blood sugar and its accompanying wave of fatigue, but I could feel the air change. The bad vibes. Blythe's eyes narrowed at me over the top of her glass of milk. Her mouth slackened as she stared openly, as I tried to keep my face composed. It was a peculiar, blank kind of look that in my experience with her immediately preceded one of hostility. An othering look. I did my best not to resemble an alien of any kind. But how could I not? I was a woman, fundamentally unknown, who had taken up residence in her life in the place where her mother used to be.

I felt for her. And I felt for myself, too, as she glared at me from behind her glasses with her father's blue eyes.

She started hunting through the tiles and began placing them in formation until she had spelled out her mother's full name on the table. Then she spelled out her father's name underneath it. Then her own.

"See, Daddy? Look."

He looked. He looked as weary as I suddenly felt. "Yes, I see."

· · ·

Go fuck yourself, read the next morning's e-mail from Blythe's mother, as though picking up from some conversation we had just left off.

In the field above the house, a set of trees has been planted. One maple tree for each of the grandchildren. That summer, Blythe's was the largest. Her younger cousin Gwen's was spindly. They pointed them out to us when we were all on a walk.

I thought that they ought to have been fruit trees, and before I could stop myself, I found myself imagining an apple tree planted for my own baby. But the apple blossoms I pictured bursting into bloom made me melancholic. I sensed they might never come. Blythe was the oldest of all her cousins, after all. I wondered if Derek would really have the energy to start all over.

After we crossed the meadow, Blythe and Gwen ran ahead to a treed hill near the road where Blythe claimed they would find the alphabet stones.

"Remember, Gwen? Remember? The alphabet stones? From last summer?"

Gwen shook her head. She was only six.

"Don't worry, I'll show you." Blythe raced her cousin partway then stopped to help her catch up. The odd, tiny hill was overgrown, with a worn wooden bench nestled among the trees. All around us, the tall grasses hummed with insect life. Blythe bent to a little heap of grey rocks that looked like slate.

"See? I told you! Here's a *D* for Derek." She placed it to the side of the pile and kept rummaging. "And a *B* for Blythe."

Gwen crouched in the dirt beside her. In a moment, she brandished one of her own and beamed with pride. "And I found a *G* for Gwen! Look!"

"That's great, Gwen."

I wasn't close enough to make out exactly how they were seeing letters on the serrated faces of the stones. Like Derek, I paced the perimeter of the hill, eager to keep the girls on the move. We had been out walking for hours, and it was time to be heading back.

"We need an *H* for Hunter," said Blythe. That's was Gwen's little brother. "And two more for Hannah and Aunt Hilary." Derek's niece and sister. As she called out the letters, she chose more and more stones out of the heap.

"We have a lot of *H*'s in this family," said Gwen. She was giddy, laughing as she carried all the special stones to a separate pile. "Don't we, Saleema?"

I smiled at her. "You do."

"Blythe, what about Saleema?" asked Gwen. "Maybe we should find an *S*."

Blythe ignored her. She was suddenly shifting the pile of rocks with a severe focus, as though working to free a trapped miner. When she got to her feet, she was holding something. Another rock. "Daddy," she said, running up to him. "Daddy, Daddy, look what I found. Can this stone be for Mommy?"

There were deer flies buzzing near my face, and I jogged down the slope to get away.

Behind me, I could hear Derek's response, mild and weary. "Sure."

"Can I leave it here in the special pile with all the other stones for our family?"

"Sure. You can do that. But we've got to head back now."

There was something primal, I decided, as we headed back to the road, about step-parents and stepchildren. A reason for the evil stepmother in the fairy tales. A child was a mascot, a reminder. And more than that, an advocate. A sleeper agent who could be programmed to destroy. I felt in my bones how easy it would be to let one's heart grow hard.

As the sun set below the cliffs in the distance, the woods grew dark, and when Derek gave Blythe a piggyback ride, Gwen slipped her hand into mine easily, trustingly.

My heart melted.

and i bet he bent u over the kitchen sink
to fuck you. i know his ways.

Blythe has straight, fine brown hair that she likes to call mousy, though I am not convinced that it is. She has sweet bow lips that she gets from her mother. Only occasionally, when her brow furrows behind her glasses and her mouth falls open in concentration, does she seem to me to resemble her father.

I turn off the music as Blythe sits down to take off her tap shoes.

"She's going to be tough on me."

The way she phrases this makes me afraid for her, and I am at a loss for words because all I want to say is *so don't tell her*. I am a novice at any sort of parenting, but even I know that encouraging a ten-year-old to lie to her mother is probably a bad idea.

"It's up to you," I say. "I mean, I don't think you should lie, but…"

I run out of reasonable things to say. I'm guessing that what will happen is that her mother will scream and swear and say terrible things. She will drink and act out. It is awfully hot in the apartment, even with all the windows open. I am grateful nobody is around to hear me floundering on the subject. "I think," I say at last, "if you didn't want to mention it, if that would be easier on you, I think that would be okay."

But Blythe is determined. It could be her excitement about the dance, or that is she set on practicing her steps while she is away visiting her mom. Or maybe she has just decided to maintain a vigilant pledge to be true to the circumstances of her own life. It's not up to her, after all, to make it easy on anyone.

But she usually tries anyway.

"Don't worry," she says. "It'll be okay."

I admire her.

It was the last day of our summer visit. Derek and Blythe had finished packing and were heading to the lake for one final swim before the drive home.

"You go ahead," I said, though the coolness of the dark water enticed me. I was packing away three weeks' worth of clothes, along with some cherished hopes about moving forward with Derek. I felt drained by the decision I had reached—that although he was waiting for an answer, I could not yet move in with Derek and Blythe. She was not ready, and neither was I. To do things right, we had to take time, even though I felt all the urgency of passionate, unprecedented love. A year, at least. It was not so long, though it felt like it.

The sun had not yet begun to sink behind the mountain when I dashed across the field, past the big metal sculpture, off the road, to the hill with the alphabet stones. I wanted to find the rock Blythe had placed in the special pile for her mother, and I wanted to remove it. I wanted to throw it to the bottom of the artificial pond, or better yet, pocket it and drop it on the side of the highway somewhere, where it could never be found. If there was some old kind of magic at work, I needed it to be influencing things in my favour.

As I cleared the road, a car passed by, probably Derek's sister, and I regretted being spotted wandering in the field in the near dark.

Self-conscious, I turned away from the side of the hill where the trees lent their shadows to the growing dusk. I felt foolish. I knew nothing was really written into the earth, nothing that couldn't be changed.

I decided to turn back. Who was I to undo a child's spell? It was probably worse luck to try to interfere.

When the MC, Derek's cousin, summons Blythe and me to the dance floor, I am running through all the steps in my head, concentrating hard on not letting her down. We have only managed to squeeze in a couple of rehearsals since she got back from visiting her mother. And it was only yesterday that we made it all the way through with no mistakes.

I hike up my wedding dress to keep from tripping, and Blythe, though I know her to be nervous, is perfectly poised. Her openness and emotional maturity never stop developing and astounding me. When Derek proposed, I was almost speechless with joy, but it was when he told me that Blythe helped him pick out the ring that I started weeping. I know that Blythe's feelings must be more complicated today, that she still mourns her parents' marriage and worries about her mom, but whatever our mutual jumble of feelings, I know that right now we are thinking exactly the same thing.

> *Buffalo buffalo, step turn step! Buffalo buffalo, step turn step!*
> *Shuffle hop step, shuffle hop step, shuffle hop step, shuffle hop*
> *step!*

Later, after we've taken a bow, and Derek and I have slow danced, when the floor heats up with faster music and all our friends, Blythe confides that she feels shy about dancing when the steps aren't choreographed.

"But I've seen you," I say. Once, the three of us had all started dancing in the kitchen to the Beastie Boys. "You're great. Plus, it gets easier the more you do it."

Before the hour is out, Blythe has grabbed the microphone and challenged a little boy to a dance-off. Everyone watching is clapping and whistling and shaking their heads with delight as these two miniature dancers flail their arms, jiggle their hips, undulate their torsos, and give it all they've got in perfect time to the music. I can't stop cheering at the top of my lungs.

I know it will not always be easy to be a stepmother—it may even get very hard—but for this moment, there is this remarkable girl, spinning on the floor, utterly fluid and lovely and free. And I am clapping and laughing and full of amazed pride and admiration.

Wicked

SUSAN OLDING

Once there was a gentleman who married, for his second wife, the proudest and most haughty woman that was ever seen.

The night I met you, it was—if you'll pardon the expression—colder than a witch's tit. Your dad and I had just finished the main course of our first shared meal. Our first *date*, as it turned out—but I only learned that later, for at the time, I was married to somebody else and your dad was my teacher, and neither of us had romance consciously in mind. But over the wine, we'd shared confidences, discovered connections. There was a spark, a sense of fit. And my feelings...my feelings confused me. I told myself I was imagining things. I told myself that it meant nothing. But my icy hands and thumping heart told a different story, and as the truth of that realization hit me, I became afraid. Your dad stood up to clear the dishes. I stared at my reflection in the window. You opened the door, shouted a greeting, and galloped up the stairs, a gust of crisp air heralding your arrival.

You were twelve years old. You'd been to see a movie with your friends. You wore braces with bright elastics, striped Pippi Long-stocking leggings, an oversized sweater, and a crown of gold-brown ringlets that trembled whenever you laughed or took a bite of your citrus tart. A small person, somehow you seemed to fill the room, the way light fills a room, changing our perception of every corner. And your eyes! Not blue, not green, but aquamarine, like the water in Barbados. Or the way I imagined the water in Barbados. I'd never been there.

There were a lot of places I'd never been. Beginning with this one.

I knew nothing about children. I hadn't spoken to a twelve-year-old in the twenty years since I was that age. So I had no idea what to say. Instead, I gulped my wine, nodded stupidly, and smiled too much.

My awkwardness didn't infect you. Still at that glorious stage before girls lose their spunk and start to wilt under the scrutiny of strangers, you held back nothing—sharing your opinions about the plot, the setting, the acting, the hairstyles, and the jokes of the film you'd just seen, followed by similar reviews of your courses, your teachers, your pets, and even your friends. After a while, you leapt up and ran to your room, returning with a book, which you opened to the Torah passage for your Bat Mitzvah. As the candles dripped yellow wax onto the cloth, you explained it to me.

Later, when your dad and I exchanged more details about our pasts, I learned that I wasn't his first love interest since your parents' separation. There'd been somebody before me. One Sunday morning, rushing in unexpectedly from your mother's place to pick up something you needed for a homework assignment, you'd been startled to encounter her at the breakfast table. Pale, fine-boned, clad in a frothy negligée—even now when you recall her, your face clouds over.

Covered up as I was in wool turtleneck, jeans, and boots; angular and fair-haired—instead of dark, ruby-lipped, and smelling of perfume and cigarettes—I must have seemed safe in comparison. But the situation felt the opposite of safe to me. Later, your dad told me that if you hadn't liked me, he'd have ended our fledgling relationship then and there.

Fledgling. On the cusp.

Like you. Even your name means "little bird."

So long as the father was at home the child was treated with kindness and affection, but the moment he went out the mistress was very unkind to her and treated her badly.

Never, in all the time I was growing up, did it occur to me that one day I might become a stepmother.

Not once.

Yet hundreds of women become stepmothers every year. In fact, there are thousands of stepmothers in Canada alone—not to mention, fourteen *million* in the United States, many of them as badly prepared as I.

I'd never had a stepmother. There were none in my extended family. Few of my friends had stepmothers, and those who had them wished they didn't and rarely saw or spoke about them. So to me, they were a mysterious species. Sure, I'd seen them on TV and in the movies. Growing up when I did, I could hardly have missed *The Brady Bunch.* But TV and movies had never influenced me all that much. I was a book-loving kid who'd grown into a book-loving woman, which meant that my deepest, most powerful, and most ingrained ideas about stepmothers derived from fairy tales. And we all know what kind of picture they paint.

To compensate, I tried to be nice. Nicer than nice. Nicer than *me*. Looking back, I think I was more present to you then than I am sometimes today to my own daughter.

Nine months after our first encounter on that winter night, I was more or less living with your dad, and you spent half of each month with us and half with your mother. The weeks you stayed at our place, I made sure to be at home when the school day ended. Most afternoons, you'd walk in the door to a freshly made snack. Muffins. Homemade soup. Sometimes hot chocolate.

"That's wicked!" you'd crow, between bites. "Do you mind if I have a bit more of that? Is it okay if Olivia comes over? Could you help me with my homework?"

I helped with other things, too — errands your parents were too busy to perform. Like taking you shopping for clothing or shoes — including your Bat Mitzvah outfit, a purple dress, as I recall. We had to get it hemmed; you stood on a block of wood in the back room of a tiny Montreal Street shop. The seamstress pulled, tucked and pinned, looking to me for approval.

I picked you up after your rehearsals or practices; I organized your Halloween treats. I signed the forms you had to return to the school. I even attended parent-teacher conferences. And this made sense. Your mother and father held demanding jobs; I was looking for work. My afternoons and evenings were more available than theirs. It was easier for me to undertake these little tasks.

But…but…but…I hardly knew you! I was utterly inexperienced! I might have been on the other side of thirty, but I felt like a kid myself. I looked like one, too — you told me so. And sometimes I felt unequal to my new responsibilities. You'd ask for permission to go someplace or do something, and I'd wonder whether I should allow it. You'd whisper something about boys or bras or your deepest beliefs, and I'd be stunned by the enormity of the trust your parents had bestowed on me.

In those days, there weren't many how-to guides for step-parents. The sole example I could find at our local library offered little in the way of usable advice and plenty of dour pronouncements. Stepmothering, it warned, was not for the faint of heart. It was a difficult, thankless, and often heart-wrenching role. And the most challenging situation of all was for a younger, childless woman to marry the older father of a pre-teen girl. A fledgling.

There was a king and a queen, and they had a daughter, and the queen found death, and the king married another. And the last queen was bad to the daughter of the first queen, and she used to beat her and put her out of the door. She sent her to herd the sheep, and was not giving her what should suffice her.

Since I couldn't figure out how to be a stepmother, I decided that I *wouldn't* be a stepmother. Besides, officially, I wasn't one. Your dad and I weren't married, and your mother wasn't dead. You didn't need mothering. So I styled myself your older friend. Like an aunt, perhaps. A young aunt. Or maybe a cousin.

You made it easy for me. You were an easy kid. Bright, responsible, and—most of the time—happy. Sure, there were days when you'd come home from school in tears and crash straight into your bedroom without a word of greeting. But you always came out an hour later, ready to talk about whatever was bothering you. Recalling the outsize moods of my own early adolescence, I understood and felt instantly at home with you. And I enjoyed our time together. We shared a love of animals. We shared some significant values. We giggled at the same things. Blessed with what the social workers and therapists would call a "good fit," we quickly fell into comfortable patterns.

Friday nights, we'd watch movies and eat gelato. You liked Julia Roberts and Jennifer Grey; *Mystic Pizza, Steel Magnolias, Dirty Dancing.* Girl stories. Perfect for sharing with another girl. Still, I worried that I was stealing your special time with your dad. For years, the two of you had been watching movies together. Now there was another body squeezed between yours on the couch—and you'd had no say in the matter.

But it didn't seem to bother you. You seemed to welcome me. You even seemed to like me. *Like* me! Recall: I'd never felt the pure affection of a child before. I hadn't known I wanted it. Hadn't known I craved it. But now that it fell on me, all unexpected, it felt like pure benediction.

Was it eighth grade when you got to play the Wicked Witch of the West in your class's annual theatre production? You had the narrow face for the part. But watching you, all I could think was how *good* you were.

"What is that useless creature doing in the best room?" asked the stepmother. "Away to the kitchen with her! And if she wants to eat, then she must earn it. She can be our maid."

Too good to be true?

If I'd been too nice to be *me*, you'd been too nice to be *you*.

The truth came out when I was least expecting it.

Your fifteenth birthday, and your dad and I were treating you to a weekend of theatre in Toronto. By this time, I was working as a teacher, and you were in high school. We must have left Kingston late in the afternoon, right after school ended, hoping to reach the city in time for supper. Along the roadside, golden leaves spun through the soft grey air. But within the metal box of our Nissan, the atmosphere was anything but mellow.

How did the argument begin? I can't recall. All I know is that my mildest comments made you bristle, and however sweetly I smiled, you shot me the kind of scornful looks that teenagers typically reserve for their own parents.

This was uncharacteristic. Unprecedented, even. I'd seen you angry. I'd seen you confused. But I'd never known you to be rude. What was going on?

You wouldn't or couldn't say. Instead, you scowled. Twisting in your seat, you set your face against me, staring out the window.

So much for the happy birthday weekend we had planned. Your dad and I exchanged a worried glance. He shrugged.

At last we heard your body shift against the seat. You straightened your spine, steeled yourself to speak. And when the words came, they came in a passionate blast. "You are *not* my stepmother," you said. "*Not!*"

My stomach clenched. Right away, I knew what had happened.

A few weeks earlier, entering the crowded staff lunchroom, I'd cleared a place to eat. Beside me sat a new colleague, recently transferred from your school. Between gulps of stale coffee, amid the clattering of plates and the beeps of the microwave, she launched into a story involving you and your friends.

I know—teachers aren't supposed to gossip. But they do, and this one was, and she wasn't aware of our relationship.

Had she come to praise or to blame? I didn't know. But to save us both possible embarrassment, I thought it best to inform her— *fast*—that I was close to you. And so, although I'd never allowed the word to pass my lips before, had never allowed myself even to *think* it—I told this woman I was your stepmother.

The minute that word left my lips, I felt uneasy. Uneasy—and even soiled. Somehow, obscurely, in the back of my mind, I knew—must have known—that my use of the term would bother you. But what else could I do? I had to say *something* to warn her.

"You should have said that you're my dad's partner!" you shouted at me now.

And usually, that's exactly what I would have done. But in this case, it would have felt wrong. My relationship with your dad wasn't the issue.

What made the word so threatening? Why, after so much together-ness — so much *love* — did it bother you to hear me use it to describe myself? And why, after all this time, did I feel so uncomfortable when I claimed it?

Once upon a time there was an old couple. The husband lost his wife and married again. But he had a daughter by the first marriage, a young girl, and she found no favor in the eyes of her evil stepmother, who used to beat her, and consider how she could get her killed outright.

"His daughter may *like* you," my ex-husband had said, in the hor-rible months following our breakup. "But you'll never be her mother."

There was the crux of it. I would never be your mother. And though this hadn't bothered me then ("I *know* that," I'd answered, witheringly) it was beginning to bother me now. Because by this time, I was thirty-five, and wondering whether I'd ever be *anyone's* mother.

As early as our first weeks together, your dad and I had talked about having children. But we didn't want to rush. Having failed at our first marriages, we wanted to ensure that our relationship was stable. We wanted to ensure that *you* were stable. We knew it had been difficult for you to accept that your mom and dad would never reunite. It seemed both kind and wise to give you time and space to adjust.

That was all very well, in theory. But in the meantime, my biological clock was ticking. And in the following years, as we struggled with unexplained infertility, sometimes I wondered if we'd simply waited too long.

Did I blame you? No — of course not, any more than you blamed me. You knew I wasn't the cause or the catalyst of your parents' breakup. If I had been, you might not have felt as free to like me as much as you genuinely did. But if I didn't cause their breakup, I must have symbolized its permanence and the loss of your dream of the perfect, intact family. Perhaps that was why, when it came right down to it, for all our apparent closeness, you could not allow yourself to see me as anything more than a glorified babysitter.

Your anger in the car that day ignited the only real disagreement we ever had. Before we reached the city, it was over. Within hours, we were feasting in some favourite restaurant, looking forward to the upcoming play. We never referred to the incident. It was as if the conflict had never happened. But, however many verbal dances I had to perform, I never again used the "s" word. Strange, how much it hurt sometimes, to avoid it.

One step removed might be as close as I would ever get to motherhood. Maybe I wasn't even as close as that. After all, if you couldn't bear to hear me call myself your stepmother, I could hardly lay title to the role.

"I'll tell you what, husband," answered the woman, "early tomorrow morning we will take the children out into the forest to where it is the thickest; there we will light a fire for them, and give each of them one more piece of bread, and then we will go to our work and leave them alone. They will not find the way home again, and we shall be rid of them."

I never did get pregnant. Instead, after years of futile attempts, your dad and I adopted. You were the first in the family to meet the baby. Do you remember? At the time, you were a student in Vancouver. We stopped there on our return from China. The photos show you bouncing Maia on your knee. Her plump Buddha cheeks shine pink with heat rash and pleasure; yours glow with the bloom of youth and hope. You'd always wanted a sister. I'd always wanted a daughter. And here she was. Delivered, as if by some fairy godmother's wand, to bring us closer together.

Two years later, you came home for the holidays. Your braces long gone, your curls a little less golden, you'd graduated from university, travelled the world, and returned with new commitment to the vegetarianism that you'd flirted with at age twelve. Now you were heading to Poland for a teaching job. But before that, you wanted to visit with your family—including your sister. A sister you loved in theory but hadn't seen a lot of. A sister who, by the time you arrived, had left her biddable babyhood far behind.

The first evening of your visit, you took your place at the table with a satisfied sigh. Cooking and eating together had always been one of our chief joys as a family. A time for sharing stories, solving problems. A time for pleasure and happy unburdening. You must have been looking forward to it.

I strapped Maia into her high chair. She screamed.

"It smells delicious," you said.

Maia screamed again.

Your dad set a bowl of steaming pasta on the table. Another scream. You opened your mouth to say something. She let out yet another ear-hammering wail.

Throughout the meal, it never let up.

I asked you a question about your upcoming journey; Maia banged her tray with her spoon, so that none of us could hear the answer. You asked for more food, and she rocked so heavily in her chair that instead of passing you the salad, we leapt up to make sure she wasn't about to tip herself over. She yanked her bib off so it had to be put back on, she spilled something and I had to get up and tend to her, she needed more water, she needed more food. In short, every single time you looked for a bit of adult attention, your dad or I or both of us were engaged with your new sister.

Back in those long-ago teenage years, you sometimes used to accuse your dad and me of "ganging up" on you. Accustomed as you were to attention from only one parent at a time, you'd writhed under our combined focus, which felt too intense and overbearing. Now, on the verge of a huge move and life transition, that level of attention and engagement was precisely what you sought from us. But with a three-year-old in the room, you'd never get it.

And Maia was no ordinary three-year-old. As a child who had undergone significant trauma, she was more active, more emotional, more prone to tantrums, and much more needy than other kids her age. The truth is, at that stage of her development, she was an emotional vampire; it took every scrap of energy, ingenuity, and careful planning your dad and I could muster just to keep her on a relatively even keel —by which I mean restricting her hour-long rages to no more than two or three a day.

Over the next week, as this reality dawned on you, the atmosphere in the house became more and more strained. You wanted, you really *wanted*, to like Maia. But you weren't truly interested in children, and you were awkward and self-conscious around her. Sensing your discomfort, she became even more demanding. So after years of living among strangers in strange cities on a student budget—and with the prospect of more of that to come—instead of the conversation and coddling you craved, instead of a *break* from it all, you came home to tumult and tension. Crowded out of your own home, I can only imagine how lost and lonely you must have felt.

Poor fledgling, shoved from the nest.

Then she summoned a huntsman and said to him, "Take Snow-White out into the woods. I never want to see her again. Kill her, and as proof that she is dead bring her lungs and her liver back to me."

Ten years later, I came to Toronto on my own for a long overdue visit with you. Without your dad, without Maia, the two of us could talk more freely. And, wedged together in a noisy Spadina restaurant booth, chomping on salad and crispy tofu (for, like Elphaba in *Wicked*, you'd become an animal-rights activist), talk we did. The way we hadn't talked for many years, I realized then, with a pang.

We'd both been busy—you working, studying, and travelling the world. Me, working, writing, and mothering. We hadn't intended to let a gulf of distance grow between us. We'd tried to keep in touch, but our meetings had become less frequent, our attention more and more divided. And I hadn't known it, but I'd been missing you.

Now a graduate student, for the past several years you'd been involved in an on-again, off-again long-distance relationship with an older man. You loved him, you respected him, you trusted him. But there were complicating factors—not least of these his young son, to whom you'd become a one-step-removed, not-quite stepmother.

A recent, painful visit to their home had persuaded you that it was time to end things for good. But you feared the loss, and at thirty-two, you wondered where your life was going. No money, no job, and no real prospects for work, no man, no children. Meanwhile, your friends were all zipping ahead in their careers and starting families.

"I feel so…I don't know. I just never thought it would *be* like this," you said. "I'm not sure what I imagined, but somehow I thought I'd have it more together by now. You know? And then I wonder, why *don't* I? Everybody else seems to manage it."

I remembered my first year with your father. No money, no work, my friends all scattered in distant cities. A painful divorce in process.

No guarantee that this new relationship would last. And the shame. Such shame. I used to shiver on the couch under a blanket. How could I have messed things up so badly?

That was the year I baked you muffins. The year I stopped whatever I was doing each afternoon to take you wherever you needed to go. The year I listened to you, putting aside my own grief and fear to tend to you.

At the time, this was a stretch for me; I was used to living solely for myself, without regard to anyone else's needs. Some days I had to swallow tears; some days I had to fake a smile when you walked in the door, so you wouldn't see how stressed and anxious I was. Yet how I had benefitted from that exercise, I saw now. How it had made me grow, and even bloom. How lucky I had been, to have you.

"You know," I said, "I was thirty-two when your dad and I got together."

A small crease formed between your eyes. "You're kidding."

"It's true."

You set down your cup. "You mean...when I first met you, you were my age?"

I nodded.

"But I thought..." Your voice trailed off. You bit your lip. There was a pause. "I thought you were a *grown up*!"

Our eyes met. We started to laugh. We laughed so hard the tiny table shook.

Then you looked at me again. For the first time in a long time, we saw one another.

The queen took fright and turned yellow and green with envy. From that hour on whenever she looked at Snow-White her heart turned over inside

her body, so great was her hatred for the girl. The envy and pride grew
ever greater, like a weed in her heart, until she had no peace day and night.

In the old stories, there is never enough. Never enough food,
money, beauty. Never enough love. Stepmother and stepdaughter
are locked forever in competition for whatever each can grasp. The
loser lies in a poisoned sleep; the loser wears the iron shoes. For the
"step" in stepmother derives from the Old English *steop. Steopcild,*
meaning orphan. *Steupa,* meaning bereft. *Stief,* meaning pushed out.

Pushed from the nest.

How lucky we are to live in more fortunate times.

These days, you and I are living once again in the same city. Every
few weeks, you set aside some time for Maia, taking her for bike rides
and walks with your mother's dog. You join us for family suppers. You
call her up to gossip. The two of you sit giggling together on our couch,
playing Mad Libs or watching movies. With twenty years between you
—the same age difference that separates you and me—you are not
quite a generation apart. Just far enough apart to make you a perfect
older friend. Like an aunt. A young aunt, or maybe a cousin.

Once you borrowed a pair of your mother's skates and the three
of us—you, me, and Maia—snuck away from the holiday meal
preparations to spin around City Square for an hour or two in the
fading afternoon light. Hoping for some aerobic benefits, I sped off
on my own for a few laps, circling the rink at a faster pace. You and
Maia skated together, your faces turned toward one another, cheeks
ruddy in the cold, arms linked as you guided each other across the
ice. Watching you, I thought of the two of us, twenty years earlier, on
a different winter night.

Later, it started to snow. On the way home, the streetlamps came
on, and we had to step delicately to avoid the hidden patches of ice.

Robin

ALISON PICK

We did this on purpose, so why am I so blown away? The efficacy of our bodies, the speed. We are *newlyweds*—old-fashioned word—married six weeks. I peel back the foil of the pregnancy test, squat over the toilet, and take aim. One line means not pregnant, two means pregnant.

The first line appears.

Then, ten seconds later, like an arrow showing the progress toward a fundraising goal, a second line inches up the screen.

I look away, look back.

The second line is still there.

My phone is not on the desk, not on the table in the hall. "I'm having a baby!" I shout to the empty apartment, then take up ransacking, yanking clothes out of drawers, dumping the contents of my purses onto the bed.

The phone is in plain view on the dresser. My husband, Degan, picks up. I hear traffic in the background. "I'm on my bike," he says.

"You're riding your bike and talking on the phone at the same time?"

"It's fine. It's a side street."

"Pull over," I say.

He sighs.

"I think I'm pregnant!"

"Because your boobs hurt?"

He doubts me. To his credit, he's heard this before.

"I took a test," I say, smug.

Loud horns in the background.

"I thought you were on a *side* street."

"You're serious?" he asks.

Degan begins to take slow deep breaths, a kind of prevenient, precautionary Lamaze. I check the second pink line to make sure it hasn't disappeared. "Oh my *God*," I say.

"Breathe with me," Degan says. "Breathe."

The next day, I drive to Midland and give a reading with the poet Anne Simpson. She announces, apropos of *nothing*, "When I was pregnant all I wanted was steak." Her eyes find mine. How does she know?

Back in the city, I visit Dr. Singh. Her hair is pulled back into the high bouncy ponytail of a cheerleader. She tests my urine, confirms the double line's augury.

"We're going to Europe," I tell her.

"When?"

"On Friday?"

Surely, this isn't allowed.

"Am I okay to travel? To fly?" I ask.

"So long as you feel up for it."

I feel up for it, I tell her. I feel *fantastic*.

. . .

There are things I have wanted in my life, things I have longed for. To have a book published. To be married. But this particular longing is different. Only in its consummation do I realize its extent, like a vast continent whose hinterlands I've remained consciously unaware of. Like many women in their early thirties, I've spent the past decade bracing against pregnancy, trying not to capitulate to its allure. The abnegation has gone on so long that I have come to believe myself incapable. Only now that I am pregnant and therefore undeniably fertile can I acknowledge how I long for a child. There is nothing I want more in the world's farthest reaches.

I'm myself, an average person boarding a plane, and then, all at once, I'm someone else. Somewhere high over the Atlantic, a transformation occurs, sudden and complete, an eclipse of the moon, a slap across the face. "It's just jet lag," I tell Degan when we land in Vienna. But I'm so tired he has to drag me out of the airport. I lie like a dishrag in the front lobby of a tanning salon while he figures out the directions to our hotel.

I sleep for fifteen hours. When I wake, Degan is dressed and shaved. He hands me a coffee—I flinch and push it away.

His eyes widen.

We visit the rooms where Sigmund Freud saw patients and the bustling *Naschmarkt*. Degan tours Schubert's apartment; waiting outside for him, I fall soundly asleep in the stairwell so that when he emerges he mistakes me, briefly, for a vagrant. At dinner, I scarf down a roast chicken and a huge plate of spaghetti. Six weeks pregnant. The hunger is for the new person I'm growing inside me, and the new self, the mother I'm becoming.

. . .

Our baby is a girl. How do I know? I just do.

I make up a silly song, and sing it under my breath: "*My little baby. Oh! My little baby...*" It's a lullaby, and a hymn, and a mantra.

We take a train to the Czech town of Brno where I read in an author's festival. After, we go for drinks. Ken Babstock, another writer at the festival, tells us about his new baby son. He is changing so fast: an argument against the continuity of the self. I picture our girl multiplying herself inside me, adding cells like rooms every second. Each day, I get an e-mail detailing her development. This week, she is blueberry sized.

The waitress brings a plate of dumplings towering with bacon and cheese.

"Is that pasteurized?" Degan asks.

I put down my fork.

Ken grins a half grin. He knows.

Our next stop is the capital city, Prague. Because of an article I have been commissioned to write, we are put up in the republic's most resplendent hotel. I spend my days curled on the bed in the fetal position. Hair in the bathtub drain makes me retch. The scum on the nozzle of the toothpaste. The lavish buffet is lost on me. I emerge from the room twice daily to eat off the "beige menu": dry bagels, dry toast, bananas.

Degan explores Prague while I head off cross-country for the second time, researching. My article, irony of ironies, is about beer. I am to tour the country's famous microbreweries, sampling the wares.

"Alcohol of any kind is prohibited!" my daily e-mail warns cheerfully. I turn away glass after glass, bile rising hot in my throat.

The tours themselves cover hectares of hallways. I race after my guides, through a pea-soup fog of malt and hops and billowing steam. I gag and sweat. It's as though I'm being trained for a marathon, maybe, or for some more ancient relay involving armour, a crossbow, and a unicorn.

August is on the verge of expiring by the time we arrive back in Toronto. There are babies everywhere: in the airport, on the bus, at the grocery store. I ogle their plump legs, their fists, unable to peel my eyes away from their auspice. I'm nine weeks pregnant. So nauseous I could weep. Dr. Singh calls to schedule a check-up. "How was your trip?" she asks brightly.

"I feel a little...sick."

She smiles brightly again. "That's normal!"

It means, she reminds me, that the pregnancy is progressing. My baby has taken up residence in her rooms.

That evening, we go out for drinks. Lynn Coady's leafy back porch is crammed with writers. Alissa York eyes my apple juice. "You're not pregnant, are you?"

I shake my head emphatically: *No.* But she knows.

As though the baby has heard my remonstrance, when I get home I find blood in my underwear. I gape at it in the same way that I gaped at the pink line on the pregnancy test: something of intimate, immediate consequence that at the same time feels remote as a star. I look away, look back. It's still there. Not the blood of a menstrual period—not quite—but any blood at all is reason for consternation.

I bleed steadily for a week, unable to think of anything else. Dr. Singh's reassurance that spotting is "normal" is met with flat-out disbelief. Finally, in face of my relentless wheedling and cajoling, my midwife agrees to send me for an ultrasound. The technician squirts jelly on my stomach, brandishes her magic wand. "Let's see if we can hear your baby's heartbeat," she says.

Wait.

What?

My *baby?*

My baby's *heartbeat?*

On the screen is a blizzard, fierce wind and snow. And then a tiny flashing blip, a flicker, like some kind of beacon.

"There it is!" The technician beams, as though she's never seen this before.

"My little baby. Oh! My little baby…"

Tears roll down my face, into my ears.

I am sent home with a photo of our dreamer, a whisper of an image as ethereal as the minute being itself. When Degan gets home from work, we lie on the bed. He presses his face to my tummy. "Hi there, little one," he murmurs. "Your heart is beating really fast. We don't know what we're doing. But we're getting ready for you to arrive."

September 8 is my thirty-third birthday. My bleeding has stopped. I'm still nauseous, but nothing like before. I'm out of the gates, out of the first trimester, thirteen-weeks pregnant to the day. Everyone says now I can relax, which means, I guess, that I can stop worrying about a miscarriage. Only I haven't been worrying at all since I'm not going to have one. Not with everything we've already endured.

Degan suggests it's time to share our news. Obviously, the whole world—the world composed of writers—already knows. Still, I send an e-mail, and am floored by the answers that flood back. Why are they all so happy for us?

I haven't been worried, but all at once it's true: I'm going to be a mother. We're going to have a *child*.

Wednesday morning, my nausea reappears, a stomach sickness more sharp and barbed than the one I've grown accustomed to. Degan finds me on the bathroom floor with my cheek pressed against the cool tiles. He leads me to bed, tucks me in. "Rest," he says. "I'll call you from work. And try to get out for some fresh air." He lifts my chin with his finger so I'm looking him in the eye. "Promise?"

I nod weakly.

I sleep for three hours and wake with the intent to do what I've been told. My bike has a flat tire, and filling it seems like a manageable goal. I heave it down the cement steps from the porch of our building to the sidewalk. The late summer air is dense, the edges of everything hazy. The bike feels inordinately heavy, but the garage is only three short blocks away. I start pushing the bike and begin to shake and perspire. When I reach the intersection I've been heading for, I realize the garage is still another block away.

When I eventually get there, I crouch in front of the counter, hanging on to my stomach, sweat pouring off me. A kind stranger fills my tire with air. The hill facing me on the way home looms like a ghoulish apparition, too steep to ride, so I'm again resigned to the Sisyphean task of pushing. The day is bright and boiling hot. And then, oddly, freezing cold. When I at last reach the apartment, I'm confronted by the steep concrete stairs. I have no memory of how I manage to get my bike up them. When I'm finally crashed out on the bed, I call Degan and tell him I feel bad. *Really* bad.

In the week after, he replays my messages and cries.

I sleep all afternoon. That night I have a fever, low at first, but rising. Degan calls our midwife, Hedrey. She tells us to come in to her office the next morning. We'll see if we can hear the baby's heartbeat.

We get to the clinic, brimming with toddlers and breast-feeding pillows and women in overalls. Degan checks a book on morning sickness out of the lending library. It has a single, sad-looking soda cracker on the cover.

Maybe I just have really bad morning sickness?

I lie down in an examining room decorated to look like a bedroom, with brightly patterned curtains and photos of babies on the walls. Sun slants hotly through the windows. I lift my shirt; Hedrey places her Doppler on my belly.

I wait for the sound of the heartbeat, but there's nothing. Only the eerie *whoosh* of my own blood through my veins.

Hedrey averts her eyes, concentrating. She moves the instrument lower, just above my pubic bone, where my stomach, in the last week, has started to protrude.

Still nothing.

I crumple the edges of my skirt in my wet palms.

And then, suddenly, there it is. The galloping hoof-beats, fast and steady. *Da-dun, da-dun, da-dun…*

Hedrey beams. "Hello baby!"

I look over at Degan, his blue eyes wide, full of tears.

. . .

The baby is fine. The baby is fine. I repeat this to myself as Degan drives us up Bathurst on the way to see Dr. Singh. *The baby is fine*...but such a high fever isn't good for her. We need to try to bring my temperature down.

Degan stops at a red light, and I call Mum and give her the update: The baby is fine! But I'm still feeling awful.

After the brief respite of the midwife's clinic, there's a paroxysm of pain. I hunch over in the passenger seat, my knees tucked up to my chest. I hang up the phone and a sound escapes my lips, a cry I at first don't recognize as coming from my own mouth. Degan reaches for me, holding my shoulder awkwardly with one arm while turning the car on to Eglinton with the other. The jabs are sharpening, converging. I cry out again and pull my knees in closer.

In the elevator on the way up to the doctor's office, I double over as though I'm about to vomit. The elevator door dings open and I run down the hall to the bathroom, my whole body clenching and squeezing. I throw myself into a stall and slam the door behind me.

When I pull down my pants, my underwear is soaked with blood. In the crotch, a cylinder of thick red jelly.

I crouch over the toilet. Cramps, then a river of shit, and then more intense cramps. Not cramps. *Contractions.* My insides are falling out, big chunks of red splashing beneath me.

I finally manage to stand, minutes or hours later, rising on wobbly legs as though I've just been born. The toilet bowl is full of blood, and feces, and something else my eyes flinch away from. I force myself to look back. I *want* to see my baby, all thirteen weeks of her—her eyelids, her fingerprints, her ears. But from beneath me there's a roar, the automatic toilet flushing.

My little baby. Oh! My little baby...

Every bit of her gone, swallowed away.

A gurney has appeared, magically, in the hall outside the bathroom, accompanied by two ambulance attendants. All I've ever wanted is to lie down. They insert an IV. I am wheeled into the elevator, then out onto the street where I blink in the bright sun. Passersby turn their heads as I'm lifted into the ambulance. From somewhere far away, Degan's voice: *I'll meet you at the hospital.* A siren starts up, announcing our procession. I'm a queen being carried through the streets on horseback. Traffic parts around us.

For the second time in a week, my ears are wet, filling up with tears.

At the hospital, morphine. Oxygen tubes in my nose. A male nurse with a pin through his eyebrow says, "You've lost a lot of blood. Your blood pressure is still very low. Without that IV you would have needed a transfusion."

Through a thin curtain, a man's gravelly voice: "I normally drink three bottles of wine a day. But I went cold turkey on Monday."

His doctor asks, "Do you ever hear voices? On the TV, say, talking to you?"

His wife chimes in: "He's paranoid about his boss at work."

To my right, another woman who took all her husband's heart medication. She keeps repeating, "It's okay; it's fine. You don't need to help me. I don't want to live."

I'm moved to a different room. The nurse with the eyebrow ring appears again, asks, "How are you feeling?" I roll onto my side, wipe my cheeks.

"We need to know your blood type," he says. "But your father gave us the rest of the info."

"The info?"

"Your address and birthday. Those things."

Should I correct him? "I think you mean my husband," I say.

"No, I mean your father. He's in the waiting room."

"That's my husband."

"It's your father," he says.

"My father lives in another city."

The nurse shrugs.

"How much morphine did you give me?" I ask.

The man in the waiting room is, in fact, my father. He came into Toronto for an errand earlier in the day. But bad news travels like dominoes falling, and now he's here with me. Not an angel, not exactly. But close.

Dad smoothes the hair back from my forehead. I have a sudden visceral memory of the Lily of the Valley he would bring to my bedside when I was a girl, a small vase on my dresser. The lush, heady fragrance in the long spring evenings: *Beauty is here. Beauty survives.*

Later—hours or days—my father leaves. Degan, who has been conferring quietly with a doctor in the hallway, appears with a wheelchair. He pushes me down into the bowels of the hospital. We are shown into a dark room where an ultrasound technician is tutoring his trainee.

He mumbles something; there's a long silence, and I realize he's talking to me.

"Pardon me?"

"Get on the table," the technician says.

Degan corrects him under his breath: "Get on the table, *please.*"

He helps me up tenderly, as a mother might help a child just learning to walk. I arrange my hospital gown over my legs, but the technician yanks it back up. He squirts a glob of jelly on my stomach, and moves the wand across my flesh. The screen appears gray, an undifferentiated stretch of snow. This time there is no blinking beacon.

I flush with the ignominy of what my body has done.

Degan's eyebrows are up, though, and he's smiling. "I think I *see* something," he says.

I can hardly stand his hope. He has been waiting for this moment, for *his* first glimpse of our child, and now his heart imagines what his mind knows isn't there. Because, of course, this is not the ultrasound he's been looking forward to. This is something different altogether.

Later, a doctor arrives with the results. The fetus, the egg sac, all the "products of the pregnancy" are gone. We gather up my blood-soaked clothes in a plastic bag. I am given a skirt from the hospital's lost-and-found and a new shirt: some other woman's clothes. Degan drives us home. Along Spadina, night has fallen swiftly. Streetlights and pizza joints. Two of us, where this morning there were three.

I sleep the whole next day. When Degan gets home from work, he tidies the bedroom while I cook rice and cut vegetables. There is a mushroom that has a smaller mushroom fused into its side. I chop the mother and baby apart without mercy. Tears in my eyes while I stir-fry.

Saturday morning, we make raspberry smoothies, and French toast with challah. I move around the kitchen, my head in and out of the fridge, with no nausea whatsoever. After swearing I will never again — *never again* — drink coffee, I brew a pot and guzzle it with relish. The hormones are draining out of me like broth through a sieve, my body giving up the task it has been performing so diligently for the last thirteen weeks.

Degan says, "I want to look at the ultrasound photo." He cradles it in his palm, slight as a moth's wing. We peer at the charcoal smudge against the field of darker grey. Who was she? Who would she have become? Someone. A person. We'll never know.

In the evening, we bring candles into the bedroom and lie together in the low flicker. We read a bit. I cry. Degan eventually falls asleep, but I'm awake and alert, a hole in my chest the wind is whistling through.

I understand for the first time — really understand — the thin membrane between death and life. Everyone will die. *Everyone* I love. It's banal, and obvious, and earth shattering.

I get up from bed and pad through the dark apartment. A sliver of moon just visible through the kitchen window. The quiet hum of the dishwasher finishing its work. In my study, I reach for the ultrasound picture; it is not on the table where we left it. I look beneath papers, between pages of books. When I still can't find it, I panic, ripping through drawers and turning out pockets. If I can't see the photo, I will die.

It's there, all at once, in full view on my desk. I cry with relief and despair. The little grey blur. The inkling. All I'll ever know of my daughter.

On Saturday morning, my friend Aviva comes over early. We go to a Shabbat service held in someone's home. There are maybe twenty others, mostly strangers to me. We chant single lines of liturgy, weaving them through the morning like strands of golden thread. The last chant is from the Song of Songs, "Zeh Dodi, v'zeh Rayee": *This is my Beloved, this is my Friend.* As we sing, we circle around each other, looking each other in the eye. Seeing, being seen. Such raw power.

After, the leader asks, "Does anyone need to say Kaddish?" Kaddish is the Jewish prayer for the dead, which does not mention death, but praises God's name. It is recited when someone has died, and therefore, by definition, been alive. So my baby doesn't count.

The circle is quiet. The leader looks around at us all, his eyes falling for a long moment on me, holding Aviva's hand, tears on my cheeks. "I'll say it for us all," he decides. And he begins: *"Glorified and sanctified be God's great name..."*

There is nothing to be done, and so we do nothing. We bear the pain, which is much worse than I could have imagined. The offense of the phrase, "You can have another." What would I want with another? I want *that* baby, *my* baby.

Oh! My little baby...

Several weeks later, it comes to me that she needs a name. That in her absence we can still evoke her existence; that a name serves as an anchor for memory.

I've been thinking about *Robin*. The bright blue eggs, the scarlet feathers, the sudden flurry of departure. A name good for a girl—or a boy, in case I was wrong. I might have been wrong.

Degan agrees; it's his idea to plant a tree. A living memorial where a fleeting spirit might rest. We choose a spot on the hillside at the cottage. The day is warm, the black earth fragrant. Degan digs a hole. I crouch down beside it. And then, in the tall grass and tangled weeds, a small abandoned nest.

The nest fits neatly in the grave. On top if it, we lay the medical report from the day of the miscarriage, and the ultrasound picture in lieu of the tiny body. I've tied them together with a pale blue string. We position the tree, begin filling the hole. But first we add a letter saying goodbye. We've signed it, for the first time ever, *Mum and Dad.*

It was an uncommon miscarriage, a statistical anomaly. I was through the first trimester; the baby was *fine*. Fine, and twenty minutes later, gone. There's no point in trying to understand.

There is another baby now. A child, almost three years old. It would be easy to end with her, her mouth wide open, chewing up the world. But I don't want to. Robin was the child that made me a mother. A lost child, but a child nonetheless.

When I am asked about my kids, I say I have a daughter. Sometimes, if the asker is really listening, I say I had another one before her. With a strong heartbeat, with fingerprints. With see-through eyelids and a pair of tiny wings. I still miss that baby. Does it sound strange? I do. And sometimes, on a rainy afternoon, when there's Van Morrison on the stereo and something sweet baking in the oven, when the living room is a cozy clutter of toys and books and crayons, I feel a quiet gaze on my back. When I turn, no one's there. But I know she's hovering in the shadows behind me, eyes wide with awe, watching the life we almost had.

The Post-Maia World

HEIDI REIMER

The first person I thought of after I gave birth to my second daughter was the woman who gave birth to my first daughter. Still throbbing from two hours' pushing, stupefied at my body's life-producing power, I wobbled to the bathroom on my midwife's arm and realized, *My god. So this is what she did to bring Maia into the world.*

In my bond with my newborn, there was no choice. I had been ambivalent about motherhood, her conception wasn't planned, but our connection to each other was primeval, animal, beyond rationality; it grew through nine months' gestation, an umbilical cord between us, a birth canal, a mouth on my breast, hormones clamouring, "You are mine and I have never loved anyone before you!" She was bone of my bones. She had inhabited me. I was gobsmacked and humbled, in the first days of her life, by how little I had understood motherhood before her. Lying blissful hours with my babe on my chest, I wept as the secret of the universe revealed itself to me. Pushing a human being out of your body—feeding her from your breasts—giving and sustaining life: nothing was more powerful. I had made *a person*! I would never do or become anything more important than this.

But first there was Maia, my niece, daughter of my teenaged brother and his teenaged girlfriend, fifteen months old when she made me a mother, nine months before I gave birth to her cousin-sister. Gestation with Maia was five days long. My husband, Richard, and I went to plays, restaurants, films, cramming into those days everything we loved about our life that was now ending. On the subway home, we sat together speed-reading parenting books. On day five, I drove five hours to pick her up.

On her first night with us, after we'd installed her bed in the space originally designated as my Room of My Own (and oh, the symbolism of that displacement), she cried, disoriented and insecure. I settled her into my lap in a rocking chair and gazed with such sympathy at this strawberry-curled, blue-eyed child who looked nothing like me, who had been shuttled from caregiver to caregiver, mother figure to mother figure, taken from her rural home and brought here, to a noisy street-facing apartment in Toronto, to me. Arbitrarily, artificially, suddenly, to me. I held her, and I summoned all the love she'd known, or should have known, or I hoped would one day know, gathered it like each scrap was a solid, vital object I could invoke for her protection, and I wove it into a song to wrap around her as I rocked: *Mama loves Maia, Maia loves Mama.*

I used Mama because my own mother and all the mothers ever modelled to me were "Mom" and "Mommy," and to declare myself suddenly one of these felt absurd and fraudulent.

Did I love her? Yes, I did. I had been conflicted, but I had chosen her. As for Maia's feelings about me, I was aware as I sang that it was not my presence she was whimpering for. She clung, I suspected, only because I was the one familiar point in an unfamiliar environment.

Papa loves Maia, Maia loves Papa. In truth, she cried whenever Richard walked into the room.

Daddy loves Maia, Maia loves Daddy. Daddy was my brother, who was tortured by the decision to relinquish her care, but after his relationship's disintegration, in the face of personal challenges of his own, he knew he couldn't raise her himself.

Grandma loves Maia, Maia loves Grandma. My mother had been Maia's guardian, the closest she'd had to a mother for the past five months.

Auntie Marja loves Maia, Maia loves Auntie Marja. Maia adored my sister, who lived beside my parents and was an active and devoted mother to her own two children. She had considered becoming Maia's mother and seemed to me infinitely more suited. Weeks from this night, Maia will skin her knee and Marja will be the one she runs to.

I did not sing her first mother's name, but her first mother was in my mind, the woman with Maia's strawberry-blonde hair, the woman who birthed her and breast-fed her and wore her in a sling, who we all thought was managing so well despite youth and inexperience and a lack of mothering in her own life, who gave it her best and could not give any more. I thought of her, especially, and of Maia's loss, her incalculable loss.

In the months of vacillation over the Maia Decision, I had felt I was determining not just whether I would become the mother of my niece but whether I would become a mother at all. It was a question I'd never decided, was always able to leave for the future, focusing on other dreams whose fulfillment I worried would be endangered by child-rearing. But I did not believe I could say no to an existing child and go on to produce offspring of my own. If I was willing to mother, I needed to say yes to mothering Maia.

My instant heart decision had been, "Yes! We are Maia's parents!" But over months of consideration, doubt and fear dogged me. We gave ourselves a deadline: at the beginning of June, I would travel north to my parents' home, stay two weeks, help my mother with Maia, and decide.

On the morning I was to leave, my suitcase packed, my ride waiting, I took a pregnancy test.

Richard insisted the adoption decision be separate from the fact of our pregnancy, but I couldn't compartmentalize the motherless child in my parents' home and the future-child in my uterus. After months of intellectual to-ing and fro-ing, my body had beat out my mind and, with one stunning pink line on a plastic wand, declared I was becoming a mother. If life would be dumped on its head in nine months' time, why not immediately? If one child, why not two? In my terrified moments, the unexpected pregnancy felt like a trap. In my peaceful ones, it was sweet confirmation, the universe aligning to point me toward my next stage of life.

"I've never believed biology equals parenthood," Maia's mother told me in the discussion that convinced me she was sure. "Just because Maia was born to me doesn't mean I'm meant to be her mother."

"She will feel like your own," said friends whose adoptive daughter had come to them at five days old. "Caring for her will feel no different than if you'd given birth to her."

She did not feel like my own. Caring for her felt like babysitting, except I wasn't getting paid and the parents were never, ever coming back. A bomb had exploded in the centre of my identity and my days had shifted, almost instantly, from measurable progress toward creative and intellectual goals to aimless circles around a playground track. I longed for a community to help me make sense of my new self, but my experience fit neither conventional motherhood narratives nor the usual adoption story. I cried all the time. *I think I'm experiencing the adoption version of postpartum depression,* I wrote. When I spoke honestly about how difficult it was, one friend was brave enough to ask what no one would think to ask the brand-new mother of a biological baby: "Do you think maybe you shouldn't be doing this?" I collapsed into bed when Maia fell asleep, first-trimester exhaustion a bag of bricks pressing me down, and wept that I was no more fit than Maia's real mother. And, yes, *real* was how I thought of her because I felt completely fake. I may have been thirty-one to her seventeen, I may have been married, but I too felt overwhelmed and incompetent, fearful, resentful, in mourning for the termination of a life I had loved. She, at least, had given birth to Maia. What was there to say that I was, that I should be, Maia's mother?

There was the gut-punch of connection at our meeting, an inexplicable recognition that this three-month-old and I belonged together. There was my giddy preoccupation, like a girl freshly in love, when Richard and I visited her at age one, just after her mother decided she couldn't raise her. There was the night she bit me and I swore and raged and then, cradling her clinging body, decided I wanted to be the person she could bite and still be unshakably loved.

There were these things. I clung to these things.

"Is this your first?" people asked as my pregnancy began to show. Always, I blanked. Yes. No. I wanted to claim this pregnancy for what it was, the first time my belly had ballooned and I felt internal flutters and heard the astonishing whoosh of a second heart beating inside me. It was all very new and very first, and I wanted the right to be a normal woman having her first baby. But I also had this little girl at my side, and I wanted to affirm and legitimize my connection to her, too.

"No," I said.

"Yes," I said.

And finally: "First pregnancy, second child."

But mine was a first pregnancy without the first-pregnancy benefit of no one to care for but myself. Play music to my belly? Read it stories? I was too exhausted running after the child on the outside and too desperate to squeeze in some non-mothering activities to help me recognize myself. After a day feeding, diapering, soothing, and entertaining a toddler, the last book I wanted to curl up with at night was *Your Pregnancy Week by Week*.

I was well into my second trimester before I gave the pregnancy the focus my first-timer friends had given theirs from the beginning. I carved out time for prenatal yoga, for relaxing with birthing hypnosis tracks, for an intimate ceremony to welcome our unborn baby ("I sense a confident spirit," said my sister), for the reading and presence and preparation I'd always hoped I would bring to pregnancy and birth should I experience them. We bought Maia a book about becoming a big sister. She rubbed cream into my belly and said, "Baby? Baby?"

And then, Aphra was born.

Maia's entrance into my life was my own birth as a mother, an arduous and premature labour. I was coming to terms not only with my new instant child but with the change in my own identity and focus. By the time Aphra arrived, I had transitioned into motherhood and embraced the new parts of myself, so that my primary response to this new person could be joy.

But my joy was laced with guilt. I had never gloried in Maia's existence the way I gloried in Aphra's. As Maia's mother, motherhood had not revealed itself as the apex of human achievement it felt like in the early days as Aphra's. "Maia must never know," I sobbed to Richard on day three, the day my milk came in and he found me weeping. "What's wrong?" he asked, stricken, and I bawled, "I just love Aphra so much!" ("Day 3," said my midwife's notes, "you can expect to be a little emotional.") I could stare for hours at Aphra's naked body, in amazement at its perfection, at the fact of her flesh-of-my-fleshness, the wonder that this human being had grown in my body and possessed my long narrow feet and brown hair. I had never stared this way at Maia.

It was my dark secret: I did not feel the same toward my adopted child as toward my biological child. This difference transgressed any adoption tenets I'd heard. I felt I ought to curb my overwhelming love for Aphra because of it. I was by now undeniably Maia's mother, her nurturer and guide, the one who met her physical and emotional needs. When strangers commented on her curls, I forgot they didn't come from me. But we had missed fifteen foundational months together. Fifteen months with Aphra meant seeing daily developments in her personality and a deepening of the bond between us. More than that, my connection to Aphra was rooted in physicality, a primal bond I could neither withstand nor fabricate. My body was everything to her — recently her home, now her source of nourishment and continued life — and my instincts responded of their own accord, keeping her close in waking and sleeping, guarding our space as ferociously as any animal. My bond with Maia was intellectual and emotional, but it was not animal, and I didn't know the difference until I was walloped by this mother-bear passion for my baby. Now I mourned what I hadn't known I'd missed out on with Maia.

I insisted, in that first year, on speaking the truth about my experience of motherhood. The image of the happy martyr mother, fulfilled solely through relationship to her children, had produced much of my motherhood trepidation, and I'd had to search for new models to reflect my reality.

You're obviously thriving in motherhood, friends commented on my Facebook pictures. *You're a beautiful mother*, said a woman who'd watched me with my children for two minutes. *How's motherhood?* others asked breezily, as though inquiring into the weather. As though there were only one answer, and sometimes they provided it for me: "Oh, you just love it!"

I did not just love it.

I had my Hallmark moments, every saccharine cliché real and fully felt inside me, my heart open, my love fierce, my satisfaction and gratitude surprising and deep. But I also had moments when I wanted to catch the first bus back to my child-free life. I yelled more, cursed more, became gripped with stronger rage, more roundly overwhelmed and undone and beleaguered than ever before. I smashed objects against floors and pounded my fists into walls. Mothering was the hardest thing I'd ever done. I was becoming the fullest and richest and most complicated me I'd ever been. "I just love it" didn't cover it.

I heard a friend rhapsodizing about her baby—her first, single, only baby—and about her love of motherhood, and I thought she could not be telling the truth.

Could she be telling the truth?

Yes, I realized, she could. Because if I separated adoption-while-pregnant from my experience, if I had only my normal pregnancy, my idyllic homebirth, my delightful infant, a manageable parent-child ratio, me and my husband and our daughter, giggling and chattering and learning to pull herself up and walk and talk, it's possible I would be rhapsodizing too. It's possible my experience would be simple and joyful, without the nuance and complexity, without my need to resist the belittling and one-noted deification of mothers. It's possible—is it?—that I would be deifying motherhood too.

Because—for the record—having one baby is one thing. Acclimatizing to the idea of parenthood through nine months' gestation, expanding step by step into this new thing called mother, following one child through each phase: this is one thing. Instantly assuming the care of a toddler and catapulting one's self into the life of mother while doing all of the above is not the same with a little extra. It is on a whole other planet.

Because, also, Maia is a volcano. An active volcano, perpetually on the verge of eruption. Maia is challenging.

Our eldest daughter is filled with pain. It surfaces at every provocation. A stubbed toe, a stuck zipper, or a torn page are enough to send her to the floor shrieking and weeping. She cries as though releasing tears for all the hurt she has ever known.

She is anxious, highly sensitive, easily frustrated, and inflexible, with a happy-to-enraged transition time of half a second. She struggles to integrate change. Noise and crowds and unfamiliar settings overwhelm her. Often I live in a state of held breath, hoping Maia will keep it together, and if she does not, that Richard and I will. Every excursion to friends' homes began, for a time, with Maia in tears at the door, until I learned I must carry her into new situations, my arms around her, bolstering, comforting, reassuring as she faces new faces, new environments. My baby, my confident spirit, crawled ahead, fending for herself, while I shored up my toddler with my love.

. . .

I happened to be reading Lionel Shriver's *The Post-Birthday World* in the final week of the Maia Decision. Shriver's character faces a life-altering choice, and the novel chronicles both possibilities in alternating chapters, two different but not altogether dissimilar lives running alongside each other—one if she said yes, one if she said no. In both versions, the character senses an unlived life paralleling the one she's in and is plagued by the what-ifs of the option she did not choose.

I longed for my own *The Post-Birthday World*, a choose-your-own-adventure I could read to the end: here is my life with Maia; here is my life without Maia.

So huge a decision as adoption, so decision-like a decision, can conjure that ghostly other life as biological birth does not. I glimpse it in my peripheral vision, that parallel unlived path, that unconfessable, unwanted back door. Adoption is like any decision—marriage to this person, acceptance of that job, a move to this city: you chose it, it wasn't born to you, and you could have chosen otherwise. Should you have?

There was nothing accidental about becoming Maia's mother, nothing organic or outside my control. I was faced with an option, I weighed the variables, and I said, "Yes."

When I have to drag Aphra away from the drumming festival we're both enjoying because Maia is crying that it's too loud, when another family dinner is upset by Maia's meltdown, when the stress of living with this explosive child strains my marriage as nothing else has, when Aphra is dancing so adorably at a concert that strangers are videotaping her but I can't watch because I'm rushing to attend to my screaming older child, when again and again my attention and energy and emotional reserves go to Maia, when again and again I put Aphra's needs on hold because she can handle it and Maia can't, I have thought, in a cavern of my mind, *what if there were only one?*

I wish I did not have this fork in the road to return to.

In Shriver's novel, neither life is better than the other. Neither choice is clearly right. They both hold pain and joy. Just different pain, different joy.

If I can sometimes fantasize my life without Maia, I can't, hypocritically, imagine hers without me. I come across the term "adoptive mother" and bristle. What? I'm her *mother*! There is no one else who has nurtured her through every challenge, who has worked so hard to understand the need behind her behaviour and meet it. There is no one else who has devoted more, sacrificed more. There is no one else who has cried when she is happy, listening to her animated chatter and longing for her to gain access to this happiness more, often, always.

She is four and a half now, and she is like Botticelli's Venus: curvy and plump, alabaster skin, red-blonde curls spilling down her back. She is volatile, histrionic, needy. And the person she wants most in all the world, the person she needs—with a sucking, consuming, bottomless need—the person she loves, is me.

When she is secure, her best self emerges: a sweet, strong, engaged girl. She loves baking, watches how-to videos on YouTube and then teaches me. She sits at my desk and announces, "I need privacy! I'm writing a book!" She paints and bravely delivers her artwork to the neighbours' mailboxes while I wait on the sidewalk. Outdoors, digging in her garden, picking flowers, she is lost in contentment. She and Aphra dance and invent and squabble, run screaming barefoot down the street in summer rainstorms, their love and partnership intense.

Sisters so entwined it seems impossible either could be who she is without the other.

I feel tremendous empathy toward Maia's introversion and sensitivity. I am an introvert, too; being around people drains me, too. I rear with protective fury when acquaintances use on her the same dismissive "oh, she's shy!" I got as a child, and I am impressed by the self-knowledge with which she will say, "I need alone time now," and choose to eat by herself when we have company or to stay in the kitchen away from the party, icing the cake and inserting candles with great seriousness and focus. A cuddle with a story is her preferred means of righting herself after an upset. She is more like me than Aphra is, Aphra the self-assured and outgoing, two words I have rarely applied to myself.

I am in love with Aphra, a feeling as effortless and unstoppable as breathing. My relationship with Maia is more akin to an arranged marriage: I made a choice I believed was right, and through that choice, over time, a bond solid and close and beautiful has grown. A connection inextricable. If I am sometimes aware that this love was a choice, if that choice is sometimes taxed, so, too, are my relationships with almost everyone I love. Of the several people integral to my existence, Aphra is the only one who came from my body.

I watch them, four and two, running naked through the sprinkler in our back garden. Their bodies fascinate me: Aphra's, in part, for its fusion of Richard and me, his dark complexion, my long limbs, our characteristics combined in this package of vitality; Maia's enchants for its difference from mine, a rounder shape, a paler shade, traits that come from her birth parents but are, to me, entirely her. And I realize, watching her, that I love her for her, and no other reason. Those hourglass curves, that belly, that hair: they are not an extension of me. They are powerfully, fully Maia.

She still asks me to sing her song. "Sing my song too!" echoes Aphra, but Aphra doesn't have a song. Aphra has never needed one. I sing Maia's song and she listens intently. I have added people to the song, new friends, newborn cousins, but *Mama* always comes first.

I believe I will always be singing Maia her song. Until the time she is confident enough, secure enough, grounded enough to create her own.

We have photographs of the day I met Maia. A series of four that someone snapped, a year before anyone knew it was a meeting of mother and daughter. In the first, my brother and his girlfriend have just stepped through my parents' patio door to the kitchen. My brother is handing Maia to my mother as I approach, a tautness and purpose in my body. Then I am reaching for her. Then I am looking down on her in my arms, and in the fourth photograph, I am beaming, tears glistening, squeezing her tight as Maia nestles into me. Her first mother is in the background, looking away.

I was overcome that day. I couldn't stop crying. I was not a baby person, but I couldn't stop crying over this baby. It was like we'd known each other in another life, like a psychic thread bound us and when we looked into each other's eyes, it sparked with awareness and recognition. She was mine. I was hers. We belonged together.

I knew it that day. I chose her. But also, from that day, there was never a choice.

Confessions of a Dilly-Dallying Shilly-Shallier

KERRY RYAN

I'm gutless.

As in, without instinct. You know, that mythical bodily organ, the built-in Magic 8-Ball that sniffs out danger, steers you to Mr. Right, provides steady footing when your mind is at sea. There's just an empty, fleshy sack where mine should be. (I keep it filled with cookies.)

Not to be confused with *guts*, plural. As in nerve, pluck, grit—all those attributes associated with orphan children of literature, female CEOs, bungee jumpers, and the like. Guts I have, though they're often dormant.

And not to be confused with *gut*, singular, as in belly. I've got that, to a varying extent, too. (See cookies, above.)

Of course, there are worse things to be have been born without. Thumbs, say. Or eyelids.

But life without gut instinct isn't easy; it's made me a chronic waffler. Unless the question is chocolate or vanilla, decision-making is agony for me. I fail in every regard: swiftness, certainty, satisfaction with end result.

There are few questions I hate more than "Hot enough for you?" but one of them is "Well, what does your gut tell you?" This is confounding to someone who only ever hears the question echoing back through her innards. If I really, really listen hard, I might be able to hear an "I dunno. Maybe." To listen to my gut instinct is the least helpful advice a person could possibly give. If I could hear my gut, friend, I wouldn't be asking you for help.

I'd love to have that magical assistance with decision-making. It would be simpler, more efficient, and less annoying to those who tire of my hemming and hawing. It would also free up a lot of time. I could finally learn how to knit.

But, then again, relying on gut instinct seems like a bit of a cop out. Sure, it may be that I'm jealous of those who have extrasensory entrails, but how can a person be held responsible for a decision that wasn't made with her brain?

Isn't having someone always telling you what to do (even if that voice is coming from within you) a little too easy? Society doesn't generally give a lot of credence to people who act on voices they hear in their heads. What's so different about following a voice in your digestive tract?

⊙

Sometimes, a good long, luscious opportunity to ponder can bring me a lot of pleasure.

To me, one of the very best things about the invention of the Internet is that you can check out a restaurant menu online, hours or days before your reservation, debating between, say, Duck Confit with Sour Cherries on Brown Butter and Parsnip Purée or Soft Polenta with Crispy White Beans and Grilled Eggplant. Now that's delicious deliberation!

This is, however, high-risk behaviour. Frequently, I'll arrive at the restaurant to discover the online menu hasn't been updated. Or, worse, there's some fabulous-sounding special! And there I am, paralyzed by indecision and/or the many glasses of wine imbibed while I make up my mind.

But who cares? (Aside from my dinner companion and his growling stomach.) It's just a meal, right? No biggie. Ha!

There's nothing that disappoints me more than having a meal I've selected and paid for turn out to be a soggy, stodgy, over/underdone, or otherwise inferior dud.

A bad restaurant decision will take up residence in my body. It'll hang like a storm cloud soaking through the rest of my day. (And maybe even the following, depending on the price.) It'll hang in my belly (with the confit). It's The Worst.

And that's probably the most inconsequential decision in the world. So you can imagine how I react when I have to make a real, potentially life-changing decision. Like whether or not to have a baby.

◉

I write poetry for a lot of reasons but the reason I write poetry instead of novels, or even short stories, is that I don't have the patience, the stamina, or the ability to plan for the future, as is required in longer-form literature.

When I was in school, I hated being asked what I wanted to be when I grew up. I never had any idea. Still don't. I cringe at the bank when an adviser brings up my financial goals. Beyond planning my next vacation, I never think about the future at all. I live in units of four to six months, tops. I don't even like thinking about the next season, unless it's spring.

Not that I'm exactly living for the day, mind you. I eat vegetables and go to bed at ten o'clock, even on weekends. I'm mostly thrifty. So in a sense I can plan: not to get cancer, not to be cranky at work tomorrow, not to go broke. But really, preventing those kinds of disasters is a crap shoot anyway.

Planning for the future means *deciding* what you want that future to be, then *deciding* how to make it happen. Instead, I flail around, letting things unfold. It's not a bad system. I have a job that hardly ever makes my stomach hurt and from which I get five weeks' vacation. I have a husband who makes me laugh and hugs me a lot. I have a house and a garden and friends and family, and I like them all. I've published two books of poems and done lots of other cool things.

None of that was *planned*. I went on a date with a guy who seemed nice. I applied for a job I saw in the paper. I wrote a few poems. And now, here I am. There must have been a gazillion incremental steps in between that would make a great montage in a movie, but I don't remember, or didn't notice, what they were.

And that's the other reason I can't write fiction. I have no idea how plot works—in a fictional character's life or in my own. I can describe a scene in minute detail, draw comparisons through poetic device, but make something happen? Create a progression of events? Nope, I haven't a clue.

I can't think of a more significant plot point to write into my life than becoming a Mom.

⊙

I may lack a gut, but I'm not missing a biological clock—at least in the fertility sense. I'm thirty-six, and I know my eggs are approaching (or might have passed) their best-before date. But having a time limit doesn't make the decision any easier.

I've revised the due date for this decision project approximately a thousand times. When age thirty-five came and went last year and I still had no clear feeling of *yes*, it seemed to me that must mean *no*. But *no* wouldn't rest; the question kept coming back, zombie-like. So, if the answer isn't *no*, does that mean it's *yes*?

After spending years working on this question without real progress, I'm beginning to realize that what I hate more than the idea of making this decision is having it made for me. I suppose that waiting out the clock is a kind of choice, but it's not one that gives me any sense of resolve.

My biological clock takes the form of an inner sadist, constantly harping. She's becoming more shrill as time goes on.

Decide! A curly-headed babe poking under the Christmas tree or an aging couple carefully unwrapping junk on a silent night? Decide! Now! Skipping footloose and fancy-free down a New York City sidewalk or trundling an SUV-sized stroller around a Winnipeg Transit bus. Decide! Decide!

Of course, it's not just my decision. I have a lovely, supportive husband who always —infuriatingly—insists: *whatever you decide.* He isn't indifferent; he has registered his desire to have a kid. But he knows the decision has far different implications for me than it does for him. So he never pushes, never even brings it up. The question sits patiently between us, but it's waiting for me.

When we do talk about it, I become more anti-baby than I actually feel. Since he's all for a kid, I feel it becomes my job to defend a child-free lifestyle. But, to be honest, my protestations are sounding more and more hollow. For example, not having a child because that child will one day throw up, which will make me throw up—which I haven't done since I was ten and I have since developed a phobia about—isn't really a good reason not to continue the species.

Plus, I have to remind myself, we'd *both* be parents. I can shirk puke duty.

My husband has a high threshold for boring, repetitive tasks, like skipping stones and hitting stones into water with sticks. Anything stone and water related. He's incredibly patient, positive, and caring. He'd make a great Dad.

But, he's also emphatic that, more than wanting a child, he wants me. It's so heartening it makes my throat gob up. Sometimes I want to tell him to make the decision for me, but I know I'd resent him for it, either way.

A few months ago, mid-waffle, I was whining to him about my limbo state. *It would be so much easier*, I moaned, *if I were to get pregnant by accident. Then I wouldn't have to make a decision.*

At which he snorted, all too keenly aware of my stringent, double-barrelled approach to safe sex, *You'd never let that happen by accident.*

True enough. Because allowing something to happen is also a form of making a choice, albeit a sneaky one. Throwing condoms to the wind is a decision, too.

⊙

I know that making a decision to have a baby isn't the same as making a baby. For every media story about a forty-year-old celebrity with a baby bump, there are three about how difficult it can be to conceive once your age no longer rounds to thirty.

At the best of times, my period is wonkily unpredictable. Last year, it stopped altogether for about six months.

It was delightful—no cramps, no irrational tears, and I saved a lot of money on tampons. But when I finally went to the doctor to find out what was up, the first in what would become a series of tests showed that my ovaries had stopped functioning entirely. Wha...?

This would later turn out to be a mix-up at the lab (there was a very elderly woman having bloodwork done at the same time as me—I wonder if her doctor was as surprised at her results!), but it felt like one last wake-up call after hitting snooze for too many years.

And that's part of the problem. If the decision is *yes*, I can't qualify it with *some day*. If the decision is *yes*, it's go time. Yikes!

⊙

In addition to lacking a gut, I'm also without maternal instinct. I was a youngest child with two much older sisters—I have only ever been the mothered, not the motherer, and three times over at that.

I was a star babysitter as a teenager, I've been an aunt (albeit from afar) for ages, and I've kept most houseplants alive, but I don't think of myself as a nurturer.

I find myself envying women with children—not so much envying the kids but women who have, seemingly, a natural inclination to be mothers. I remember a friend telling me, well before she met her husband and had a child, "I am so ready to be a Mom." I've been waiting for that kind of confidence to strike, but I know it'll never happen.

Do you have to have a maternal instinct from the get-go, or does it kick in with your breast milk? And if not, can you wing it, or is your child destined to become a serial killer?

If I'm going to be a Mom, I want to be a good one. But does that mean I have to want—more than anything else—to be one? Do I have to be dying to be a Mom, dreaming of being a Mom, obsessed with being a Mom? And does it mean it's the only thing I should want to be?

If a baby were suddenly thrust into my life, I think I could do a decent job of being a Mom. I also think I could be a good not-Mom. My happiness and fulfillment don't depend on the presence or absence of a child in my life.

It seems to me that being, or not being, a Mom is the one thing a woman should feel really certain about. But I just can't get on board with either option.

⊙

This ambivalence about motherhood is a huge weight on me. Surely, *normal* women don't feel this way. But, then again, I've never felt I belonged to that group (which I associate with wearing mascara and carrying purses).

It doesn't mean I don't care about having a child. It means I care equally about having or not having one.

I've always been blessed/cursed with the ability to see both sides of an argument. (I've never had a fight with anyone in my life, but I was pretty solid member of my high school debating team.) In a lot of ways, this is a really good thing. I can empathize with almost any point of view, I have insight into all facets of a situation, and I can be flexible in my thinking. And I can almost always find a bright side.

But it also means that I don't know how to commit to one option over another, so I often don't.

Not having a child is the default setting. It's easier than having one; it requires zero effort. But I can't think of anything worthwhile that requires zero effort.

In my experience, it has only been the difficult things, the frightening and risky things, that have changed my life for the better. Three years ago, I decided to take part in an amateur boxing match. The training process was gruelling; I ached, complained, and cried daily. But stepping into that ring is one of the things I'm most proud of, and I will be forever.

The thought of having a baby mostly terrifies me. So does the thought of having a teenager. But reading bedtime stories, creating new traditions, seeing the world fresh through little eyes, making and being part of a family—that all sounds amazing.

I can think of lots of reasons not to have a child, but being too scared is the lamest one of all.

⊙

The thought of starting a family brings with it a sky-darkening flock of questions and what-ifs. The humungous: what if we have a baby with serious health problems? The unbearable: what if the stress of having even a healthy baby causes irreparable damage to my relationship with my husband? The small, yet still important: what if I don't have time or brain power to write anymore? And very worst of all: what if I don't like being a Mom? What if I regret it?

I have a hard enough time making a standard decision. How is it possible to make a decision when the big question explodes into a swarm of so many pesky little ones?

But lately the question has shifted away from the *yes/no* dichotomy. Right now it's this: at the end of my life will I regret the things I've done or the things I haven't?

⊙

I write because I'm driven to create, to make something no one else can or will. I love sending little bundles of words out into the world to wobble around on their own. My poems look, sound, and act like me.

I know that hardly anyone reads poetry and almost no one reads mine, but it doesn't matter. My poems are my contribution to the world, my *Kilroy wuz here*. My books won't live forever, but they will have a life that's larger than mine, and I like the thought of that.

I couldn't tell you how to write a poem, or even how I write one. It's a mystery to me. It's not that a poem appears magically—it's hard work; I just can't explain it.

I may be lacking when it comes to gut and maternal instincts, but I do have a poetic one. It alerts me to poem-worthy ideas and pushes me to dig in and do the work, even when the work gets hard. I trust it.

So I'm going to channel that poetic instinct—the only gut I can muster—to help me make this decision.

I will work it until it gleams, but it will never feel perfect.

It may appear simple, but it will be infinitely complex under a surface only I can see.

It will be a demonstration, if not of confidence, then of courage. If not of *gut*, then of *guts*.

And it will be mine.

How to Fall

CARRIE SNYDER

I have four children.

In retrospect, it seems a lackadaisical oversight to have produced four dependents without considering the implications—financial, emotional, marital, to name but a few—and purely because I wanted to, but the truth is that I never weighed in advance what it would mean, nor, more precisely, how it might change me. I am the eldest of five. There were times, it must be said, when our family's size seemed ever so slightly extravagant—namely, when all seven of us were cruising to the beach in a Honda Civic hatchback, with a picnic and a giant watermelon thrown in for good measure. We also did a European holiday in a Volkswagen Jetta, from Belgium to Spain to Switzerland, when three of us were teenagers. I'll leave it to you to imagine the seating arrangements. But those are good memories. In my own family, on some very basic level, I must have wanted to replicate that level of chaos, adventure, and unavoidable interdependence.

Yet *wanted* is not a strong enough word to capture my desire to be a mother.

I do not think of myself as a careless person, but my path to motherhood didn't follow even the semblance of a thoughtful, detailed plan. Every stage was enacted on an emotional level, with unconscious urgency. Act first, analyze later (or never). To be frank, until asked to write on the subject, I'd never given more than half a thought to why I have four children. I might have answered that it was quite possibly this simple: I have four children because I kept on wanting to have more, even after the first, the second, and then the third.

Why four? Why stop there? I can only say that when I was done, I knew, and then I was as certain as I'd been all those years before, when I knew I would do everything in my power to be a mother.

Motherhood is associated with self-sacrifice, and as a mother of four, it may be assumed I have a self-sacrificing character, but I'd like to present another perspective. Sacrifice implies making offerings against one's will, losing out on chances, making choices that benefit others, rather than oneself. That was never me. All along, I've associated motherhood with emotional wealth, with richness of experience, an expansive and expanding adventure. Add more fascinating and unique personalities to the mix, and the adventure grows that much more unpredictable, overwhelming, challenging—and I mean that in the best way possible.

I've always relished a challenge.

In these parts, in early twenty-first-century, middle-class, urban Southern Ontario, being mother to four children puts me in a category special enough to draw the occasional lifted eyebrow of surprise, which I always take as a compliment—*You* have four children! Yup. But I'm not bragging. (And you're probably not complimenting me either.) There wasn't much to it, let's agree. All it took was fertility, luck, and an overwhelming biological imperative that I had no desire to override.

The subtext of our exchange might go something like this. You: "*You have four children?*" Me: "Yes, all planned." You: "But you appear to be educated." Me: "I also have a career. And I exercise. I'm really pretty happy." You: "Um, okay, if you say so." Me: "Shoot, I hear crying—that sounds like real crying. Uh-oh, looks like blood!" [dashing off] You: "Good luck to you, lady."

But is there a subtext to the subtext? Because if I am to slice into my motivations with a scalpel of brutal honesty, I'd have to confess: I am kind of bragging. Just a little. But you already knew that, didn't you? Because you, with your one kid or two kids or three kids, are feeling ever so slightly irritated by the whiff of superiority I'm giving off. I get it, I do. I was the kid in class who always had her hand up ("Me! Oh, pick me! I know the answer!"): the shameless overachiever.

Uncomfortable things happen to shameless overachievers. We set ourselves up. We take risks, push the limits, grab for more and more and more, showing off, until it's suddenly too much. And then we topple. We fall.

Oh, mother-of-four, how your children will behave in ways that embarrass you publicly; how you will behave in ways that embarrass them publicly. How your chore charts will crumble to dust; how your disciplinary pronouncements will humble you, one after another. How your kid may be the bully, or may be bullied, and how you will miss the signs before heartache comes crashing your way. How there will be lice, fleas, and even bedbugs.

Ah, *schadenfreude*, there you are.

I don't think that I knew, before motherhood, what motherhood would ask of me; but I don't think, either, that advance insight would have stopped me. On some level, you've got to be willing to fall—don't you?—to attempt any performance so complicated and so visible.

. . .

Why four? Was it ever so slightly because most of the people I know *don't* have four kids? See—I win! When SouleMama, the popular home-schooling homesteader (whom I know only through her blog) announced she was having her fifth baby, I had a little moment. She'd overachieved me. I was irritated by the whiff of superiority but also impressed. I wanted to yell: "Seriously!? Are you shitting me? C'mon now! How do you do it?"

Maybe we're always impressed (and irritated) by the person who appears to be managing just that much more than we can, or imagine we could. *Appears to be* is the magical phrase in that sentence. Who knows how others are living their lives, really? Who knows what kind of a day SouleMama's really having, behind her lovely photographs? And who knows what kind of a day I'm really having, behind what you glimpse as I herd my offspring across a busy street? Maybe I'm swearing under my breath. Maybe I can't wait for the babysitter to relieve me. Maybe I'm blissfully occupied. Even I couldn't tell you for sure.

There's a flip side to the picture I'm drawing of competitive overachiever. I'm also the mother of four children because I didn't know what else to be, for a while. For nearly a decade, in truth.

I was married at an age that now looks very young: twenty-four; my husband was twenty-nine. I remember an older colleague, mother to two toddlers, urging me to wait on the babies: "There's no hurry." But I couldn't relate. This wasn't about hurrying, this was about getting started. We allowed one year, almost to the day, after our wedding. I was twenty-five and I wanted to be a mother. *Now.* And so it was—we were fortunate and fertile. At the age of twenty-six-and-a-half, I birthed a plump, squalling, red-faced, red-haired alien. Video evidence shows a peaceful young woman serenely rocking, patting, and bouncing an infant who is invariably screaming his lungs out in alarming fashion.

We'd produced a colicky soul, but it was as if I hadn't even noticed. More accurately, this was the baby I'd been expecting. I had myself been a colicky, red-faced, red-haired soul who had tortured my parents and turned out quite well. I suffered no qualms about either my son or my parenting, even when, during an appointment, a doctor hollered at me (over top of this amazing infant's hearty screams), "Can't you get him to stop crying?"

Why no, I thought, surprised. *It's what he does—it's his defining characteristic. And aren't you impressed by his incredible lung power?*

I've heard of women who suffer anxieties about caring for their children, who read every self-help book and question their choices constantly; that was not me. When it came to childcare, I trusted my instincts, almost casually, right from the very beginning. I knew my son would stop crying, and he did. At around four months, he turned into a champion napper and jolly little fellow. Mothering this first child, and those who followed, was never a stressful undertaking. The role felt—*feels*—comfortable, familiar, known.

My own mother stayed at home. It was her sincere hope that her daughters would build healthy, independent careers (the message being: so we could leave our husbands, if need be, which she never felt secure enough to do). But when I became a mother myself, no one understood my impulse to throw aside all other considerations better than she did—and I needed someone to understand; the truth is, birthing all these children at a relatively young age cast me largely out of step with my peers.

. . .

I spent the better part of a decade either pregnant or breast-feeding or both, co-sleeping, diaper-changing, and starting but never finishing a series of conversations with other mothers over cups of coffee at playgroup. In the rare photo from this era that includes me, I have much larger breasts, I am likely to be wearing something unflattering and/or dripped-upon, I am holding a baby or two, I look mildly exhausted, and I am grinning from ear to ear—pride beams for my children, who are in the fore.

And though I can't deny the milky, sleepy, intense boredom of the stay-at-home lifestyle, I can't deny, also, that I loved it. Because I did.

Have I mentioned that I'm a feminist?

It was the feminist in me who yearned to be respected for choosing to have children, and for choosing to stay home with them; and I knew that I wasn't respected, and I resented it. When meeting new people, I would deliberately neglect to mention that I was a writer because I wanted to be appreciated—to be found worthy of interest—for my ascendant mothering self. I considered myself a social scientist conducting research: how does the general public respond to a *mere* stay-at-home mother? Results were predictable, and infuriating. People were polite: never unkind, but disinterested. Why should I have been surprised? Stay-at-home motherhood is work without measure: no salary, no job reviews, no raises, no bonuses, no promotions, no objective rewards that others can see—that we ourselves, the stay-at-home mothers, can claim, either. A tough job for an admitted overachiever, more than a little bound to a system of rewards.

In retrospect, I see something fairly complex going on here. My feminist principles were intact—genuine and righteous: I wanted to transcend the shallow system of social and cultural compensation and demand respect for honest labour, yes. But my intense defensiveness and hurt was also personal. *I was afraid.* I craved legitimacy and respect for my mothering self in part because I feared it might be my only self—and I did not want it to be.

I was caught up in a self-fulfilling prophecy but blind to my own collusion: the more I called myself a mother, and not a writer, the more I believed it myself; I was mother, not writer.

Even though I'd given birth to the perfect family—a boy and then a girl, seventeen months apart—I'd wanted even more babies. Was this because I could imagine succeeding at no other job or role? Because it was a relief to be good at something? Because I needed to be needed? Did I fear that, without babies, I'd be purposeless, adrift? These were troubled years, I'll confess. After the birth of my second child, I published a book of fiction, my first. The second book would take another eight years to produce, and its multiple gestations and wrong turns and dead ends, and the time lost to these barren attempts, would come close to crushing my confidence.

"What am I going to do with my life?" I would ask my husband, one of the few who witnessed my cycles of angst. "Should I just quit trying to write? Should I go back to school? I just want to do something useful!"

The tangle of anxieties is almost too uncomfortable to unravel, but here is the thread of career-suicide fear (mixed with anger that motherhood/career should ever be an either/or proposition), and here the thread of letting-down-all-womanhood shame, and here the thread of maybe-serial-motherhood-is-just-an-excuse-for-dearth-of-talent terror, and here is my-husband-makes-the-money-and-I-spend-it dependence (and resentment).

Deep down, I feared aimlessness, a lack of ambition and clarity of vision outside of caring for my children.

Then something happened.

. . .

Rather abruptly, I outgrew immersion-style, all-or-nothing motherhood. Here was the family I'd imagined having. Here was the challenge of repetition and daily drudgery, and it was not, after all, the only thing I was good at, nor was it all I wanted to do. I lifted my eyes and saw the end of diapers and breast milk and it looked, suddenly, not so terrifying after all. In fact, life after babies was downright inviting, a mecca of possibilities available to those who sleep through the night. Yoga. Triathlon training. Starting *and* finishing conversations with friends. Freelancing. Completing and selling a second book. Perhaps, most tellingly, I embarked on a daily self-portrait project that aimed the lens on a subject that hadn't been the centre of attention for a decade: myself. I called it "my 365," and my husband, quietly, hated it.

"Just working on my 365!" I'd say blithely, late into the evening, kids in bed, in answer to his hopeful, "What are you up to?" I can hear it, and I would have hated it too had the roles been reversed.

You can probably predict what happened next: our lives got messy. We'd entered the danger zone that lurks in most marriages, when partners begin behaving in ways that are not predictable, that defy past behaviour and patterns. It was a deeply uncomfortable transition, a fundamental shift in power. We'd spent a decade occupying traditional roles of husband (breadwinner) and wife (caretaker), even while we'd imagined ourselves enlightened, untouched by the stereotypes. He was an active parent; I made time for my writing. We tried. But the proof was in the pudding: when I explicitly cleared paths for myself away from the children, away from him, too, *he was afraid*. His fear made me angry.

But we don't get to change in isolation. We change in relationship.

It would be narratively pleasant to pin our struggles into a tidy moment of breakthrough, but I can't. We could not solve our problems immediately, with a round of couples counselling, as we would have preferred. Instead, we had to be patient. We had to trust that it would get better.

The only way out was through.

Here's the good news: having four children prepares a person for deeply uncomfortable transitions — and by transition, I mean those threshold moments of change, which can be as simple as walking through the door after school (potential for meltdown: high!) to as complex as changes in identity (potential for meltdown: high!). By my unscientific estimate, getting through the transitions is at least half of parenthood: learning to recognize that change, no matter how big, no matter how small, is disruptive, and disruption can be helped along by understanding, by recognition, by humour and, in the case of after-school meltdowns, sometimes by snacks. But it needs to be got through. There's no going around it.

Change is constant.

We are not who we were, exactly. And yet, we are.

Parenthood is a funny thing. It's not about self-sacrifice, though we may pretend that it is. More accurately, it's about being needed and being needed by four children is a powerful joy. But parenthood is about something else, too. It's about recognizing when we're not needed. Accepting and recognizing such doubleness may be the key to surviving what parenthood demands of us: that we be open to change, open to being wrong, open to missing the cues, open to looking ridiculous, open to being broken-hearted, open to apology, open to altering course.

There is great freedom, as well as genuine pain, in arriving at this understanding. The ambitious overachiever in me wants to believe that I am necessary and mothering young children is an excellent way to feel absolutely necessary. But I'm no longer so necessary—not in the same visceral, milk and blood way I once was. And that's okay; really, it is.

It means that I can be a strong mother and also so many other things. It means that I can throw myself in deep (to just about any project or idea) and still let it go. And that is a lesson worth learning, over and over, as all good lessons must be learned.

Each pregnancy seemed like it might last forever—that languorous stretching of time that happens when one is sublimely occupied and does not wish to imagine being otherwise. But, of course, each ended in birth, and birth is the first separation between mother and child. So it goes from there, a series of small goodbyes, invisible barriers settling between each lovely layer of intimacy.

I could never have had enough children to prevent this from happening.

No matter how I got here, this is where I am: mother of four, thrown into the emotional wild. It's dangerous territory, chaotic, unpredictable, exhausting, potentially crushing. It's also a place where I am free to be sentimental, confessional, silly, overwrought, outrageous, truthful, needy, unvarnished. I love living here. I hope I get to stay even after my four children are grown and gone from home.

Because—I know what it means to relax fully and deeply inside a moment that will at any instant collapse. Because—I forgive and am forgiven, regularly. Because—I've learned how to fall.

You Make 'Em, I Amuse 'Em

PATRICIA STORMS

But for some bizarre reason, many people find it odd that I did not choose motherhood.

You make picture books for kids— You'd be the perfect mother! Why don't you have kids??

It's usually these same people who think that motherhood for them is a ticket to publishing their own writing.

Will you illustrate all these stories I wrote this weekend? My children ADORE them, so I know they're GREAT!!

Some of the most successful creators of kid's books did not have kids, which was probably a good thing...

Margaret Wise Brown

Well, I don't especially like children, either. At least not as a group.

Dr. Seuss

You make 'em, I amuse 'em.

Maurice Sendak

CHILDHOOD IS CANNIBALS AND PSYCHOTICS VOMITING IN YOUR MOUTH!

Which means: You don't have to have kids to write for kids. You just have to remember what it was like to be a kid.

Yeah... I remember all those fantasy games I played with my sister... we pretended to be chipmunks and wolves and foxes and dogs and bears and groundhogs and we wrote songs and poetry and plays about all these animals and we had burping and farting contests and wrote comic strips about poo... Ha ha ha hee hee hee hee hee....

Now really — would you want me to raise YOUR kids?

Mommy Wrote a Book of All My Secrets

SARAH YI-MEI TSIANG

Rapunzel, to me, has always been more about maternity than hair. The story gives us two mothers: the birthmother who trades her newborn child for lettuce and the adoptive mother who traps that same child in a tower, away from the world.

I've always wondered about those moments before Rapunzel's birthmother gave her up. Here is what I picture: Rapunzel's mother, torn apart and exhausted. She holds a small infant who pulls at her breast until her nipples crack and bleed. Her milk flows creamy pink, and her blood stains that small, open mouth. Her entire life centres around the wet bodily functions of breasts and mouth, until she can no longer remember what it is to be alone. Who she is. And then here comes the witch, calm as a windless day. Her hands are calloused and competent. She stands tall as a tower, implacable and filled with a clear, singular desire. She looks at the baby as though she knows what to do with it. When Rapunzel's mother hands over the child, it feels as natural as breathing. Like surfacing from the water just as her lungs were about to burst. Nothing but air and the empty sky before her.

As mothers, our identities are irrevocably changed in that moment when we meet our children. We know that everything has changed, but we don't know *how*. The endless possibilities are frightening and overwhelming. The day after I had my daughter, I remember having a vivid dream that I was attending lectures at the university campus and I kept forgetting my newborn in her car seat everywhere I went. In the dream's climax, my pink and shining newborn looks up at me and says, "I hate you, Mommy," and I reply, "You're right to hate me."

Infants are infinitely demanding. They hold the belief that they are one with their mothers and cannot demarcate where their body ends and their mother's begins. In an exquisite poem by Sheri Benning, "Why I'm Afraid to Have Children," she writes, "because I would rather give up my life than my self and you will demand no less." Infants don't ask that we give up ourselves; infants assert that we are but a part of *their* selves, an appendage, say, or a large and vital organ.

And yet, even as you know that your child sees you as part of him- or herself, even as you stand, bouncing for hours at a time, a hot fuzzy skull pressing into your shoulder, you know that this state is one of impermanence. *Children grow up so fast*—if you're a mother, someone will say this to you at least twice a week. And after the first grasp, the first tooth, or the first time your child sits, or totters away from you, or says your name, you yearn for the time when they couldn't—you feel that phrase in your bones like the ache of a remembered wound.

Motherhood is a study in conflicts, which is why it attracts me as a writer. It was, for me, the first time I yearned for two identities at once. I wanted to be the dedicated mother who made her own playdough, and I wanted to be the kind of woman could take the time to sit and think for more than three minutes. I wanted more time with my child at the same time that I wanted to run screaming from the house. The belief of an infant that she is one with her mother is a belief that can be hard to deny in those first, heady months. There is no other relationship that we begin so passionately and then spend teaching our beloveds a way to leave us.

As a stay-at-home mother for most of my daughter's life, I was privileged to be able to spend just about all my time with her in the early days. I could decode the garble that was her first language because I could understand her every reference point. Our first real separation, when Abby was three, was at a daycare for a few hours a day, and I'll never forget the first drop-off. We had talked about it with Abby for quite a long time, letting her know that I would go away and then come back. I set her up with a toy and when she was engaged with it, I slipped out the door. Of course, there was no explanation that my three-year-old would understand for the concept of trust. It has to be earned; it has to be exemplified over and over again. That first time I left, she had no way of truly knowing that I would be back. For Abby, I think this was truly the moment when it struck her that she and I are separate beings. We are not a single line but rather temporarily parallel lines on a track of divergence.

When I came back for her a few hours later, I peeked in. She stood forlornly at the table, looking off into the middle distance. She was so beautiful it took my breath away. I had spent those hours feeling sick with the separation, intensely wanting to know what she was doing, wanting even just to feel the curve of her soft cheek one more time. When she spotted me, she immediately broke down into the most desperate, soul-crushing sobs I had ever heard. She could barely contain her relief, and the despair that she carefully bottled up all that morning came pouring out. Dropping her off the next morning was one of the hardest things I have ever done. As I pried her off me, every fiber of my being wanted to snatch her up again and run away, to the mutual safety of our shared home.

The experience of leaving her for even a few hours gave me barrels of sympathy for the witch in Rapunzel. Her beautiful adopted child, perhaps the first love of her life, that small packet of intense desire. Here is what I picture: the witch, that other mother, holding a child who reaches up, strokes her cheek with small, soft fingers. The other hand laid on her breast, possessively. The hours spent surrounded by Rapunzel's powder-and-milk smell, the way the child searches her out even in her sleep, cries without waking if she is left alone. The day the other mother watches that child take her first, tottering steps away from her. Who wouldn't want to build a tower around her?

I'm caught between these two mothers, between wanting a minute alone in the bathroom and then being overwhelmed by how my daughter can skip away from me, go to a friend's house without looking back, while I linger on the porch, trying to find excuses to have one more minute with her. I'm caught between the identity of the birthmother and the witch, both desires so strong that they seem to define who I am in those moments. How do I redefine my own identity and help to shape my daughter's identity, all the while carving out room for us to grow apart, into independent beings? I suspect that just about all mothers deal with this internal conflict, and all of us likely have our own outlets. As a writer, I search out conflicts, and this mother-conflict both animates a lot of my work and simultaneously raises some unavoidable ethical questions.

I write about my daughter a lot, in both my fiction and my poetry. Writers tend to come back again and again to relationships, places, or ideas that hold a certain mystery and ambivalence for them. For me, it's my daughter, but it sometimes fills me with a free-floating guilt, an unease that what I am doing walks the line of ethical. And it's not just me who shudders a little bit with the thought of exposing my child through my writing.

Years ago, I was invited to do a talk and poetry reading at Queen's University. I did my reading and then the talk naturally came around to the ethics of writing about someone who cannot give permission. I joked that I might start giving my daughter a cut of whatever stories or poems I sold that mentioned her.

One woman, sitting in the corner, shook her head and piped up: "Selling your daughter's story without her consent and then paying her after the fact? How is that different from prostituting her?"

I wanted to laugh it off, but the laughter stuck in my throat. I tried to prattle on a bit about how writing is always a creation and not a direct representation of a person.

The woman wouldn't have any of it. "Isn't it," she said, "simply using her soul and not her body for your personal gain and without regard for her?"

I was being identified as the witch, the fairy-tale villain full of cackles and spite, and not as the loving mother I had created in my imaginings. My writing was being seen as a way to build towers around my daughter. I was no mother at all, but a villain who preyed on the young. I could suddenly see the woman as a villager, angry torch in hand, standing below this precarious tower I had built.

Was it true? All the while I was bravely urging my daughter out into the world, apart from me, was I, in fact, trapping her, immortal, filled with the passions and tragedy of childhood, within the walls of my writing? She has no say in this, and no way down from the tower, either. As the writer I am the one who can call her to let down her hair. Did I set the boundaries of her voice with my own?

On the whole, I know that what that woman was saying was hyperbole of the worst kind. And yet there is a certain nugget of truth in it that all writers would like to avoid. We cannot give voice to a character based on someone real without silencing, at least in part, the person who inspired us.

This was brought home to me the time my daughter heard me on the radio. I was reading from my new book, *Status Update*. My husband, who was with my daughter, recounted that she was listening keenly throughout the broadcast, laughing at some of my sillier images and looking pensive at other moments. Until I got to a poem about us, about how quickly our children become themselves, and as I blithely read the poem over the air, my five-year-old daughter suddenly, breathlessly, began to sob. She was inconsolable. When my husband could finally calm her down enough to speak, she blurted out, "Mommy wrote a book of all my secrets."

I had exposed her, without meaning to. The poem seemed innocuous to me, a straightforward account of my love for my daughter. But it is an intense thing to realize that you are *seen*: you are thought about and interpreted and represented. While the poem was about the divergence and separate experience of our identities, it was also an intimate portrayal of who Abby is. It was her first lesson in the fact that you cannot love without exposing yourself. A lesson for me, too: that it is both a responsibility and a privilege to write about the ones you love.

Writing about my daughter is my way of trying to grope toward the truth of ourselves and our relationship. I think of how my daughter learned language, mimicking not only the words, but also my mannerisms, my tone, my cadence. This is what I would like to do to her as well, to find a way inside her voice. Of course, I cannot. In many ways, writing about her only serves to remind me of the expanse between us, the real and untraversable distance between our two lives and identities. But perhaps it is the *trying* to broach that distance that is important, bridging the separate islands we have become in the years since her birth.

There may be no real way to inhabit the voice of another, but it is the struggle to do so that makes us grow and create. Whatever else writing is, it's an attempt to express something true, and while anything well intentioned can turn out terribly, I believe we are well positioned to write about our children when our desire to create stems from that wellspring of love.

This joy of creation is something we share with our children, something that allows us to define our world together. This is how I can find balance in my mothering: by showing my daughter how I see the world and trusting that she will share with me her own vision of the world and voice to express it. By trusting that my voice can be a beacon to wide open spaces rather than a trap.

My daughter's voice is already developing into its own poetry. At the age of two and a half, while we were playing in the baseball fields by our home, Abby was twirling and twirling, creating a sandstorm around her, when she proclaimed, "I'm going to make up a poem." Then she threw some sand up in the air and recited:

> In the morning air
> I was dropping so much time
> In the evening air

My girl, writing her own book of secrets. She is a complex, mysterious, and amazing person. It's unsurprising that I can find no end of inspiration from her life. I wouldn't dare attempt to define her, but I will likely spend my entire life trying to get a little closer to understanding the whole of her.

Footnote to the Poem
"Now That All My Friends Are Having Babies: A Thirties Lament"

PRISCILA UPPAL

I must, I suppose, resign myself to the fact that we will
    never again
be able to throw what used to be called "an adult party"
    (though, of course,
no one actually acted like adults). Now I must prepare

for diaper changes, breast-feedings, time-outs in the
    middle of martini-making,
discussions of diaper changes, breast-feeding, time-outs
    in the middle of dinner,
dessert, after-dinner liqueurs, the only sex chat
each pregnant woman outdoing the other with how horny
being blown up like a balloon makes her feel, premature
    labour
always the result of taboo, non-recommended, eight-
    month fucking. Now that all

my friends are having babies, I should be more
    connected, I would think,
to my own womanhood, and how amazing bodies are
that can hold, sustain, shoot out life right there, onto my floor
in all its strange handness and footness and foreheads red
    with sweat
mouths wide with yawn, glee, or being. I thought I might
    even return
to religion, apprehend some sense of a holy order,
    harmony, even hierarchy.

(I'm sure you can already tell this didn't happen. So, what
    did?) Now that all
my friends are having babies, I am beset by a most
    curious fear
during the day, in the wee hours of morning, when I am
    brushing my teeth
or cleaning a CD. It can happen anywhere, I tell you,
    anywhere. My breath

stops, my ears tingle, the backs of my knees go cold as
    ice. I know now, more pointedly,
that I am going to die—these children are going to kill,
    not only me, but
my friends, my colleagues, my neighbour with the
    glorious rows of gardenias
and impatiens, my GP, my beloved cats and their
    neutered siblings. We are nothing

to these babies, rolling on the floor making Play-Doh pies
    or building forts out of Lego,
pushed around in strollers with ribboned hair or Velcro
    shoes, drinking juice from
sippy-cups and crying, kicking at the concrete, cat walling
    a daffodil, demanding a video,
tying a skipping rope to a chair, beating a piñata, or
    kissing my cheeks.

Holy, perhaps, but irreversibly deadly. And their lips
    know not what they will say.
And nobody cares that I am taking a stand and remaining
    childless — you couldn't
pay me enough to take one on, not on this planet where
    we let our non-biological
children die, and keep dying, as long as they die quietly.
    And they might be holy too.
And the clouds waltz by and keep coupling as if nothing
    has happened.

—PRISCILA UPPAL

⊙

Out of place in our kitchen, in steel-toed boots and black dress shirt and slacks, Chris stomped on two bags of ice while I placed the glass top-hat ice bucket on the dining room table.

"I'm never forgiving Jennifer for this."

It was not the first time Chris had said this in the last week, once he discovered that he was actually *invited* and most surely *expected* to attend Jennifer's baby shower, but this time he looked like he meant it.

"It's bad *enough*," he stomped, "that we can't throw *adult* parties anymore and people keep showing up with *babies* attached to their hips without warning and then expect us to fly around the house putting away every *knife* and *vase* and *cat toy*, but I would like to know when it suddenly became *necessary* to subject men to *baby showers!*"

"I think the ice is broken," I replied, tearing the plastic cover off a veggie platter of celery and broccoli and carrot sticks.

"Seriously," he went on, picking up the bags of ice and splitting them open with his hands. "What woman would seriously think that men—straight men—want to spend the afternoon talking about baby milk and baby diapers and sippy-cups? Are we going to have to sit there through the gift opening? I don't think I can take it. You think Ray is going to last the afternoon? I think we should be able to take a walk while that is going on."

"Just try not to drink too much beer," I warned, mixing sour cream and herbs.

"Oh, I'm drinking as much beer as *necessary*. Ray too. I'm never forgiving Jennifer for this." Cold water spilled through his hands onto our recently mopped floor.

Chris wasn't put out that we were hosting yet another party. We are frequently called upon to host parties, as we actually own a house in a fairly central Toronto location and are adept at organizing guest lists and hors d'oeuvres and cases of booze. If I might be so bold as to say so, we are also fun, gracious, and generous hosts. We throw lots of parties, from an annual BBQ for my former students, to a We-Survived-the-Holidays party once the new year rolls around, to Halloween events, to any excuse, really, to break out some bubbly and toast another rotation of the planet Earth.

Chris wasn't even put out that we, the communal "we" as in "we" who own this house, would be hosting yet another baby shower. "We" had hosted them before. Several. Although I guess it depends on what you mean by host. For baby showers, it meant that Chris helped out by picking up bottles of wine and cases of beer, grocery shopping at Loblaws, and even by cutting slices of baguette and rectangles of cheese. But it also meant that he went to a movie matinee—usually some excessively violent horror flick I had no intention of ever seeing—and I was left to the afternoon delight of ladies sipping champagne and soda water, nibbling on salmon rolls and chocolate brownie bites, and to snippets of discussions Chris and I both dearly dreaded—baby milk and diapers and sippy-cups.

I say *snippets*, because this is indeed why "we"—or "I"—started offering to host baby showers for our recently impregnated friends: so I could spend the majority of the party hiding in the kitchen. I can't stand the conversations about breast-feeding and nipple peeling and baby diarrhea and teething toys and food brands. And I especially can't stand the conversations about pre- or post-delivery sexual intercourse that every woman seems to want to trot out as some kind of badge of honour to prove how incredibly sexy being pregnant actually is.

Well, not in my world. I discovered that instead of making faces of disgust or discomfort as my friends dissected the differences between different breast pumps or offered up another steamy little anecdote about how to have sex bent over when your man can't get his arms around your voluptuous figure, my time would be much better spent, and more politely spent, refilling glasses, heating up mini-samosas, and recycling wrapping paper.

Sippy-cups may be boring, but breast-feeding and baby spit and stretched labias are disgusting. I wasn't one of those girls who cele-brated when the Period Fairy arrived, and I'm still less than impressed once a month when I need to succumb to tampons and panty liners. I don't think pregnant women are beautiful. I think they look extremely uncomfortable and are possibly delusional. I can't imagine looking forward to sore breasts and morning sickness and a human being taking shape inside my body, fed on the same food that I eat. That's just plain gross. That's the stuff of horror films and alien invasions. I know this likely makes me seem juvenile, but I have enough trouble getting needles in my arm or cleaning the cat litter. When I think of conceiving, delivering, or tending to a newborn baby, I feel nauseous. Physically and, if it's possible, emotionally nauseous.

Poor Chris. This would be his first initiation into the horror of women discussing babies. I felt sorry for him. It wasn't right. Whoever decided men should now be invited to baby showers was certainly a sadist. Probably most pregnant women are.

Ding Dong.

"Yes, OK, you're never forgiving Jennifer," I concede as the guest of honour and her entourage of fetal well-wishers arrive.

Since the ethos of most baby showers is communal, we have arranged the chairs and couches into a circle and a roomful of women and Ray claim their afternoon perches. Chris is serving the champagne to those who can drink it, gripping the bottle's throat as if someone might replace it with a baby if he shows even a moment's weakness.

We have never wanted children. Never.

"I didn't want children either, until I met…"

"When you find the right person, yes, that's when you…"

"All of a sudden you know that, yes, he is the right man to be a father…"

I go back to the kitchen to check on the quesadilla bites in the oven.

I've heard this all before. The old "I used to think I would never have children, but then the right person came along, and then I knew I was always meant to start a family" story. I'm sure it's a real story for some people. But I've always found it an insulting one to those in the room who have had stronger convictions on the subject, both those who have always wanted kids and those who haven't. Our friends Ray and Mara have also chosen not to have kids. Why should it mean there is something wrong with our choice of partner if we simply don't want to reproduce? Why are we the only couples invited to this baby shower anyway? Are they unconsciously trying to convince us through osmosis? Sure, the child-rearing couples maintain that the partner or husband is the one taking care of the kids this afternoon. I hate to point this out, but Ray and Mara and Chris and I have actually been together the longest of our coupled friends and family. I wonder how much of this has to do with *not* having children, agreeing on this before committing to a long-term relationship.

The idea that couples change their minds on this fundamental issue unnerves me, the way that people unnerve me when they decide to convert religions, or when they all of a sudden sell off all of their worldly possessions for a clipper sailboat. I've seen far too many people break up because one member of the heterosexual pair — usually the male — was adamant about not having children and the woman was aghast that she couldn't convince him to relent. I've also witnessed the serious emotional turmoil that ensues when homo-sexual couples change their tune about whether or not children are wanted as part of their marriage and to what lengths they might go to adopt or create a child.

Meeting the right person. Hormones kicking in. Realizing one can't live forever. Fine. I understand. But what about the other reasons people suddenly change their minds on this issue, which never get discussed at the baby shower? To trap someone in a relationship. To try to rewrite your childhood. To ensure you will always have someone who loves you. (No mother believes she is going to give birth to an ungrateful child who will leave her to rot in a nursing home one day.) What about boredom? I heard a poet the other day, anticipating his first child, admit this in a poem—in a tongue-and-cheek way, of course—but the audience laughed because they could identify with the statement: *We were bored with ourselves, so we made another self.* Everyone needs a project or a hobby. Or what about a number of people who don't want to admit the reason they want a baby all of a sudden is they've realized they are never going to reach the pinnacle of their career, that work no longer offers satisfaction, and it would be more realistic to look forward to celebrating report cards and piano recitals and track-and-field meets—the future potential accomplishments of their children, rather than their own.

Perhaps it is my workaholism that keeps me childless. It's certainly a factor. I find great satisfaction in writing and teaching. Many professors do, which is why a gigantic hook is required to get us to retire. And it's also why so many children of professors are so royally screwed up. How can a child compete with graduate students? Most children don't and won't share the intense passion for the specialized fields of research of their parents, nor will they sit wide-eyed and impressed when lectures on the subject are offered. Most wouldn't choose a parent who is "away" much of the time, either on research trips or intellectual journeys inside their own heads. I know I would resent the time spent away from my computer and notebooks. I already do. I think our three cats are demanding, and I frequently have to shoo them away as they bat my hands while I type.

. . .

I bring out another pot of Tranquility Tea for the mother-to-be and the designated drivers. Mother-to-be appears suitably subdued as she devours gherkins and mac-and-cheese bites and sugar cookies. The mothers-who've-been-there are now trying to out do each other with how atypical their own birthing experience was. I linger a little, as I must admit that this part I typically find amusing. Those who choose no drug-assistance are superior to those who do. Those who homebirth are superior to those who choose a hospital. Those who employ foreign women as part of the homebirth, far away from any modern medical personnel, are superior to all, especially if they are vegetarian or vegan to boot.

"I brought a photograph of when I was pregnant with twins!"

Everyone screams with glee. Except Chris and Ray, who stuff their faces with popcorn. This isn't a movie they are used to screening.

"Oh my god!!!"

"I've never seen a belly that big!"

"Ouch! Ouch! Ouch!"

Chris and Ray's eyes go very wide and then turn to the window. Soon, I can see why. The photograph was taken the day before a medically forced labour. The subject of the photo is completely naked. I have never seen a belly that large in my entire life. It resembles one of those large rubber balls you would inflate and kick about in school gymnasiums. It looks like the photographer used a fish-eye lens. The subject's breasts, equally hideously malproportioned and faced with the encroachment of the ever-growing belly, part to both sides. Nipples as wide as my own face. Nothing is worth seeing this.

"I kept begging to be fucked so I'd go into labour, but it didn't work. But we did do a lot of fucking!"

No way. I don't believe it. And I don't want this image wedged in my mind like a puzzle to solve.

At any other bridal shower, the contest would be over, the twin lady crowned Queen of all Mothers, and we could move on to the presents. But not at this one. We who choose to be childless will not be let off so easily. There is another pregnant woman besides the day's mother-to-be in the room. She isn't quite as far along as Jennifer, and so she seems a bit more mobile as she puts down her glass of sparkling water and rises from her chair, as if she is going to excuse herself to the washroom — which she does — but not before she drops this: "I plan on keeping the baby's placenta in the refrigerator and eating it in a special ritual on its first birthday."

I don't stick around for the explanation of where in the world this practice first began or who was the first celebrity to embrace it. My stomach can't handle it. Neither can Chris's. As I retreat into the kitchen to boil more water for tea that no one has asked for, I spot Chris out of the corner of my eye, grabbing two more beer from the cooler. There's no way now he's going to let me host *her* baby shower. Ray is laughing, but he does not look happy. Not in the least.

I start to think that maybe I was lucky my mother abandoned me when I was eight, lucky she didn't think so highly of the entire birthing process that she kept my placenta as a gourmet reminder.

This isn't what most people, especially new mothers, want to hear. But I was indeed better off without my unstable mother, even if she did abandon my brother and me to the care of a single-parent quadriplegic. An adult before my time, at least I learned how to survive and take care of myself in nearly any circumstance. I was self-supporting by the age of fifteen and put myself through university with scholarships and student loans, the latter of which I paid off from my book advances. I'm one of the most resilient people I know, which I attribute to having no mother.

Having no mother is probably also somewhat responsible for my decision not to become a mother. I've witnessed some dedicated, nurturing, and inspiring mothers in my day—usually the mothers of friends I was desperate to impress so I could eat home-cooked meals at their tables on holidays and be taken on trips my father could never afford—but it's not unlike witnessing an amazingly talented acrobat or glass-blower or nuclear physicist. Impressive and awe-inducing, but far removed from my day-to-day life. I have almost no memories of what mothers do and who they are, and therefore very few emotional associations with the entire enterprise.

I love young adults, though, which is why I'm such a dedicated professor. When faced with the ubiquitous question, "When will you and Chris have children?" I always respond, "Never. I have hundreds of children at the university. Their parents screw them up and then I help them become adults." This description isn't inaccurate. My office corridor is often littered with students on the cusp of adulthood desperate for someone to offer them guidance, wisdom, support, and, most importantly, truth without bullshit. Many have loving parents. Few have parents capable of telling the truth. Not about their children and not about the hardships of life. Many know they have been loved to the point of crippling indulgence and are now struggling to shape a life for themselves as they recognize their expectations are unrealistic.

Time for presents! Dozens of pastel-coloured bags with ribbon ringlets and baby rattles and baby golden retrievers and baby trucks on the sides. Jennifer's life is one of too many unwanted surprises—even this pregnancy was not planned, although she embraced it when she realized that, being in her early forties, this might be her last chance at parenthood; and she is not keen on keeping the much-younger father involved—so she knows she's having a boy. Even in this crowd of artists and feminists, the predominant colours are blue and green. Blue baby blankets, blue diaper bags, blue nursing pillows, green onesies, green booties, green pacifiers. Chris and I have bought the boy-about-to-be a grizzly bear sleeper and a bunch of Golden Books.

Then some gifties for Mom: pink bath salts and cozy slipper socks and the inevitable black lace underwear (but Jen doesn't want a man in her life, remember?). All the women squeal as each object is plucked from a bag or unravelled from tissue. Many offer comparisons:

"If you hold the nursing pillow this way, it's so much easier..."

"Sophie the giraffe is *the* best teething toy on the market..."

"When I would get super horny, I would use this amazing lubricant..."

Happy recycler, I flatten out tissue and paper bags and start to remove used flute glasses and small plates from the living room. Chris and Ray are now both drunk. Though they haven't left the premises for a walk, they have retreated to the security of the stereo, where they laugh loudly as they debate what songs to play next—Ramones or AC/DC, T. Rex or Motörhead—in the futile effort to supplant the images that must be lodged in their brains.

I find myself contemplating, not for the first time, why it is the same group of people who will have a conniption if you don't bring your own thermos to the Second Cup, or label you a criminal for eating a hamburger, don't have any patience for the argument that the planet could be saved by having fewer babies. This might be because I was abandoned myself, or because I spent a year living with a family in foster care, or because I spent an inordinate amount of time as a child watching telethons and UNICEF commercials, but I do find it a little disconcerting how many people desperate for children to care for will only adopt as a last resort. There are so many unwanted children who are going to live loveless lives because willing mothers and fathers can't see past their own biology.

My own brother can't. He has two boys: Emmitt, five, and Hunter, two. I love them dearly. I play hockey and baseball and robots and superheroes with them. Emmitt jumps on my lap for story time. Hunter gives me high-fives and fist bumps. I buy them box-loads of puppets.

I swear I am not a child hater, not a monster, not someone lacking in nurturing qualities, not someone lacking in a wonderful partner. I am a born auntie. I am simply someone who does not wish to embody the role of mother. I am someone who thinks we pair up and create carelessly. I count on my birth control pills to keep me honest.

When the women and Ray have all left, and we've helped load up a car full of Jennifer's new treasures, Chris nurses his impeding hangover with pizza and an evening on the couch, and I take a walk around our neighbourhood. I maneuver around strollers and road hockey matches, watching the clouds waltz by and keep coupling as if nothing has happened.

Leaving the Eighteenth Floor

JULIA ZARANKIN

Excess Light

One day, I ride the elevator with a woman who accidentally finds herself on the eighteenth floor as the doors slide open.

"Why is this floor so light?"

I hadn't thought of it before. The atmosphere on the eighteenth floor is exaggerated, desperate. Every word takes on hyperbolic meaning. One wouldn't want to come here by accident.

I tell her, "It's a fertility clinic. Everybody here feels defeated, so they provide us with excess light."

"I'm so sorry," she mutters and quickly presses her desired floor.

"Don't worry about it," I say as I walk out the doors.

Preparing

A few months into our marriage, my husband and I declare the time ripe to start trying. The entryway into the world of potential motherhood begins with this verb, *to try*, and we hesitate on its threshold. I worry about how a baby would alter our lifestyle. Would I still be able to write in the mornings? Where would my writing desk go once we assembled the baby's crib and changing table, and added a Diaper Genie, wet wipes, baby powder, mobiles, and a white noise machine? Would we opt for grandparent childcare or a nanny? How would a baby affect my husband's gym routine? What if the baby knocks herself out on his 48-kg kettlebell while learning to crawl? When would we move to a better school district? Would we start with piano lessons or soccer? Would we opt for the same kibbutz-style sleep-away camp I had attended? How long would we wait before we had our second? Would my new husband still find me attractive if I couldn't manage to shed the extra baby pounds?

We put off abandoning birth control for a few months because we can't decide on the optimal time to conceive—before or after our trip to Amsterdam? I don't want to gaze at Vermeers while feeling nauseous, and we both look forward to Heineken on tap. We would start trying upon our return.

I anticipate how I would transform my baby into a polyglot as early as possible. Since my husband and I speak Russian at home, we can assure ourselves a bilingual child by preschool age and a trilingual one by the time she enters grade two (thanks to a quality French elementary school). From there, she could easily add a few more Romance languages to the equation, go on to master Latin and Greek in high school and become…a better version of myself.

I begin filing away parenting stories from my friends for future usage, read mommy blogs, and start contributing to the conversations in my mind, referring to my imaginary baby as "Emma" and even conjuring up a sibling for her named "Daniel." I am almost convinced by the invented personal anecdotes I am accumulating: "My Emma can already recognize letters! Can you believe it? At eighteen months!" "Daniel wants to take up the oboe. I didn't know he knew the instrument existed!"

Trying

I continue charting my future baby's educational trajectory until I realize that I am already thirty-five and my husband twelve years my senior, but we aren't concerned. Our conception genes on both sides are inspiring: my mother-in-law claimed to conceive so easily that even air could impregnate her, and though my mother made no such pronouncements, her track record strikes me as equally impressive.

My OB/GYN displays slightly less optimism but assures me there is still time. Start trying. Study your cycles. If nothing happens in six months, come back and see me. I return home eager to commence a new life scheduled around the verb *to try*.

I read through the etymology and definition of *try* in search of a mention of difficulties associated with conceiving, looking for an echo, a glimpse of my own experience. Instead, I learn that the verb comes from the Old French *trier*, which means "to pick out, cull," which derives from medieval Latin *triare*. I don't allow myself to fear that I may not be one of those who will be picked out.

Instinctively, I copy my friends and begin to plan for a June baby. That way, it wouldn't interfere with my lecturing schedule, and summer is a good time to get through the horrid first three months (by this point enough of my friends have been through the initial shock of babydom, the accompanying sleeplessness, and I am ready to sacrifice a hot and humid Toronto summer to the ordeal). Worst case scenario—I'd be willing to accept a May or July delivery.

I collect reading material and acquire toys. I study and annotate *Taking Charge of Your Fertility*, photocopy worksheets, and begin charting my cycles. I learn new words, consult with my husband about my luteal phase, take my basal temperature every morning, carefully consider my cervical mucus. I buy ovulation kits and, a few months later, a magic ovulation monitor that tests your saliva every morning, to which my friend attributes both of her successful pregnancies. I pay $300 to a website in Colorado for the ovulation tool and an extra $60 in duty to a brown-clad UPS deliveryman who appeared at my door. I try fighting the sixty dollars but then consider it a small price to pay for a cute, fat baby nine months from now. Between my late-night reading and ovulation monitoring, I imagine my ovaries taking on a life of their own in response to my diligent meticulous tracking.

Measuring

I begin to measure life in nine-month increments. If I have a baby in March, when should my husband begin taking driving lessons? I imagine I could drive until the eighth month, but probably not beyond then. What if it still snows in March and we end up on black ice?

And then nothing. After six months of cycle charting and saliva testing, nothing. My assumption that I'd have a child at thirty-five morphs into a desire to have a baby at thirty-six. At this point, we wonder whether something might be awry. My OB/GYN orders tests: my fallopian tubes are open and look wonderful, but my uterus turns out to be of a sub-optimal shape. But it isn't a deal breaker. People still conceive, even with a slightly tilted uterus. And then we learn that my husband has poor swimmers. There are plenty of sperm, but they are lazy. The doctor suggests a repeat test, just to make sure. A second test reveals sperm even more slovenly than the first. Maybe they are asleep? All hundred million of them?

The Clinic

We arrive at the fertility clinic on Bay Street a few months after my thirty-sixth birthday. I am in a new age rubric on all the statistical charts: the thirty-five to thirty-nine category. I can't help becoming fiercely jealous of the under-twenty-nine set, whose prognoses are better, across the board. Why hadn't I started earlier?

Why hadn't I met my husband earlier, when his sperm were better, more aggressive swimmers, with lower DNA fragmentation? Why had I wasted time dating so much unfatherly material? Where was my judgment? Why wasn't I having babies at under twenty-nine? Why had I considered getting a PhD somehow more important than procreation? Why had I mocked my mother's decision to have a baby in her early twenties? A litany of *why*s.

Hannah

We gain a new family member. The fertility nurse, Hannah (not her real name), calls me with results the afternoon of my blood tests and informs me of my FSH level, follicle count, and, later in the cycle, my LH surge.

"Your follicle is looking great, honey. Just beautiful. You're just about ready to ovulate. Please don't forget to make love tomorrow and the next day! Looking good!" She often accentuates the word *love* and turns it into luuurve, the way I'd only heard in romantic comedies.

Every evening, my husband comes home and inquires about Hannah. As a joke, we preface every intimate conversation with "Hannah says..." and after a while, it almost feels as if she is there, evaluating us. The night my husband has a migraine and we have to forego sex, I worry most about letting Hannah down.

Some days, I talk to her more often than I talk to my mother. Her disembodied, sultry voice does not match her corpulent, slightly hunched over physique, and Hannah is the first person who learns, every month, that I am not pregnant. She exhales the appropriate sigh, followed by, "Oh, honey."

The winter months of 2011 are a blur. I take the subway to Dundas station at 7:00 a.m. at least five mornings per cycle. If I'm lucky, I happen on the one lab technician who can draw blood successfully from my diminutive veins on the first try. The others poke at least four times and leave both of my arms bruised. Sometimes I stop in to see Hannah with a question; other times, I invent a pretext, just to talk to someone about this. I wonder if protocol dictates that she ask for my name every time, before plucking my file from the pile on her desk. Her eye contact feels genuine; she smiles intently and inquires what she could do for me. She has pastel-coloured framed Bible quotations on her office walls and an army of variously sized plush ladybugs adorning her desk and filing cabinet. After my second babyless cycle, she gives me a pair of thumb-sized glass ladybug magnets.

"They bring good luck," she says, pressing them into my hand.

"Really?"

"It's been proven." I put the magnets on my fridge that night.

Why

My husband and I attend various information sessions and embark on learning a language together. Our conversations revolve around my periods, which now seem more regular than ever, around Hannah's instructions on when to "make love," around trips to the fertility clinic for blood work and ultrasounds. The day I take his sperm sample to the fertility clinic for yet another DNA fragmentation test (*DNA frag*, for short), there is a delay on the subway and I call the clinic in a panic.

"I'm at Rosedale station, there's a delay, but I have the sample on me," I blurt out to Hannah before giving her my name, suddenly aware that I am on the subway during rush hour, pressed up against people I don't know who can hear and freely interpret my conversation, gripping a plastic container under my armpit, trying to keep it warm. "Oh, it's Julia. I was supposed to be at the lab 10 minutes ago."

When I finally drop off the specimen, the secretary assures me that everything is in good hands.

"Even famous people come here, you know. This is all more common than you think," she says.

We wait anxiously all week, wondering whether my husband's sperms' swimming abilities have improved after an intense training regimen consisting of months of dutiful intake of high doses of CO-enzyme Q10, vitamin E, folic acid, and regular acupuncture sessions. The dramatic improvements I had been visualizing during my morning meditations fail to materialize in the test results.

After three months of cycle monitoring and sex on optimal days, and after concluding that I am indeed ovulating fairly well (after all, I am thirty-six and the word "optimal" is out of the question for any of my reproductive capabilities; my FSH levels never appear in the ideal bracket, my LH surges too much, and my AMH hormones tip to the higher end of normal), our doctor suggests IVF. She utters the three letters quickly, staring at a spot slightly above my head, and adds that, of course, nothing obliges us to take this route, and it certainly doesn't preclude other treatments, but to her mind, it is the best way to work around male-factor infertility, which is primarily what we're dealing with.

My husband and I walk out of her office with a packet of information and an appointment for an evening IVF info session at the clinic, fairly optimistic. Maybe it's worth a shot. How bad could the three letters be? Friends of friends had done it. My osteopath's clients had done it; a blogger friend of mine had done it. All had beautiful children. Nobody pretended it was easy or didn't come with its share of trauma and side effects. But all had photos of children.

An embryologist, a reproductive medicine doctor, and a head nurse offer us cookies, granola bars, humus and pita snacks, bottled water, and a PowerPoint presentation of the ins and outs of IVF. The fertility doctor utters "pharmaceutical doses" and provides an outline of the drugs involved. The nurse talks about "the teaching," wherein Hannah would show me how to self-inject drugs over the course of a few weeks. Then they would *harvest* my eggs with a giant needle, which would—they hope—not pierce anything on the way (what could it pierce, someone asks? Well, bowels, organs, there's lots of *stuff* in there), and then, the embryologist would take over and make magic happen. We are given an inside view of embryologist Nick's (not his real name) lab, where he would connect my eggs with my husband's shy, unaggressive, and slightly slothful swimmers, and force them to pollinate. A few days later, once they've turned into hopefully viable embryos, back they go! For the particularly lazy swimmers, such as my husband's, they also offer a procedure called ICSI, wherein Nick ruptures the actual coating of the egg with a laserbeam so that the indecisive sperm doesn't have to do it alone.

We leave the clinic with our untouched cookies wrapped in napkins, an IVF DVD, and a folder full of information, including a price tag for each procedure. I already know, and my husband knows by looking at me, that the folder will end up in the recycling bin. I can't go through with this. The cycle monitoring is trying enough, and I don't think I could handle the drugs, the needles, the eventual harvesting, and the likelihood of a repeat procedure.

"Why can't we just find your sperm a good swimming coach?" I whimper into my husband's shoulder as we ride home on the subway. Why.

We meet with our doctor a week later and share our reservations about IVF, and tell her that we would like to opt for less invasive treatments.

This is the same doctor who had been recommended by friends who now have three beautiful daughters. *She's a magician*, they said. I was initially put off by her inflectionless voice and deliberate eye contact at twenty-second intervals, but my husband considered her no-nonsense style a mark of professional behavior.

"I just don't feel comfortable with this," I tell her, hoping to initiate a conversation.

"Right. No problem. We all know our limits."

Our conversation ends with another copy of a sheet she had given us at our first appointment, listing statistics of success of less invasive treatments for the thirty-five to thirty-nine age group. We are looking at a 5- to 7-percent chance of success. "Of course, you never know. Nothing precludes a spontaneous pregnancy either," she adds and glances down at her watch.

Deciding

"I don't know what to do, Hannah." I burst into her office with cotton swabs taped to both arms. Three novice lab technicians failed to draw blood this Sunday morning, and the more I bite my lip to stop myself from crying, the more the tears fog my vision.

"Sorry, honey, let's backtrack a little. What's your name?"

For the past six months, Hannah has called me on the phone more often than my own mother. She has dictated the terms of my sex life, she knows the shape of my ovaries and my hormone levels, she is the only person in my life who calls me *honey*. And she still doesn't know my name. I collapse into a chair and sob, pointing to my arms.

In the end, we decide I can skip this particular cycle, and we'd resume the following month. "Honey, have I given you some ladybugs?" she asks me as I get up to leave her office.

In a way, this is when I know things have come to an end.

I return to the eighteenth floor the next month, knowing it will be my last. The luminous floor that takes no holidays. It operates 7 days a week, 365 days a year. On weekends, I access the building through a different door and with a special code. On weekdays, I enter through the front door and let myself pretend that I am a person going to work on the fifteenth floor, at the Environment and Lands Tribunals of Ontario. A normal person. Only when I press eighteen am I reminded that I haven't been picked. Still trying.

Ending

This story doesn't have an end yet. We've taken a break from the fertility clinic for the time being, because for an entire year we lost ourselves. Not a day went by when we didn't mention Hannah. I started to resent every stroller in Toronto, not to mention the parents of every perfect baby I saw everywhere. All around me, everybody was pregnant, and those who weren't just didn't know it yet.

I had thought that motherhood was all about the planning. The chapter I underlined most actively in *Taking Charge of your Fertility* considered how to determine the sex of your baby. I wanted a baby girl, and two years later, a boy. It sounds ridiculous now—precious, almost —that I could have once been so naive.

I am not a mother yet and may never become one. I can't predict how I will feel—or even what will be—a few years from now, but I am learning to come to terms with life either way. My experiences on the eighteenth floor showed me how life often refuses to yield to predetermined expectations, no matter how many schedules, charts, plans, followed by alternate plans and amendments, my doctor and Hannah devised for me. The more I *took charge* of my fertility by archiving stories, imagining scenarios, and amassing dog-eared books and ovulation detector kits, the more any sense of tangible control eluded me. Perhaps giving up on the master plan is my first real lesson in motherhood.

Afterword

Grandmothering

MICHELE LANDSBERG

The best fictional grandmothers are tart and acerbic, veering between laconic wisdom and childishly profane outbursts, like Grandmother in *The Summer Book*, or calmly magical, like Grandmother in *The Golden Key*, or tough as nails and bony-fingered, like Grandma in *What Would Joey Do?* I grew up learning how to be from the books I read, but now that I'm a grandmother, I find myself without a fictional template that I can make fit me. Calmly magical is utterly out of my grasp. Tart has never been my style. And even if I wanted to pull off the tough act ("I just want to make sure you're in good shape before I check out," says the cigarette-puffing Grandma to Joey), I would cry before I got to the end of the sentence.

I had never thought of becoming a grandmother. Although some of my peers were already lamenting their lack of longed-for descendants, I was far too busy in my own life, hacking out newspaper columns, running to New York to be with my friends, and keeping up with feminist activism to think about it or daydream myself in a new role. Aging itself was a puzzle; no matter how relentlessly the years passed, I felt the same young self looking out of my eyes.

At fifty-four, when I was levelled by breast cancer and a menacing cascade of the treatment's malign and accidental side effects (including diabetes and a nearly fatal aspiration pneumonia), I struggled to understand the implications of my chronological age. Frequently, during that year of sickness and fear, I wracked my mind: was I so terribly young to die? Or had I, at fifty-five (I mysteriously got my age wrong for that entire year), lived a luxuriously long time and should be satisfied? Focused on my own survival, I never contemplated future generations.

Even as I lurched into my sixties, I lacked grandmotherly thoughts. And even when our older daughter proclaimed her intention to have a baby on her own, with the aid of a sperm donor clinic in New York (where she worked at the United Nations), my thoughts circled around her well-being and her happiness, and not on any potential human being.

Truthfully, it was not until the surgeon lifted the plump baby boy into the air that my shocked heart rocketed to the sky; I was in an instant dazzled and in love. If he hadn't been quickly bundled and put into my arms, I might have immoderately snatched him from the nurses. While my daughter was stitched up from the Caesarean, I was invited to sit in an adjacent room and rock the baby in my arms for an hour. Not since she, my first, had been born, had I experienced such an astonishment of love. To this day, ten years later, I have only to look at his face or into his grey-green eyes to feel the endorphins ricocheting around in my brain.

But I mislead; there are other grandsons, three more (though no granddaughters, nor likely to be) and, miraculously, they occupy that same room in my heart that seemed full to overflowing with Zev. His younger brother (same donor) is Yoav, lithe and leaping and as maddeningly skilled in argument as a lawyer. Their little cousin, Zimri Alan, is the son of our younger daughter, who resorted to technology as she neared forty when no appropriate suitors presented themselves. She has lived with us since Zimri was born. He is now a joyful three-year-old, so beautiful that I sometimes find it hard to look away from him as we sit together at the dinner table. One day, no doubt, he will be asking about *his* donor. We'll have to remind these three wonderful boys that there are other ways to be created—as exemplified by our son, who has just fathered the fourth boy in the family.

This spring, I twice travelled to the West Coast to spend time with my son, his wife, and their fantastically alert newborn baby. Toma Lee, the second grandson with a middle name given in memory of my mother, so longed for and so perfect, nestled in my arms as we were both enfolded by the fragrance of the rain forest and the hush of the ocean. Eyes, toes, spiky hair, three days old, and compact with potential. For the fourth time, I was thunderstruck by our collective luck and peril: miraculously perfect babies—and yet born into such a threatened world. But parental activism may yet help to change that future—and how odd and exhilarating to think that this baby has two parents!

Of course, it's a different and extra-privileged role, to be the grand-mother of intensely desired babies born to single mothers. Baldly, there's no partner to take up a half-share of the burden or even to come between you and the baby; the role, should you accept it, is baggy and stretchable. In my case, my older daughter was exception-ally generous in inviting my participation, probably because she was completely grown-up (in her late thirties) before venturing on single motherhood. She moved home to Toronto from New York to be close to the family, and there I was, in my sixties, with a completely new passionate focus to my life.

I proposed his name, and it was agreed upon (he was named Zev after Zelig, my gentle grandpa, a carpenter); I was normally the one on the other end of the phone or jumping into my car when there was any crisis of feeding or fever; I was the one to accompany my daughter to look at daycare centres and interview babysitters, and listed as "co-parent" on the admission forms with my phone number as the emergency back-up. (And I was the one who kept getting the flu his whole first year at daycare.)

To my utter surprise, I welcomed this role without reserve or resentment. My emotional commitment was so complete that other private joys fell utterly away. Patterns of socializing with dear friends were sloughed off with barely an apology. Writing in my garden journal, which had been such an absorbing and deeply pleasurable task — I used to come in, exhausted, muddy, and blissed out from hours of heavy work in the garden, relishing the flow of the pen as I recorded the day's doings — suddenly ended. Even if there had been time, the emotional energy for it had evaporated.

Surprisingly, there were few clashes of view between my daughter and me. (When they did happen, the pain and midnight anguish were as sharp as any I recall from youthful love affairs.) At first, my entire dedication was to "mothering the mother," a credo that formed during my early days of breast-feeding my own babies. Mothering the mother meant that I would go to any lengths to make her feel strong, capable, and cherished, even if it meant giving up my beloved book room to create a bedroom for her and her baby during her "lying-in." Luckily, she was such a natural and easy breast-feeder, and the baby so flourishing, she did not need much extra to make her feel confident in her role.

I have not, contrary to conventional wisdom, felt sidelined, disempowered, dethroned, or downgraded to be a grandparent rather than a parent, and I did not often have to bite my tongue to prevent myself from offering bossy advice. Instead, I gave the one gift to each of my daughters that I believe neither of them noticed, but without which parenting can be an emotional sinkhole. I was, for them, the one other person in the world as keenly interested in the quality of the crying, the first word, the mysterious temper tantrums, the diarrhea, the appetite or lack of it, the preferred style of sun hat.

I knew how important it was to be able to share such loomingly significant details. My husband had been leader of a provincial political party for much of the time our own three children were very young. Although I operated basically as a single mother, I never (all right —rarely) felt aggrieved or abandoned because, wherever he was, he phoned at least twice a day and shared my interest and concern about all the monumental trivia of a child's daily well-being. I knew how vital it could be to a mother's equanimity to share that burden. Even if my daughters never noticed my constancy in this regard, I knew I was giving something important in lending my total attention, and it was easy to take a back seat in any actual decisions.

Later, I assigned myself the role of the one who brought the extras —the bearer of stacks of carefully chosen children's books, provider of chicken soup or spaghetti dinners, the pumper of balloons and the planner (along with their aunt) of birthday parties, arranger of music lessons, chauffeur, and scourer of the Internet to find and record music that would please the infant and then toddler taste.

I think the older grandson also inherited from me an almost insane glee in the sound and feel of words. When he was two, I carried him outside at midnight to see the brilliant sky, and he breathed, in awe, "Starry night!"—the name of his favourite painting. He was just three when one night his mother overheard him sleepily saying aloud in bed, "Legumes...peas and beans and stuff...what an awesome word!" and then, getting wilder and more drunken on words, "Holy breading! Granola! Great outdoors! Barn! Holy Science Centre! Art gallery!" and then, quietly, "I said 'Jesus!' just like Safta."

I am "Safta" (the one who incautiously swears), having rejected the somehow suburban and patronizing sound of "Bubby," choosing Hebrew over the Yiddish name for grandmother, neither of which I used as a child. My mother, part of the immigrant generation that strove for perfect assimilation, taught me to say "Grandma" for that beloved woman who died when I was twelve. I have her image always in my mind: her kind, broad face, her gentle voice, her deep, old-fashioned bosom. She spoke very little English (thought "letta" was the singular of "lettuce"), but she lavished me with her tenderness, her brilliant cooking, her skilled dressmaking. Her quiet, unconditional love for me was the ground floor of my life.

As a Safta myself, I was the confidante and co-conspirator in raising a baby boy as macho-free as possible. My daughter, as strong a feminist as I and a lesbian, to boot, held passionate principles against gender stereotyping and all forms of societally approved violence. Together, we rebuffed the hockey-and-superhero T-shirts, pyjamas, and rain boots thrust forward by crass consumer capitalism; we parsed the popular entertainment on offer with gimlet eyes to shield him from unworthy role models. Together, we unwittingly set him up to be persecuted at nursery school, where strutting six-year-olds spotted this tenderly affectionate three-year-old as tempting prey and reduced him to tears with their playground taunts and terrorism.

So tenaciously did we explain and interpret the gendered world for him that, by the age of six, he could wryly dismiss the strutters and terrorizers as "standard boys" and resolutely forge his own path.

People tend to trade the same weary cliché about why being a grand-parent is so wonderful: "When I'm tired of them," they beam, "I can just hand them back to their parents." This nostrum always irritated me. I never tired of my grandchildren; if anything, I was and am always sorry to hand them back and to miss the next precious hours of whatever they would be doing next. Second, it's far too shallow an explanation for a joy that runs so deep. I've brooded over this. Sometimes I think the delight springs from the fact that your own children (usually) have survived and thrived, so you are not weighed down by the dread of mistake or failure that attends every tiny decision you make as a parent. And it's not necessarily the satisfaction that they will carry my genes on into the unknowable future; my genes are a rather abstract substance to me, and too many of them have turned out to be crappy (cancer, heart attack, diabetes...) for me to dote on them.

No, I can only think that love is its own reward. To own the privilege of having these fresh young creatures in my life, to accompany them as they make staggering daily discoveries, to have an excuse to share the childish happiness of Halloween or autumn leaf piles or a sandy beach. Each of them doubles and triples the amount of life in my life.

Most parents remember that they were immortal in their youth, and began to be mortal the moment their children were born—and, even more ominously, began to realize, with a thrill of horror, that their tender babes were also vulnerable to injury and death. That fear subsided as my children grew to adulthood, only to be replaced by a new spectre after the grandchildren were born. I began to hear the ominous clock of mortality ticking in the background; the more I grew devoted to these infants, the more horrified I became at the thought that I must, in all probability, "check out" before they were grown.

I bargained with the Shadow: "Just let me live till they are Bar Mitzvah," or, as that became less likely with my advancing age and the continued production of babies, "Just until they're old enough to remember me." I didn't care about my genes, but I wanted them always to remember how much they were loved.

I phrased it a little differently when I sat with my beloved friend Esther Broner, novelist and important Jewish feminist, for what we both knew was likely our last visit. We talked quietly for several hours, not bothering to turn on the lamps as the daylight faded in her tiny Upper West Side apartment. She, like me, but years earlier, had helped to raise the child of her single daughter, now a loving, idealistic, and beautiful young woman of great promise. We shared some thoughts about death.

"I can't bear not knowing how they'll grow up!" I kvetched to Esther, with tears in my eyes.

"Ah, but you do know," said Esther the novelist. "You know that character is plot, and you know the character of that little poet of yours..."

Miraculously, the moment she uttered this magical mantra, the Shadow shrunk away and has rarely returned. I still can't bear the thought of leaving them one day, but only because of my stubborn reluctance to think that all this rich and complicated happiness could end. I'll never change my mind about that.

Notes

The authors gratefully acknowledge the following works.

Foreword: The Motherhood Conversation (or "Life With a Uterus")

10 **"Could it be true...be the case."** Rachel Cusk, *A Life's Work: On Becoming a Mother* (London: Faber and Faber, 2008).

12 **"Are You Mom Enough?"** was the cover story from *Time* magazine, May 21, 2012.

Doubleness Clarifies KERRY CLARE

45 **"Oddly, the epic confusion...an explanation."** Carol Shields, *Unless* (London: Fourth Estate, 2002).

48 **"[Children's] lives start long...within our lives."** Hilary Mantel, *Giving Up the Ghost* (London: Harper Perennial, 2004).

50 **"You did not have to apologize for wanting to own your own soul."** Erica Jong, *Fear of Flying* (New York: Signet, 1995).

51 **"Yes, but real human beings shouldn't have to go through that."** Lynn Coady, *Strange Heaven* (Fredericton: Goose Lane Editions, 1998).

These Are My Children CHRISTA COUTURE

73 **"more slit-like and gaping"** *Wikipedia*, s.v. "Cervix," last modified January 17, 2014, http://en.wikipedia.org/wiki/Cervix.

302 | **The M Word**

Babies in a Dangerous Time: On Choosing to be Child-Free NICOLE DIXON

107 **an essay for *Canadian Notes & Queries*.** Nicole Dixon, "The Other F-Word: The Disappearance of Feminism from our Fiction," *Canadian Notes & Queries* 80 (Fall 2010): 9-17.

107 **"I've said it before...your asses too."** Dan Savage, "Stepdad Seeking," *Savage Love* (blog), *The Stranger*, November 10, 2005, http://www.thestranger.com/seattle/SavageLove?oid=25106. Used by permission of the author.

109 **"The Childfree Life"** was the cover story from *Time* magazine, August 12, 2013.

Primipara ARIEL GORDON

122 Ariel Gordon, "Primipara," in *Stowaways* (Kingsville, ON: Palimpsest Press, 2014). Used by permission of the author.

122 **primipara** *Webster's New World Dictionary*, s.v. "primipara."

A Natural Woman AMY LAVENDER HARRIS

126 **"untimely ripped"** William Shakespeare *MacBeth* (Act 5, Scene 8).

131 Donna Haraway, "A Cyborg Manifesto: Science, Technology, and Socialist-Feminism in the Late Twentieth Century," in *Simians, Cyborgs, and Women: The Reinvention of Nature* (New York: Routledge, 1990), 149-182.

The Best Interests of the Child FIONA TINWEI LAM

136 **systemic practice...of coercing thousands of single mothers** Kathryn Blaze Carlson, "Curtain lifts on decades of forced adoption for unwed mothers in Canada," *National Post*, September 3, 2012, http://news.nationalpost.com/2012/03/09/curtain-lifts-on-decades-of-forced-adoptions-for-unwed-mothers-in-canada/.

137 **conceived through natural means** Tom Blackwell, "Fertility dispute triggers ripples of concern across Canada after sperm donor wins paternity ruling," *National Post*, April 10, 2012, http://news.nationalpost.com/2012/04/10/fertility-dispute-triggers-ripples-of-concern-across-canada-after-sperm-donor-wins-paternity-ruling/.

140 **parliamentary committee** Testimony of Dr. Margaret Somerville, McGill Centre for Medicine, Ethics and Law before the Legislative Committee on Bill C-38, No. 010, First Session, 38th Parliament June 2, 2005, http://www.parl.gc.ca/HousePublications/Publication.aspx?DocId=1900398&Language=E&Mode=1&Parl=38&Ses=1.

140 **"unlink...bonds," "powerful feelings...biological families,"** and **"knowing who our...meaning in life"** Margaret Somerville, "Old Nature, New Science: Respecting Nature, the Natural, and Life," in *The Ethical Imagination: Journeys of the Human Spirit* (Toronto: House of Anansi Press, 2006), 146-154.

141 **"a woman needs a man like a fish needs a bicycle."** This expression is often attributed to Gloria Steinem. As Ms. Steinem herself attested in a letter to *Time* magazine in 2000, the true author of the saying is Irina Dunn, an Australian educator, politician, and journalist.

146 **"who are...psychological harm."** from Camille Bains, "Appeal court quashes ruling on right to reveal sperm donors," *Globe and Mail*, November 28, 2012, S.3.

The Girl on the Subway DEANNA McFADDEN

149 **"How warm and lovely it was to hold a child in one's lap, and the soft little arms, the unconscious cheeky little legs."** D.H. Lawrence, *Lady Chatterley's Lover* (Toronto: HarperPerennial Classics, 2013). ePub.

Junior MARIA MEINDL

166 **"Most fibroids are...pelvic exam."** Christine Northrup, *Women's Bodies, Women's Wisdom* (New York: Bantam, 1994).

170 **Second Chakra Issues** Ibid.

170 **"release the emotional...uterus."** Mary Danylak, Carolyn Dean, and Sat Daram Kaur, *The Complete Natural Medicine Guide to Women's Health* (Toronto: Robert Rose Inc. 2005).

170 **"blows to the feminine ego"** Louise Hay, *Heal Your Body: The Mental Causes of Physical Illness and the Metaphysical Way to Overcome Them* (New York: Hay House Inc., 1984).

170 **"illness is not...metaphoric thinking."** Susan Sontag, *Illness as Metaphor* (New York: Farrar, Straus and Giroux, 1978).

171 **women are increasingly "conscripted" into care** Pat Armstrong and Olga Kits, "One Hundred Years of Caregiving," in *Caring For/Caring About Women, Home Care, and Unpaid Caregiving*, ed. Karen R. Grant, Carol Amaratunga, Pat Armstrong, Madeline Boscoe, Ann Pederson, and Kay Willson (Aurora: Garamond Press, 2004), 45-75.

Wicked SUSAN OLDING

191 **"Once there was a gentleman...was ever seen."** Joseph Jacobs, "Cinderella," *Europa's Fairy Book* (New York and London: G.P. Putnam's Sons, 1916).

193 **"So long as...treated her badly."** Consiglieri Pedroso, "The Hearth Cat," *Portuguese Folk-Tales*, trans. Henriqueta Monteiro, with introduction by W.R.S. Ralston (London: Elliot Stock, 1882).

195 **"There was a...suffice her."** J.F. Campbell, "The Sharp Grey Sheep," *Popular Tales of the West Highlands: Orally Collected*, vol. 2 (Edinburgh: Edmonston and Douglas, 1860).

196 **"'What is that...be our maid.'"** Jacob Grimm and Wilhelm Grimm, "Cinderella," *Kinder- und Hausmärchen*, 1st ed., trans. D.L. Ashliman. Published on http://www.pitt.edu/~dash/ashliman.html. Used by permission of translator.

198 **"Once upon a time...killed outright."** W.R.S. Ralston, "The Baba Yaga," *Russian Folk-Tales* (London: Smith, Elder, and Company, 1873).

199 **"'I'll tell you what...rid of them.'"** Jacob Grimm and Wilhelm Grimm, "Hansel and Gretel," *Kinder- und Hausmärchen*, 1st ed., trans. D.L. Ashliman. Published on http://www.pitt.edu/~dash/ashliman.html. Used by permission of translator.

202 **"Then she summoned...'back to me.'"** Jacob Grimm and Wilhelm Grimm. "Little Snow White," *Kinder- und Hausmärchen* 1st ed., trans. D.L. Ashliman. Published on http://www.pitt.edu/~dash/ashliman.html. Used by permission of translator.

203-204 **"The queen took fright...day and night."** Ibid. Used by permission of translator.

Robin ALISON PICK

218 **Zeh Dodi, v'zeh Rayee** "Song of Songs" from the Torah.

218 **"Glorified and sanctified be God's great name..."** From the Mourner's Kaddish, which is part of the Jewish prayer service.

You Make 'Em, I Amuse 'Em PATRICIA STORMS

258 **Margaret Wise Brown: "Well, I don't especially like children, either. At least not as a group."** Joseph Stanton, "'Goodnight Nobody': Comfort and the Vast Dark in the Picture-Poems of Margaret Wise Brown and Her Collaborators," *The Lion and the Unicorn*, vol. 14, no. 2, December 1990.

258 **Dr. Seuss: "You make 'em, I amuse 'em."** Clifton Fadiman, *Enter, Conversing* (New York: World Pub. Co., 1962).

258 **Maurice Sendak: "Childhood is cannibals and psychotics vomiting in your mouth!"** Kelsey Campbell-Dollaghan, "The Creative Legacy of Maurice

Sendak," *Fast Company* (blog), May 2, 2012, http://www.fastcodesign.com/1669723/the-creative-legacy-of-maurice-sendak-in-his-own-words.

Mommy Wrote a Book of All My Secrets SARAH YI-MEI TSIANG

260 **"because I would rather…demand no less."** Shari Benning, "Why I'm Afraid to Have Children," *Earth After Rain* (Saskatoon: Thistledown Press, 2001). Used by permission of the author.

Footnote to the Poem "Now That All My Friends Are Having Babies: A Thirties Lament" PRISCILA UPPAL

267-269 Priscila Uppal, "Now That All My Friends Are Having Babies: A Thirties Lament," in *Traumatology* (Toronto: Exile Editions, 2010). Used by permission of the author.

274 **"We were bored with ourselves, so we made another self."** Jacob McArthur Mooney, "Fertility" (reading, Words Aloud 10 Spoken Word Festival at the Durham Art Gallery, Durham, Ontario, Canada, November 3, 2013). Used by permission of the author.

Afterword: Grandmothering MICHELE LANDSBERG

293 **"I just want to make sure you're in good shape before I check out."** Jack Gantos, *What Would Joey Do?* (New York: HarperCollins, 2004).

Acknowledgements

This book was inspired by so many conversations, and I thank Amy Lavender Harris and Katie Doering, in particular, for lighting the spark. Everything that followed underlined my certainty that women are amazing, and that we can make great things when we get together. I am so grateful to the incredible writers who were enthusiastic about this project and generous with their time and talent. I am grateful also to the Vicious Circle and the Toronto Women Writers' Salon, whose support has been essential.

The idea for this anthology turned into a reality with the help of the wonderful Samantha Haywood, who brought us to the good people at Goose Lane Editions. With the incredible talents of Susanne Alexander, Colleen Kitts-Goguen, Julie Scriver, and the indomitable Bethany Gibson, a good book was transformed into a great one. Their faith and investment in this project have been beyond my wildest dreams. It has been a pleasure working with all of you.

Along the way, I've been grateful for the support of Kim Jernigan and *The New Quarterly*, Jennifer Knoch, Alexis Kienlan, Heather Cromarty, Heather Birrell, Heidi Reimer, Rebecca Rosenblum, and so many other excellent friends. Many thanks also to my parents and sister for their tireless enthusiasm for everything I do—I am so lucky.

And finally, thanks to Stuart, with whom all good things are possible. And also to the amazing Harriet, who made me a mother—the most inspiring experience of my life—and to Iris, who gestated along with this book. She's finally in the world now, and she makes us all so happy.

Contributors

HEATHER BIRRELL is the author of two story collections, *Mad Hope* and *I know you are but what am I?* Her work has been honoured with the Journey Prize for short fiction and the Edna Staebler Award for creative non-fiction and has been shortlisted for both National and Western Magazine Awards. Birrell's stories have appeared in many North American journals and anthologies, including *The New Quarterly* and *Toronto Noir*. She lives with her husband and two daughters in Toronto, where she teaches high school English by day and creative writing to adults by night. Learn more at www.heatherbirrell.com.

JULIE BOOKER is a Toronto writer whose short-story collection, *Up Up Up*, came out in 2011. Her twins are finally allowing her to work on a novel.

DIANA FITZGERALD BRYDEN's first novel, *No Place Strange*, was shortlisted for the Amazon.ca First Novel Award and longlisted for the IMPAC/Dublin Award. She is at work on a second novel, *Tunapuna*, and is the author of two books of poetry: *Learning Russian*, shortlisted for the Pat Lowther Award, and *Clinic Day*.

KERRY CLARE's essays have appeared in a number of Canadian magazines and newspapers, including *Reader's Digest*, *Today's Parent,* and *The Globe and Mail*. Her essay "Love is a Let-Down" was shortlisted for a National Magazine Award and appeared in *Best Canadian Essays 2011*. She is editor of the Canadian books website *49thShelf* and writes about books on her blog, *Pickle Me This*. She lives in Toronto.

MYRL COULTER's adoption memoir, *The House With the Broken Two*, won the 2010 First Book Competition, sponsored by the Writers Studio at Simon Fraser University, and the 2011 Canadian Author Association's Exporting Alberta Award. Her work has been published in several anthologies and *Geist* magazine. Myrl lives in Edmonton, Alberta.

CHRISTA COUTURE has established herself as a singer-songwriter with sharp-shooting wit, effortless grace, and heart-on-sleeve intensity. Since her critically acclaimed debut album, *Fell Out of Oz*, and her sophomore record, *The Wedding Singer and the Undertaker*, she has explored intimate spaces with a frank confidence that avoids cliché and melodrama. In September 2012, she released her third album, *The Living Record*, produced by Steve Dawson and picked by CBC Music as one of the "Best Albums of 2012." In addition to being a touring and recording artist, Couture is a graduate of the Vancouver Film School, the managing editor of RPM.fm's "Indigenous Music Culture," a knitter, a blogger, a graphic designer, a Scotch drinker, and then some.

NANCY JO CULLEN is a Journey Prize-nominated fiction writer and the author of three critically acclaimed collections of poetry with Calgary's Frontenac House Press. Her most recent book, the short-story collection *Canary*, was the winner of 2012 Metcalf-Rooke Award. Cullen was the 2010 winner of the Writers' Trust Dayne Ogilvie Prize for Emerging LGBT Writers. She holds an MFA in Creative Writing from the University of Guelph Humber.

MARITA DACHSEL is the author of *Glossolalia*, *Eliza Roxcy Snow*, and *All Things Said & Done*. Her poetry has been shortlisted for the Robert Kroetsch Award for Innovative Poetry and the ReLit Prize and has appeared in many literary journals and anthologies. Her play *Initiation Trilogy* was nominated for the Jessie Richardson Award for Outstanding New Script. She is the 2013-2014 Artist-in-Residence at UVic's Centre for Studies in Religion and Society. After many years in Vancouver and Edmonton, she and her family now live in Victoria.

NICOLE DIXON's first book, the collection of stories *High-Water Mark*, was shortlisted for an Atlantic Book Award. In 2005, she won the Writers' Trust of Canada RBC Bronwen Wallace Award for Emerging Writers. An electronic resources librarian at Cape Breton University, Nicole lives in New Waterford on Cape Breton Island. From January to March, 2015, she'll be the writer-in-residence at the Pierre Berton House in Dawson City, Yukon. Please visit nicoledixon.ca.

ARIEL GORDON is a Winnipeg writer. Her second collection of poetry, *Stowaways*, will be published in spring 2014 by Palimpsest Press. Most recently, her chapbook *How to Make a Collage* won Kalamalka Press's inaugural John Lent Poetry-Prose Award. When not being bookish, Ariel likes tromping through the woods and taking macro photographs of mushrooms.

AMY LAVENDER HARRIS is the author of *Imagining Toronto*, which was short-listed for the Gabrielle Roy Prize in Canadian literary criticism and won the 2011 Heritage Toronto Award of Merit. She is a contributing editor with *Spacing* magazine, for which she writes a regular column on urban literature. Amy's next book, *Acts of Salvage*, explores what the contemporary city compels us to cling to or discard. She lives in Toronto with her husband and daughter.

FIONA TINWEI LAM is the author of two poetry books, *Intimate Distances* (a finalist for the City of Vancouver Book Award) and *Enter the Chrysanthemum*, and, most recently, the illustrated children's book *The Rainbow Rocket*. Her poetry, fiction, and creative non-fiction appear in over twenty anthologies. Her poems have been twice selected for BC's Poetry in Transit program. She co-edited the literary non-fiction anthology *Double Lives: Writing and Motherhood* and edited *The Bright Well: Contemporary Canadian Poetry about Facing Cancer*.

MICHELE LANDSBERG, a celebrated Toronto-born writer, feminist, and activist, wrote columns from a feminist perspective in *The Toronto Star* for 25 years. Her columns made a significant impact at the height of the women's movement and she won two National Newspaper Awards, including the first ever given for column writing. She also wrote columns for *The Globe and Mail* for three years while she lived in New York when her husband, Stephen Lewis, was Canada's ambassador to the United Nations. Michele has published four books, on topics ranging from children's literature to feminism to New York life, and has been awarded seven honorary degrees from Canadian universities. In 2002 she was awarded the Governor General's Medal in Commemoration of the Persons Case; in 2006, she was made an Officer of the Order of Canada, and in 2014, the Canadian Journalism Foundation announced a joint award (with the Canadian Women's Foundation) to be called The Landsberg, to honour a journalist who shines a light on women's equality issues in Canada.

DEANNA McFADDEN's professional writing career has involved abridging classics for kids, publishing a few poems, writing some very odd short stories in university, hacking it up for the Internet, and completing one unpublished novel. During work hours, she develops content and manages an e-book program for a very large publishing house. At home, she's happily embedded in a family unit that consists of one amazing boy and an equally amazing husband.

MARIA MEINDL is the author of *Outside the Box: The Life and Legacy of Writer Mona Gould, the Grandmother I Thought I Knew*, winner of the Alison Prentice Award for women's history. "The Last Judgment" was published in 2011 by *Found Press* and "Rules," an essay, in an anthology on death published by *Creative Non Fiction*. Her essays have appeared in *The Literary Review of Canada*, *Descant*, and *Musicworks*. She has made two radio series for CBC *Ideas*: "Parent Care" and "Remembering Polio." She teaches movement classes in downtown Toronto. www.bodylanguagejournal.wordpress.com.

SALEEMA NAWAZ is the author of the short story collection *Mother Superior* and the novel *Bone and Bread*, which won the 2013 Quebec Writers' Federation Paragraphe Hugh MacLennan Prize for Fiction. Her fiction has appeared in journals such as *PRISM International*, *Grain*, *The New Quarterly*, *Prairie Fire*, and *The Dalhousie Review*. Her short story "My Three Girls," won the 2008 Writers' Trust of Canada/McClelland & Stewart Journey Prize.

SUSAN OLDING's *Pathologies: A Life in Essays* won the Creative Nonfiction Collective's Readers' Choice Award for 2010. Her poetry and prose have appeared widely in magazines such as *CV2*, *Event*, the *L.A. Review of Books*, the *New Quarterly*, and the *Utne Reader*. She lives with her family in Kingston.

ALISON PICK's most recent novel is *Far to Go*, winner of the Canadian Jewish Book Award for fiction and nominated for the Man Booker Prize. Rights have been sold internationally, and the book has been optioned for film. Pick was the 2002 Bronwen Wallace Award winner for most promising unpublished writer under thirty-five in Canada. She has published one other novel, *The Sweet Edge*, and two poetry collections, *The Dream World* and *Question & Answer*. She is currently on faculty at the Humber School for Writers and the Banff Centre for the Arts. Her memoir *Between Gods*, from which this essay is loosely excerpted, is forthcoming from Doubleday in 2014.

HEIDI REIMER's short stories and essays have appeared in *Literary Mama*, *Little Fiction*, *Stealing Time: A Literary Journal for Parents*, *Hip Mama*, and *Outcrops: Northeastern Ontario Short Stories*. She is the co-creator with her husband, Richard Willis, of the solo show *Strolling Player*. They live in Toronto with their two daughters. www.heidireimer.ca.

KERRY RYAN is the author of two collections of poems: *The Sleeping Life* and *Vs.*, which was shortlisted for the Acorn Plantos Award. She has had poems published in anthologies as well as a number of journals, including *The New Quarterly*, *Prairie Fire*, *The Antigonish Review*, and others. And now, suddenly, she is someone's mother.

CARRIE SNYDER is the author of two collections of short fiction, including *The Juliet Stories*, which was a finalist for Canada's 2012 Governor General's Award for Fiction. Her debut novel, *Girl Runner*, will be published in Canada by House of Anansi this fall. Carrie lives in Waterloo, Ontario, with her family. She blogs as *Obscure CanLit Mama* (carrieannesnyder.blogspot.ca/).

PATRICIA STORMS is an award-winning editorial cartoonist and author/illustrator of children's books and humour books. Her cartoons have been published in numerous magazines and newspapers, including *Reader's Digest*, *The Town Crier*, *The National Post*, *The London Times*, *The London Evening Standard*, *The Chronicle of Higher Education*, and *Canadian Notes & Queries*. Her newest picture book, *Never Let You Go*, has been described as "profound" with "exuberant illustrations" and has been published in numerous languages. She lives in Toronto with her husband and two fat cats in a cozy old house full to the brim with books.

SARAH YI-MEI TSIANG is the author of the poetry books *Status Update* and *Sweet Devilry*, which won the Gerald Lampert Award. She is also the author of several children's books, including *A Flock of Shoes* and *Warriors and Wailers*. Sarah's work has been published and translated internationally as well as named to the OLA Best Bets for Children 2010, Best Books for Kids & Teens 2011 & 2012, and the Toronto Public Library's First and Best Book List (2012). She is also the editor of the anthology *Desperately Seeking Susans* and the forthcoming *Tag: Canadian Poets at Play*.

PRISCILA UPPAL is a Toronto poet, fiction writer, memoirist, essayist, and playwright, and a professor of English at York University. Among her publications are nine collections of poetry, most recently, *Ontological Necessities*, *Traumatology, Successful Tragedies: Poems 1998-2010, Winter Sport: Poems* and *Summer Sport: Poems*; the critically acclaimed novels *The Divine Economy of Salvation* and *To Whom It May Concern*; and the study *We Are What We Mourn: The Contemporary English-Canadian Elegy*. Her memoir *Projection: Encounters with My Runaway Mother* was nominated for the Hilary Weston Writer's Trust Prize for Non-Fiction and the Governor General's Award for Non-Fiction. *Time Out London* dubbed her "Canada's coolest poet." For more information, visit priscilauppal.ca.

JULIA ZARANKIN'S stories and essays have appeared in *PRISM International*, *The Threepenny Review*, *The Antioch Review*, *The Dalhousie Review*, and *The Globe and Mail*. She was awarded first runner-up in *PRISM*'s nonfiction contest, longlisted for a CBC Literary Award, and recently awarded a residency at the MacDowell Colony. In her former life (which ended in 2008), Julia worked as a Russian literature professor at the University of Missouri. Now she lives, writes, and watches birds with gusto in Toronto. Learn more at coyot.es/birdsandwords.